PRAISE FOR
WAR IN 140 CHARACTERS

"Regardless of how things factually unfold on the ground, an army of twenty-first-century operatives has arisen to shape and manipulate the perception of the masses. In a highly insightful and timely journey, author David Patrikarakos investigates this world and rhetorically asks 'If a bomb lands in a village and nobody tweets about it, did it actually happen?' Packed with insights from Patrikarakos' years as a journalist, *War in 140 Characters* deftly explores the intersection of warfare and information and what it means for the future of our world."

—Marc Goodman, *New York Times* bestselling author of *Future Crimes*

"An important, somewhat scary book, built around a series of fascinating profiles, on how social media is changing issues of war and peace, eroding the concept of the nation state, and making the truth harder to find. It is all the more scary in that Putin and ISIS seem to understand and exploit this new world better than the West, and Trump appears to want to emulate rather than challenge the demagogic strategies and dishonest tactics they deploy."

—Alastair Campbell, author and strategist, former director of communications and strategy for Prime Minister Tony Blair

"Reporting from the conflict zones of Eastern Europe and the Middle East, David Patrikarakos goes beyond descriptions of places he visited, people he met, and situations he encountered to find common threads that define the new state of war. Inquisitive, thoughtful, and wonderfully written, this is a book for all of us, who whether we want it or not, find ourselves in the cyber trenches of the new global war, and have to learn how to fight and live in the world it has created."

—Serhii Plokhy, author of *Lost Kingdom*

**WAR IN 140
CHARACTERS**

DAVID PATRIKARAKOS

WAR IN 140 CHARACTERS

HOW SOCIAL MEDIA IS RESHAPING CONFLICT IN THE TWENTY-FIRST CENTURY

BASIC BOOKS
New York

Basic Books
Hachette Book Group
1290 Avenue of the Americas, New York, NY 10104
www.basicbooks.com

Printed in the United States of America
First Edition: November 2017
Published by Basic Books, an imprint of Perseus Books, LLC, a subsidiary of Hachette Book Group, Inc.
The Hachette Speakers Bureau provides a wide range of authors for speaking events. To find out more, go to www.hachettespeakersbureau.com or call (866) 376-6591.
The publisher is not responsible for websites (or their content) that are not owned by the publisher.

Print book interior design by Amy Quinn.

The Library of Congress has cataloged the hardcover edition as follows:

Names: Patrikarakos, David, 1977– author.
Title: War in 140 characters : how social media is reshaping conflict in the twenty-first century / David Patrikarakos.
Other titles: How social media is reshaping conflict in the twenty-first century
Description: First edition. | New York : Basic Books, [2017] | Includes bibliographical references and index.
Identifiers: LCCN 2017022137 (print) | LCCN 2017027790 (ebook) | ISBN 9780465096152 (ebook) | ISBN 9780465096145 (hardcover)
Subjects: LCSH: Information warfare—Case studies. | Social media—Political aspects. | Propaganda—Technological innovations. | Online social networks—Political aspects. | Arab-Israeli conflict—Mass media and the conflict. | Ukraine Conflict, 2014—Mass media and war. | IS (Organization) —In mass media. | Cyberspace—Political aspects. | War and society.
Classification: LCC U163 (ebook) | LCC U163 .P375 2017 (print) | DDC 355.020285/5678—dc23
LC record available at https://lccn.loc.gov/2017022137

ISBNs: 978-0-465-09614-5 (hardcover); 978-0-465-09615-2 (e-book)

LSC-C

10 9 8 7 6 5 4 3 2 1

To my father, who changed the
course of everything

CONTENTS

ACKNOWLEDGMENTS

As ever when writing a book, the list of people to whom I owe thanks will be long yet almost certainly incomplete. Most immediately, I owe a huge debt of gratitude to John Jenkins and Huston Gilmore, true scholars, both of whom took time out from their own intellectual pursuits to read through the manuscript and help improve it immeasurably. Rebecca Greig—one of the finest journalists I know—brought both her time and editing skills to answer my endless questions with endless forbearance; the text is all the better for her input. Alan Ramon Ward and Bryn Harris also took the time to read sections of the book, for which I am extremely thankful.

Emile Simpson, whose work was a great inspiration for me, also took the time to read the manuscript and give me the benefit of his expert opinion, which again, proved invaluable.

Thanks must also go to my editors at Basic Books, Lara Heimert and above all Leah Stecher, who was on hand throughout the process and whose excellent advice and edits I almost universally incorporated into the book. My agent, Peter Robinson, was also always there to provide advice and support throughout. Writing a book that has taken me from Gaza to Siberia has been a difficult process, and their unfailing patience and guidance were vital to bringing this work to fruition.

I must also mention the various people who helped me on the ground, from Mohamed in Gaza to Elie in France to Andrey in Russia. Again, their assistance was vital to making this book what it is, and I am grateful.

Lucy Cockcroft was an unyielding source of support and encouragement, for which she has my eternal thanks. I am also grateful to all the staff at Café Diplo, where I spent so many hours working on this book—guys, you are great. I must also thank Kristyna Foltynova for her quick work that, at times, saved this book by allowing me to travel to places I so desperately needed to go. Gratitude goes also to Dave McAvoy, who helped me with Arabic translation where necessary, and of course to all the experts who I interviewed and whose thinking helped inform my own.

I could never have written this book without the unfailing support of Anna Zaika, to whom I owe so much. Thank you, Anya. Thanks also to my brother, Phillip, and to my father, without whom I never would have been able to undertake all the necessary research. You saved me, guys.

I must also thank my mother and Rene for all the support and kindness they have shown me throughout my life, enabling me to do the things that make me happy.

I would like to thank the editors at *Mashable*, the *New Statesman*, *Foreign Policy*, the *Daily Beast*, and the *New York Times*, who have kindly allowed me to reproduce for the book excerpts from articles I have previously written for them. I thank them also for the opportunities they have given me to write for them and for helping me to improve my prose over the years.

Finally, and perhaps most of all, thanks must go to the stars of this book: the characters profiled, all of whom gave their time generously to help me tell the story of twenty-first-century warfare and social media's role at its heart.

David Patrikarakos
May 2017

INTRODUCTION

July 5, 2014:
The occupied city of Donetsk, in eastern Ukraine

I woke up and, as always, immediately checked my phone. What I saw astonished me: Twitter was reporting that Ukrainian forces had driven pro-Russia separatists from their stronghold in the nearby town of Sloviansk. The rebels were now fleeing to Donetsk, the self-proclaimed capital of the separatist enclave. Tweeted photos of the escaping convoy taken by passersby confirmed the story. I checked the BBC and other traditional news outlets for coverage but found nothing. The truth, however, was plain to see all around me: the city was in lockdown, its streets almost empty. Nobody was enjoying the weekend sunshine. I made my way to the city's occupied central administration building, which was now serving as the People's Republic of Donetsk (DNR) headquarters. Outside, several tattooed militia members guarded the entrance, fiddling listlessly with their Kalashnikovs. After a cursory search of my rucksack, they allowed me to enter. DON'T BE A PIG. CLEAN UP AFTER YOURSELF: the exasperated-sounding sign, taped to a pillar, looked over an archipelago of rubbish strewn across the building's lobby. I made my way to the elevator.

In November 2013, Ukrainians had taken to the streets to protest President Viktor Yanukovych's refusal to sign a trade agreement that would have strengthened the country's ties to the European

Union. In what became known as the Euromaidan revolution, the people rose up and took to the streets, eventually forcing Yanukovych to flee to Russia in late February 2014. Now the country was on the brink of civil war. Waves of protests, both for and against the new government, had rippled across eastern Ukraine after Yanukovych's fall. In March, Russia took advantage of the instability across its border to annex the Ukrainian territory of Crimea. Galvanized by this act, pro-Russia separatists (backed by Russian forces) proceeded to take control of several eastern cities and towns, including Donetsk, throughout April and May. Now all journalists needed official accreditation from the newly proclaimed DNR's press office to work in the city.

The office was housed on the fifth floor of the DNR headquarters and run by Claudia, an efficient woman trying her best to organize interviews with separatist officials. Information on the situation, she explained, was scarce. It was true that several thousand DNR fighters led by Igor "Strelkov" Gurkin, the head of the separatist militia, had left Sloviansk in convoy and were on their way here, though she had no idea where they were now or when they would arrive. Reports of the rebel exodus were only just emerging on the BBC and CNN. Twitter had, yet again, beaten mainstream media to the news.

Everyone in the office was discussing worst-case scenarios. In front of Claudia's desk sat two men in their early twenties, one with tousled dark hair and a slack jaw, the other a dirty blond with a partial squint. Their functions remained unclear. "What's the drill if all electronic communications are cut?" said the dark-haired one. "We use birds, right?" His friend grunted in agreement. "What were they again?" he continued. "Chickens, swans?"

"Carrier pigeons," came the reply.[1]

A few days later, my interviews done, I filed a piece on the recent events. Scrolling through Twitter, I saw pro-Kremlin accounts out in force once again, spinning the loss of Sloviansk as best they could. The rebels hadn't retreated but were merely "strategically relocating"; the battle against the "fascist junta" in Kyiv continued. I saw fellow journalists take abuse for reporting the facts of the retreat, often from anonymous accounts with a strong pro-Russia bent. More striking, as ever, were the pro-Russia narratives that filled this corner of the Internet: stories of Ukrainian atrocities (a three-year-old boy crucified by the Ukrainian army was a particularly notorious example), accounts of the machinations of the country's government and its affiliates that had no basis in truth.[2] Pro-Russian users were keen to show the so-called fascist nature of the Ukrainian side, uploading false stories of the far-right militia Pravy Sektor terrorizing Odessa's Jewish population; all were shared and retweeted thousands of times.[3] It wasn't propaganda I was witnessing, it was the reinvention of reality. And social media was at its heart.

This is a book about war. But it is also a book about stories, the narratives of conflict and the conflict of narratives. I first became aware that the nature of conflict had changed when I entered eastern Ukraine in the spring of 2014 and realized that Twitter contained more up-to-date information than the *New York Times* or NBC. Individuals, not institutions, became my primary source of information on the ground. As summer drew in, the terrorist group Islamic State (more commonly known as ISIS) exploded into global headlines when it took Iraq's second-largest city, Mosul, on June 10. Then in July, Israel launched Operation Protective Edge and another Gaza war began. As a Middle East specialist, I followed events closely in the region while continuing to report from Ukraine. It didn't matter that I was in Kyiv or Donetsk, far from English-language media; Gaza's bloody destruction was smeared across my phone and laptop on the dozens of videos and photos that filled my Twitter and Facebook feeds each day. As Islamic State continued its rampage across Iraq, more horrific images came in, posted by bystanders, participants, and state organizations alike. War had never been so close, visceral, or ubiquitous. Social media, I understood, had opened up for individuals vital spaces of communication once controlled exclusively by the state.

I began to understand that I was caught up in two wars: one fought on the ground with tanks and artillery, and an information war fought largely, though not exclusively, through social media. And, perhaps counterintuitively, it mattered more who won the war of words and narratives than who had the most potent weaponry. I realized, too, that while the Kremlin's information war regarding eastern Ukraine sought primarily to target disaffected eastern Ukrainians, it was also—just like the public information streams of the Israel Defense Forces (IDF) and Hamas and Islamic State—aimed at a global audience, as opposed to the "enemy" population, as has been traditional in wartime.

The US Joint Forces Command defines so-called hybrid war, which in traditional institutions is regarded as the latest development in conflict, as warfare that "simultaneously and adaptively employs a tailored mix of conventional, irregular, terrorism and criminal means or activities in the operational battle space."[4] What I was seeing went beyond this definition—this seemed like a new kind of warfare altogether. At its center, one thing shone out: the extraordinary ability of social media to endow ordinary individuals, frequently noncombatants, with the power to change the course of both the physical battlefield and the discourse around it.

Everyone, it seemed, could now be an actor in war. I was, I realized, witnessing a form of virtual mass enlistment. It is instructive that of the eight major characters profiled in this book, four are women, and three of those are civilians. War, which for millennia was an almost exclusively male domain, has been opened up in ways that were previously impossible. In December 2016, a seven-year-old Syrian girl, Bana Alabed, made global headlines by tweeting about the destruction that Syrian president Bashar al-Assad had rained down on her home city, Aleppo. Her tweets, written in imperfect English, had more power to shape the argument surrounding Syria's civil war than the state's propaganda machine did.[5]

I decided to write this book while lying on my bed in a bleak room of the Ramada hotel in Donetsk, listening to the sound of shelling on the city's outskirts. I have seen modern warfare up close, and it is clear that the old frameworks of understanding it are now insufficient. We are in need of a new conceptual framework that takes into account how social media has transformed the way that wars are waged, covered, and consumed. We need to better understand the twenty-first-century war.

In this century, "if we want peace, don't prepare for war; rethink it," writes Emile Simpson, author of *War From the Ground Up: Twenty-First-Century Combat as Politics* and a former British soldier who served three tours in Afghanistan.[6] My experiences of war in Ukraine and my study of the Gaza conflict together with the rise of Islamic State forced me to do just that—and this revealed three trends to me. First, power has shifted from hierarchies or institutions to individual citizens and networks of citizens. Second, the narrative dimensions of war are arguably becoming more important than its physical dimensions. And third, the conflicts I was examining were not "traditional" state-on-state wars. Instead, modern conflict tends to either take place between a state and a non-state actor (as with, for example, Israel and Hamas, or Iraq and Islamic State) or exist somewhere in the nebulous region between the boundaries of war and peace (as I witnessed in Ukraine).

Twentieth-century thinking on conventional conflict is largely based on the ideas of the Prussian military theorist Carl von Clausewitz, who conceived of war as something like a straight military fight between sovereign states. The battleground was as clear as a boxing ring, and the enemy was obvious. Military victory was easy to determine, and once it was achieved, the victor imposed a political settlement on the loser. The defeat of Germany in World War I, and the

resulting Treaty of Versailles, offers a perfect (albeit egregious) example of this process.

We live in a post-1945 security system that was designed to reg-
ulate war out of existence.[7] Following the atrocities of World War II,
there was a nearly unanimous desire among the major powers to create an international order where the use of force between major states
would be almost impossible. Organizations like the European Union
and United Nations were formed with this intention at their heart.
The emergence of nuclear weapons has also made it harder for states to
compel their enemy to do their will, for fear of possible escalation. The
post-1945 security order has, therefore, seen a decline in state-on-state
conflict and an almost total absence of (direct) war between two major
powers. But the urge to fight predates civilization itself—it cannot be
regulated out of existence. War, like a virus, must mutate to survive.

Clausewitzian forms of war do, of course, still exist today. In Sri
Lanka, as Simpson points out, the government militarily crushed its
insurgent enemy, the Tamil Tigers, and forced them to the negotiating table.[8] But what I was seeing, from Ukraine to Gaza to Iraq, was
the gradual erosion of this type of war in favor of looser, more open-
ended conflicts. Russian president Vladimir Putin had no interest in
defeating Ukraine militarily (which he easily could have done) and
forcing it to accept Russia's annexation of eastern Ukraine. Likewise,
Israel had no intention of defeating Hamas militarily (which it easily could have done) and forcing it to finally accept Israel's existence.
With Islamic State, too, I observed a new form of conflict. Unlike terror groups of the past, its only demand is that Syria and Iraq, and
then the rest of the Middle East and beyond, dismantle their states
and join its caliphate—something that is self-evidently impossible to
compromise on. The conflict, therefore, cannot be resolved through
negotiation. Without total victory (in this case requiring near annihi-
lation) by one side over the other, it will never end.

Clausewitz observed that war is the continuation of politics by
other means, but in Ukraine conflict was the practice of politics itself. Rather than militarily defeating Ukraine, Moscow seemed most

concerned with getting eastern Ukrainians to subscribe to a political narrative: namely, that the Kyiv government—a "fascist junta"—was out to persecute Russian-speaking Ukrainians. This was because its ultimate objective was not the defeat of Ukraine but its destabilization, for which it needed to divide the country's population. In essence, its military goal was political. Whereas in war as it is traditionally understood, information operations support military action on the battlefield, in Ukraine it became clear that military operations on the ground were supporting information operations on TV and in cyberspace. The boundaries between politics and war, it appeared to me, had become blurred—and the boundaries between war and peace even more so. After I left Ukraine, I sought out Emile Simpson, who told me that during his time in Afghanistan the goal of the coalition forces ultimately became not to defeat the Taliban with superior military strength but to convince the local population not to join its insurgency. "War as we traditionally understand it, as military fight distinct from peace, still exists," he explained. "However, the *general tendency*, driven by the information revolution, is away from that paradigm and towards open-ended, networked conflicts that occupy a gray zone between war and peace."[9]

Simpson confirmed to me something I had already noticed: what has changed is not the practice of war—soldiers still shoot at soldiers, tanks still fire on tanks—but the context in which it takes place. US secretary of defense General James "Mad Dog" Mattis may have been right when he declared that "Alex [*sic*] the Great would not be in the least bit perplexed by the enemy that we face right now in Iraq."[10] But this statement refers to the unchanging experience of combat, not the shifting context in which war is now fought, which has been altered beyond all recognition by the information revolution and the speed and interconnectivity it has brought to the world.[11]

Moreover, Simpson identifies "coercive communication" as a crucial element of warfare because the concept of defeat always involves a political message that has been successfully communicated to the loser: defeat equates to the perception of having lost, and the consequent acceptance of the victor's terms.[12] The key distinction between traditional and contemporary warfare is the extent to which coercive communication tries to achieve that political goal via a military victory on the battlefield. In Sri Lanka it was clear: a straight military fight resulted in the winner imposing its will on the loser. But at the time of writing, the military conflict in Ukraine remains "frozen," existing neither in a state of outright war nor in one of peace. And in response Ukraine's allies in the West have taken advantage of an interconnected, globalized world to amplify modes of "coercive communication" against Russia (such as financial sanctions) that bypass the battlefield. The degree of global financial integration that exists today means that the capacity to wage war through nonmilitary means has never been greater. The boundaries between war and peace are crumbling, and this new status quo threatens international stability; if war has increasingly become the practice of politics (and its attendant economics), it has no clear end because politics never ends.

Thus do the more open-ended conflicts we see today have far greater potential to slip into outright war involving multiple states. I believe that the world is facing a greater prospect of wide-scale war now than at any other time since 1945. The Cold War that followed the end of World War II was underpinned by a balance between the world's only two superpowers, the Soviet Union and the United States, that largely ensured an (admittedly uneasy) peace, or at least negated the threat of major war between multiple states. That world order no longer exists—and the globalized world that has replaced it has introduced new challenges into the sphere of conflict.

At the center of these challenges stand not just globalization and the information revolution but more specifically social media and networking technologies. According to think-tank researchers Emerson T. Brooking and P. W. Singer, around 3.4 billion people now use the Internet. Each day they send roughly 500 million tweets and upload nearly seven hours of footage to YouTube per second in up to seventy-six different languages. Facebook has 1.7 billion active accounts, giving it a larger "population" than China, while Twitter and

Facebook are the platforms from which the majority of Americans get their news; indeed, 59 percent of American Twitter users rely on the service to follow news events as they happen in real time.[13] And nowhere do news events happen as dramatically in real time as they do in times of war.

This book takes as its starting point the premise that social media has helped to dismantle traditional information and media hierarchies, and in so doing has given birth to a new type of hyperempowered individual, networked, globally connected, and more potent than ever before: a uniquely twenty-first-century phenomenon I term *Homo digitalis*.[14] The result is that social media has irretrievably changed the way that wars are fought, reported on, and consumed. I use Andreas M. Kaplan and Michael Haenlein's definition of social media as "a group of Internet-based applications that build on the ideological and technological foundations of Web 2.0, and that allow the creation and exchange of user-generated content."[15] Put simply, Web 2.0 describes websites that emphasize content Internet users themselves can create—such as discussion forums, messenger applications, tweets, videos, et cetera—using online services such as social media websites or blogs. It stands in contrast to the first generation of websites, where Internet users were largely relegated to merely passively viewing content.

The twentieth-century nation-state traditionally held primacy in two areas, from which it derived much of its power: its near monopoly on the use of force, and its dominant control of information flows.[16] Web 2.0 has endowed people with two crucial abilities to disrupt this power: first, they can actively produce content on social media platforms with almost no barriers to entry, and second, through the use of these forums they can form transnational networks. Both of these abilities enable them to fill roles traditionally occupied by nation-states and to shape events around the globe. At his home in Baltimore, I met Alec Ross, former senior advisor for innovation to ex-secretary of state Hillary Clinton, who articulated this phenomenon unequivocally to me.

> I believe that when most people talk about shifts in geopolitical power they do so on a geographical basis, how power is moving from West to East, from the United States and Europe to Asia, or from the global North to the global South. Now, whether that is true or not is a debatable proposition, but what I don't think is a debatable proposition is that power is moving from hierarchies to citizens and networks, and connection technologies enable that shift in power—defining a hierarchy as the nation-state, as a large media organization, or other such things. And the kinds of capabilities that would have once been reserved for large media organizations or for nation-states have suddenly become available to networks of individuals.[17]

He was right. It is unthinkable that the Arab Spring uprisings of 2011, which began when a Tunisian street vendor named Mohamed Bouazizi set himself on fire in response to harassment from police on January 4, 2011, could have happened without social media. The images, caught on camera phones and uploaded to social media platforms, sparked violent demonstrations that led to the overthrow of President Zine El Abidine Ben Ali just ten days later. The images spread internationally, causing outrage in Egypt, whose people rose up and overthrew the dictator Hosni Mubarak. Demonstrations soon followed in Syria. It was during the Arab Spring that *Homo digitalis* was first revealed.

Homo digitalis is especially dangerous for authoritarian states, which rely even more than liberal democracies on controlling information flows. Without near monopolies on these flows, it is impossible for states to project power (especially in war or protest situations) the way they once could. And because these new social media forums are structurally more egalitarian, many delight in holding up the Internet as the ultimate tool against tyrants.

This idea is what the author Evgeny Morozov terms "cyber-utopianism"—the belief that "the Internet favors the oppressed rather than the oppressor . . . a naive belief in the emancipatory nature of online communication that rests on a stubborn refusal to acknowledge its downside . . . [by failing to acknowledge] how authoritarian governments would respond to the Internet . . . how useful it would prove for propaganda purposes, how masterfully dictators would learn to use it for surveillance, and how sophisticated modern systems of Internet censorship would become."[18] In Ukraine, the truth of his words was plain to see: while Ukrainians uploaded photos of Russian military hardware crossing the border, the Russian state used the same platforms to spread its counternarrative. *Homo digitalis* may challenge the state, but the state will always fight back.

New media has expanded the arena of conflict into the virtual world, which is becoming every bit as "real" as the fighting on the ground. Whether you are a president, a soldier, or a terrorist, if you don't understand how to effectively deploy the power of new media, you may win the odd battle but you will lose a twenty-first-century war, or at least a major part of it.

The need to understand this idea is urgent. It's clichéd but true to say that the twentieth-century nation-state is dead. But it is important to remember that this nation-state was atypical in its centralization, especially in its ability to control information flows by encouraging people to consume state-sanctioned TV, newspapers, and radio. In creating new venues that allow people to communicate outside these traditional state hierarchies of communication, social media platforms have spawned a political reversal: a regression from centralized communicative modes to the more chaotic network effects of an earlier age. Before the twentieth-century nation-states emerged, statehood was a looser and more decentralized affair (in 1860, for example, only half of France's population spoke French as a first language).[19] The effect has been to destabilize classic forms of war. The "new wars" I witnessed seemed, in their fluidity and chaos, to be more like the wars of the early modern period—before states became as centralized and powerful as they are today—than like the wars of the twentieth century.[20]

As Alec Ross observed from his experience of working in the White House: "I think the Internet is the single most disruptive force for the sovereign nation-state since the concept was founded with the 1648 Treaty of Westphalia. I don't think the Internet is going to take an eraser to state wars, but it is inherently anti-state."

Once again he is right. What I experienced in Ukraine, and saw in Israel and with the rise of Islamic State, was an ability not just to build networks but to shatter them. Social media is both centripetal and centrifugal. Just as I witnessed it bring people together to support Ukraine, I watched the same platforms further divide eastern Ukrainians from their fellow citizens in Kyiv. As Facebook and Twitter once united Egyptians against Mubarak, the same tools now divide Coptics, Salafis, and the Muslim Brotherhood within Egypt, as social media gives them all a voice and—now bereft of a common enemy—magnifies their existing sectarian conflicts.

Social media shatters unity and divides people in two overarching ways. The first is obvious: it sets them at loggerheads with one another as Facebook and Twitter make direct engagement (and therefore confrontation) between opposing camps far easier, especially during times of crisis like war. The second is more insidious. The majority of young Americans now receive their news from social media.[21] And what they receive depends on whom they "friend" or follow and the type of content they post. Social media platforms are not impartial; they are capitalist enterprises designed to make money off their users. As we cocoon ourselves in online bubbles of like-minded friends and followers posting content we find agreeable, so the Facebook algorithm feeds us yet more content that, based on our online habits, it calculates we will like. This is designed to keep us on their forums for as long as possible to allow companies to advertise specific products to us users based on what they know we like.

This results in what is known as "homophily" (meaning literally "love of the same"), in which individuals bond with like-minded others, who reinforce their worldview—which is then exacerbated by algorithms that feed them desirable content. Ten years ago, both pro-Israeli and pro-Palestinian sympathizers would have watched CNN (with its required standards of impartiality and objectivity). Now each side receives its news from preferred sources that reaffirm existent opinions. The result is a homophily on each side that reinforces prejudices and exacerbates hatred of the other. Thus does division grow, thus does war become easier.

History shows us that with each new major evolution in information technology comes a period of great instability, often leading to conflict. The invention of the printing press in the fifteenth century brought subsequent wars of religion to Europe. Once it enabled mass publication of the Bible, which was subsequently translated from Latin into the vernacular languages of states, the Catholic Church no longer became the sole mediator between the text and the people. Everyone could bring their own interpretation to it—and war ensued. The 1920s saw the mass expansion of radio, which, a mere decade later, gave the demagogues of the 1930s platforms on which to flourish, leading ultimately to World War II. November 2016 saw the election of Donald Trump, arguably the most demagogic US presidential candidate in history, who employed Twitter as one of his primary campaign tools. Like the printing press and then radio and TV, social media has opened up new venues of communication, but the degree to which it has decentralized the transmission of information means the extent to which the state can impose a single interpretation of events has decreased even further. This is both a force for good, in that it brings greater transparency, and a force for ill, in that it is destabilizing. As social media makes almost every action visible through a share or a tweet (especially in wartime), both governments and the traditional media have seen their role as the gatekeepers of information recede in favor of wildly differing interpretations of events—and the spread of outright falsehoods.

The problem we now face is twofold: the boundaries between politics and warfare have never been so blurred, and politics has never been so unstable. The rise of social media, an inherently destabilizing technology, has coincided with a time of crisis in the West, which, since the early 2000s, has seen the systematic discrediting of its major institutions. In 2003 its leading politicians took a coalition to war against Iraq to seize nonexistent weapons of mass destruction. In 2008 its financial sector's irresponsible behavior led to the Great Recession. Edward Snowden's 2013 revelations that the US National Security Agency had been spying on its own citizens further discredited the security establishment. Along with the longer-term trend of a declining trust in mainstream media in Europe and North America, these forces have combined to create an environment of widespread mistrust of the "establishment" that has allowed nationalist demagogues, like Geert Wilders in the Netherlands and Marine Le Pen in France, to rise across Europe, and Trump to win the US presidency. Coterminous with these trends has been the rise of postmodernism within our academic institutions and its lack of belief in a knowable "objective truth," which has allowed the lies of both the Kremlin and Trump to flourish. We live in a postmodern age that has brought forth postmodern politics and war. The trend toward the regressive and chaotic has rarely been more pronounced in our lifetimes.

At the end of 2016, "post-truth" was named word of the year by Oxford Dictionaries. It was defined as "relating to or denoting circumstances in which objective facts are less influential in shaping public opinion than appeals to emotion and personal belief."[22] This reflected a year in which Donald Trump was on record as having told the most lies of any US presidential candidate in modern history, and in which the Brexit campaign advocating Britain's departure from the EU was largely based on a slew of misinformation and half-truths. According to Oxford Dictionaries president Casper Grathwohl: "It's not surprising that our choice reflects a year dominated by highly-charged political and social discourse. Fuelled by the rise of social media as a news source and a growing distrust of facts offered up by the establishment, post-truth as a concept has been finding its linguistic footing for some time."[23]

The costs of this are plain to see. The meaning of truth itself is changing in contemporary politics and, more dangerously, in conflict, at a number of levels. First, the death of the idea of an "objective truth" allows Russia—through the use of its propaganda—to erode trust in *all* sources of truth, allowing for so-called fake news to infect real news. Second, social media catalyzes both centripetal and centrifugal forces in the shaping of information: stories go viral, but you also have endless versions of events and information overflow, both of which stretch truth like an elastic band. Third, the definition of a story is changing: now a tweet can itself be the story, not just a means to tell it. Finally, new rules are being created, and the state is often behind *Homo digitalis*. This explains geopolitical phenomena like the Arab Spring and the rise of the terror group Islamic State, which would have been simply impossible fifteen years ago.

This is why it is imperative to examine the changing nature of warfare now. In the run-up to World War I, none of the great powers wanted conflict but, through miscalculation and error, drifted into it. Everything I experienced in Ukraine and saw in Gaza and in the rise of Islamic State made me believe that we may be heading in that direction once more. It is both urgent and imperative for politicians, policy makers, and the general public to understand the ways conflict has changed: twenty-first-century war requires a twenty-first-century response. This book is part of that response.

To do this I have traveled thousands of miles across three continents to detail how *Homo digitalis* is redefining twenty-first-century conflict. Each individual story highlights an emergent theme. Starting with Israel's 2014 war against Hamas, the early chapters examine the archetypal twenty-first-century asymmetric war, pitting a state versus a non-state actor, and explore both the power of *Homo digitalis* to take on a democratic state through the promulgation of powerful narratives and the state's attempts to battle it with narratives of its own. The clash between individual authenticity and institutional corporatism looms large here, as do the differing importance of visual and verbal messaging and legacy media's receding ability to act as gatekeepers of information emerging from war zones, as illustrated by the image on this book's jacket.[24] The book then moves on to the Ukraine-Russia war to detail the murky world of gray-zone conflicts, where reality is reinvented to serve the ends of a new kind of dictator. In response, *Homo digitalis* uses the power of social media both to directly impact the battlefield and (from thousands of miles away) to affect war at the narrative level, using newly available investigative tools to discern the truth in wartime more rapidly and efficiently than even intelligence institutions. Finally, I arrive at the culmination of twenty-first-century conflict: the surreal brutality and chaos of Islamic State, powered by the dark side of *Homo digitalis* and by Islamic State's ability to use social media to radicalize and to recruit, rapidly and transnationally. Set against this are the disadvantages that sclerotic state bureaucracies face in countering the unprecedented volume and sophistication of the group's propaganda. The culpability of mainstream media in Islamic State's propaganda battle and the nature of social media companies as capitalist enterprises that de facto enable the group's virtual war are also considered. Within these chapters, numerous other themes will be explored to present an intimate and detailed portrait of twenty-first-century war and the people and technologies that are reshaping it.

1

THE CITIZEN JOURNALIST:
STORIES VERSUS GUNS

The first thing you notice about Gaza is the children: playing in the road, riding bikes, squealing in ragged groups, kicking soccer balls, or just sitting on the sidewalk.[1] Occasionally they half-heartedly ask passersby for money. Many wear the jerseys of famous soccer players. The names of impossibly wealthy superstars emblazoned across their spindly backs seem almost mocking, hinting at lives they will never have and chances they will never be given. The irony is as acrid as the dust is pervasive. Cars scuttle in and out of back streets. Donkeys attached to carts invariably driven by middle-aged men weave in and out of traffic, hauling agricultural produce throughout the city center. Selling their fruits and vegetables, these vendors form a vital part of the lifeblood of Gaza's economy. Cars honk in annoyance at the donkeys' languid trot through roads half paved with Saudi and Qatari money: a mixture of potholes and smooth cement. Whether the money has not yet fully arrived or has been stolen by corrupt officials is unclear.

By now you are aware that you have arrived at a place unlike any other on earth. I entered through Erez Crossing, a concrete monolith that separates the Hamas-controlled Gaza Strip from Israel to the west. Once through the Israeli checkpoint—a succession of security booths and revolving bars—I walk approximately a mile and a half through an open-air corridor enclosed with wire netting. On either side of me I see the landscape through a mesh of wire: bright green shrubbery dots a vista of sand and dirt and gray rock. I pass two concrete blocks defaced by blue Arabic graffiti. One reads AL-QUDS INTIFADA (the words literally translate to "Jerusalem" and "tremor"), referring to the uprisings that Palestinians have conducted in both Gaza and the West Bank against Israel's occupation. The other says simply PALESTINE.

I arrive at the Gaza side. Such is the hatred between Israel and Hamas, the Palestinian resistance movement that now controls Gaza, that the two parties won't even have corresponding checkpoints, and I enter through one manned by Fatah, the official party of the Palestine Liberation Organization, which controls the West Bank. Lines of blue plastic chairs are spread across an uneven concrete floor. I make my way to the counter to have my documents checked. Nearby, a vending machine sells cans of Pepsi. I'm approved and walk into the torrid heat to catch a taxi to what really matters: the Hamas checkpoint. Here I meet my fixer, Mohamed, a broad, stocky man—his physique the result of many hours spent in the gym. Mohamed has contacts in Hamas, and after some perfunctory questioning I am allowed through.

This part of the world has a turbulent history. In 1947 a United Nations resolution divided Palestine into Jewish and Arab states (as well as a third, international zone containing Jerusalem and its surrounding areas). The following year, Israel formally declared its independence over the territory allocated to it by the UN. A coalition of five Arab countries immediately invaded the new Jewish state, attempting to strangle it at birth. During the resulting war, Israeli forces captured large swaths of territory and increased Israel's area. However, the Israelis failed to take control of two areas of "original" Palestine—the West Bank and Gaza, which were held by Jordan and

Egypt, respectively. Two decades later, during the 1967 Six-Day War, Israel captured both.

In 1987 the Palestinians launched the intifada, or uprising, against the occupation of their two territories, during which emerged Hamas, an Islamist movement. Hamas rejected the Oslo peace process of the 1990s, instead using suicide bombings within Israel to attack the state. When the Oslo process collapsed, the second intifada, bloodier than the first, emerged to unleash waves of suicide bombings in which Hamas played a leading role. Israel continues to occupy the West Bank, but in August 2005 Israeli prime minister Ariel Sharon forced the withdrawal of all Jewish settlements from Gaza. In 2006 Hamas won the Palestinian elections and began to rule over the strip.

Gaza is unique. Measuring a mere 141 square miles, it is home to 1.85 million people. It is also under a blockade by both Egypt and Israel—though Israel allows in humanitarian aid. Since it took control of the area, Hamas has continuously fired rockets from Gaza into Israel as well as sending suicide bombers across the border. Israel considers it a serious terrorist threat. Just days before I arrived, a bomb exploded on a Jerusalem bus, injuring twenty-one people, two critically.[2] Hamas admitted that the culprit, Abu Srour, was a member of its organization.[3]

Mohamed drives fast. Soon we are in Gaza City. It bustles and teems like a typical Arab metropolis. Shops are thronged with people. Bananas and apples as well as falafel and chicken stuffed with rice—a Gazan specialty—are all on display. Amid the activity, however, the city still bears the scars of the 2014 war between Hamas and Israel. It was a fifty-one-day conflict, and it was bloody. Around 2,300 Gazans were killed, with about 10,000 wounded, while 66 Israeli soldiers and 6 Israeli civilians died, with a further 469 soldiers and 87 civilians wounded. The devastation is plain to see. Destruction dots the cityscape. While many of the destroyed buildings have been rebuilt, many also bear the scorch marks of rocket fire. The traces of Operation Protective Edge (the name Israel gave to its 2014 military actions) are pervasive, as are the traces of something else: Hamas.

Near the center of Gaza City stands a monument: a rocket belonging to Hamas's military wing, the Izzedine al-Qassam Brigades. It points in the direction of Israel.

Later on, as we drive through the city, Mohamed indicates some graffiti on a wall by the main road. It is, he tells me, the work of the famous British graffiti artist Banksy. Sprayed onto the dilapidated wall, whose top bricks are crumbling, is the image of an Israeli security tower. Children swing from it in chairs like a fairground ride. Army versus civilian, the state versus children, experience versus innocence—the meaning couldn't be clearer.

I am here to investigate all of these things. I have come to Gaza to go back in time to those fifty-one days in August 2014, to hear a story of Gazan suffering. It is of the adult world of war seen through the eyes of a child, and, through the use of social media, that child's ability to broadcast it to the world.

The advent of new media brought to the Internet a revolution that was both technological and ideological. Once online services became interactive, they became two-way vehicles for people to network and socialize.[4] The social media technologies that emerged from Web 2.0 have allowed for the rise of a participatory culture, empowering users by enabling them to become what some have termed "produsers," users who can also produce content.[5] This has created two revolutionary shifts in communication practices that are especially relevant (and potent) in wartime. The first is the ability to broadcast, which, due to the reach of social media networks, can be done transnationally. A power once reserved for major institutions like governments or media outlets like the *New York Times* or CNN has transferred to the individual. Anyone who owns a smartphone can become a mini-CNN: broadcasting content that—thanks to social media networks— has the potential to go viral and reach an audience of millions.

The second shift, implicit in the first, is that this can be done with almost no start-up cost. Content that once would have required a team of cameramen, trained journalists, editors, and news anchors to reach a national or international audience can be now produced and disseminated in seconds with the sharing of an image or text in a single tweet or post. This ability so radically changes the production, flow, and consumption of all types of media, it cannot help but be a destabilizing force for existing hierarchies, like state armies, especially ones fighting insurgent forces. In a previous era, the Israel Defense Forces (IDF) would have been able to largely control the narrative surrounding wars with Hamas by controlling journalists' access to war zones, or even refusing to accredit certain journalists, as well as having an entire public relations division devoted to getting its message out. The Palestinians, conversely, could offer little by way of a counternarrative. The advent of new media has irrevocably altered this, and its importance to modern warfare could not be greater.

In the third edition of her book *New and Old Wars: Organized Violence in a Global Era*, Mary Kaldor formulates a definition of "new war," which, as opposed to "old war" (involving conflicts between states "in which battle is the decisive encounter"), involves "networks of state and non-state actors."[6] Facing an international system designed to prevent interstate conflict, nation-states now engage in battles that are mostly asymmetric. States fight against insurgent groups, soldiers fight militants, and civilians are inevitably caught in the middle. Nowhere is the disparity in military power between combatants greater than in asymmetric warfare. And nowhere is the influence of *Homo digitalis* more profound. In the Palestinian case, the power lies not in directly affecting the physical battlefield but rather in directing the discourse that surrounds it. As the boundaries between war and politics increasingly become erased, the ability to guide the narrative of war becomes ever more important.

In the twenty-first century, observes Harvard political scientist Joseph Nye, conflicts will be less about whose army wins than about whose story wins.[7] We live in an age obsessed with both postmodernism and cable TV series, where narratives are privileged over arguments, the emotive over the dry and merely rational. And in 2014, a young Gazan girl called Farah Baker was able to create, via social media, a narrative of drama and suffering—that is to say, a narrative of the most emotive and powerful kind, one that could face off against the might of the IDF in the information sphere. Farah's case illustrates, in miniature, what happens in conflicts between established armies and insurgent groups when individual, networked citizens are given access to broadcast tools with virtually no start-up cost. She illustrates how social media can level the playing field in asymmetric warfare.

Armed with only a smartphone, Farah represents an almost entirely new power for smaller, less militarily powerful nations: the ability to defeat their adversaries on the narrative battlefield. This ability is, moreover, absolutely fundamental when victory on the physical battlefield is essentially impossible. Propaganda wars are as old as warfare itself, but in twenty-first-century war, narrative conflict has

Farah Baker, Gazan tweeter. (Courtesy of Ahmed Moner Skaik)

become more than physical conflict's adjunct. It is arguably its most powerful frontier. And as the 2014 war between Israel and Hamas shows, a lone teenage girl can now battle—and threaten—the institutional power of one of the world's most powerful armies.

On June 12, 2014, three Israeli teenagers, Naftali Frenkel, Gilad Shaer, and Eyal Yifrah, were on their way home to celebrate Shabbat (the Jewish Sabbath) when Hamas operatives driving a Hyundai picked them up at a hitchhiking stop in the Israeli settlement area of Gush Etzion in the West Bank and promptly murdered them. The killings caused uproar in Israel. Calls for revenge on social media, stoked by the rhetoric of hard-right politicians like economy and trade minister Naftali Bennett (who urged war on Hamas), led to violence on the streets, culminating in the murder of an Arab teenager, Mohammed Abu Khdeir, in East Jerusalem on July 2.[8] This murder, combined with an Israeli government crackdown on Hamas, prompted the militant wing of the party to begin firing rockets at towns in southern Israel. Most of the rockets were intercepted by Israel's anti-missile system, Iron Dome, but some got through. The normally militarily cautious Israeli prime minister, Benjamin Netanyahu, decided that the time had come for action, and on July 8, 2014, he launched Operation Protective Edge against Hamas. The IDF began its Gaza campaign with air strikes, which were followed on July 17 by a full-on ground invasion.

All of this was, frankly, ruining Farah Baker's summer. A sixteen-year-old Palestinian, she had been looking forward to the summer break before returning to high school as a senior. And she had plans. The daughter of a well-known Palestinian surgeon, Baker is part of the educated upper echelons of Gazan society. That summer she wanted to learn the guitar, go to the gym to lose weight, and improve her English—things typical of teenagers around the world. But the war almost instantly put a stop to all that.

Two years later, Mohamed and I pulled up to Farah's large apartment complex in central Gaza City. He dialed her cell phone to let her know we were here for the agreed-upon interview. Could we come in? Farah said we had to wait. Her father was still in the house and had gotten sick of the endless interviews; nothing could happen until he left. As we circled her block (while Mohamed became increasingly irritated, punching in her number with his bearlike fingers) it was clear that Farah was now a big deal in Gaza. Eventually we parked a few yards down from her front door. After about fifteen minutes a Mercedes pulled out of the driveway, and then Farah appeared, telling us it was safe to enter. She led us up two flights of stairs to her apartment, where she welcomed us into her living room. Smiling and gregarious, she poured us glasses of water and invited us to sit. Then she began her story.[9]

Farah hadn't been expecting war to come that summer. There had been talk of it on social media, of course, especially in the wake of the kidnappings, but then there was always talk of war. To this day she remains convinced that she'll live through many wars—Israel and Gaza are no closer to peace, and the cycle of violence seems impossible to break. In the previous Israel-Hamas war of 2012, Farah's older sister had begun tweeting, so Farah had opened a Twitter account, too. The family's children were confined to the house for their own safety, and she was bored. She wanted to do something, so she started tweeting about the situation in Arabic because her English wasn't strong enough. Two years later, though, when the 2014 conflict erupted, her English was much improved, and as she watched events unfold, she believed that the Western media was twisting facts to make Israel appear the victim. From her living room it seemed clear that the opposite was true, and Farah wanted to do her bit to set the record straight. But because she was a sixteen-year-old girl her options in wartime were almost zero—or at least would have been before the advent of new media enabled anyone with a phone to become a broadcaster. So she decided to do the only thing she realistically could: to use the ability she now had to put her story out there and see if anyone would listen. "I am a Palestinian and the world was against us because [people] are brainwashed, so I started writing about my life, my hopes and dreams," she told me as I sat in her traditionally decorated living room that hot April afternoon. She also made the decision to tweet photos, so the outside world could see as well as read about what was happening. Everything she did was geared toward making people, especially those in the West, understand what it was like to be a Palestinian in a time of war.

Things were slow at first, but as the war expanded, so did her follower count, spiking in tandem with the war's most drastic events. She became an increasingly popular source of information coming out of Gaza—as far removed from the centralized and highly bureaucratic newsrooms of the *Guardian* or the *Wall Street Journal* as it is possible to be. In just a matter of weeks, Farah said, her followers jumped from 800 to around 200,000.[10] Today she still has around 170,000.[11] (To put this in context, the average Twitter user has 208 followers).[12] This phenomenal growth was no accident. Farah had made two careful choices: the first was to use Twitter rather than Facebook as her social media platform of choice, despite the fact that Facebook is far more popular in Gaza, and the second was to tweet in English.

At only sixteen, Farah understood, even if only instinctively, the importance of social media in wartime, especially to a perpetual underdog like the Palestinians. She understood the power it gave to a single individual and to networks of individuals, power that previously would have been impossible. She understood that Twitter, as a more public social media platform, was perfectly suited to getting her message out instantly: more people, she told me, can see what you write, and, crucially, journalists use it as a source. People on the ground tweeting photos and descriptions of events during wartime have become invaluable—especially as they often tweet or post from areas too dangerous for journalists to go. Fakery exists, of course, but when enough people tweet similar information from the same area, it provides a form of verification that has changed how wars are viewed. It allows the victims of war to gain a voice and the world to view—with greater detail than ever before—just what exactly is happening inside zones of conflict.

As the war began and the bombing started, she decided to become a citizen journalist, a civilian broadcasting what she believed to be the truth about the war. Social media, and especially Twitter, with its ability to magnify a message through retweets (especially from accounts with large numbers of followers), would ultimately give her the tools to reach a potential audience of millions without needing substantial resources or access to expensive media technology. She could become a broadcaster at virtually zero cost.

Information campaigns in wartime have traditionally focused on influencing the "enemy" population by sapping its morale, disseminating fear, or urging surrender.[13] Farah had no interest whatsoever in these sorts of tactics (and she would not have had the power to effectively carry them out, anyway). She was not even seeking to do battle with Israelis online or to convince them of the validity of her cause. Rather, her target audience was the wider world. Reaching an international, predominantly Western audience was so vital to the Gazan cause because, hopelessly outmatched militarily, the Palestinians could never hope to defeat the Israelis; their only chance was to show the destruction that was being wrought on them and pray that international outrage would rein Israel in. Put simply, their rockets could never stop Israel, but their narrative might. And in the service of this goal, someone like Farah could morph from a mere child into the most potent of weapons.

So she decided to tweet, and she made it personal. On July 21, 2014, for example, she tweeted a photo of herself holding a handwritten sign in English: "I'm Farah Baker, Gazan girl, 16 years old. Since I was born I have survived 3 wars and I think this is enough #SaveGaza." It was retweeted more than 2,500 times.[14] Farah was presenting herself to the world not as a prototypical anti-Israel Gazan voice but as an ordinary sixteen-year-old girl caught up in a horrific situation beyond her control. She began to build a narrative—to tell a story—about her everyday life under bombardment. She created a public diary that could be viewed by hundreds of thousands of people, if not millions, in real time. And the more she wrote, the more interest there was; the more followers she gained, the more questions they asked. It encouraged her to keep on tweeting.

As the bombs fell and Israeli soldiers entered Gaza, Farah tweeted hundreds of times, in the most dramatic terms. "A child martyred and many wounded" is just one example of many tweets in a similar vein, and it is instructive of the power her messaging carried: the death of a child naturally resonates powerfully with any right-thinking audience.[15] Farah was using Twitter to highlight the most extreme effects of war, to garner greater sympathy and build more public support for Gaza by showing the sheer extent of the carnage the IDF was wreaking there. In this vein, she also made sure to document, as comprehensively as the platform allowed, the reality all around her. Many of her tweets were simple descriptions or videos of what she saw and heard. "This is the car which was bombed at my house door #Gaza #GazaUnderAttack," she tweeted on July 26 with an accompanying photo of the destroyed vehicle. It highlighted the documentary quality of much of her tweeting.[16]

But it was the detailing of her emotions—her fear for her safety and for that of her family, especially her little sister, Lamar—that was by far the most powerful and popular element of her output. In one tweet, which was accompanied with a photo of her sister cutely wearing a Santa Claus–type hat, she wrote, "My 6 yrs old sister have witnessed 3 wars! #GazaUnderAttack #GazaUnderFire #PrayForGaza."[17]

The emphasis on the suffering of children was a common theme: "When u need 2 have hundreds of protests just 2 tell th world that BOMBING CHILDREN IS NOT OKAY. That's when u know that HUMANITY DIED #Gaza," she tweeted on July 28, 2014. It was retweeted hundreds of times.[18] Farah was not running a propaganda campaign in the traditional sense. She was a teenage victim of war and tweeting what she saw and heard, what she believed to be true. But it is clear that she repeatedly homed in on topics most likely to sway public opinion—that is to say, topics where the Palestinian narrative war was at its strongest.

The Israeli military and Hamas each kept a tight leash on journalists, whom they had to accredit in the first place. And of course some places were just too dangerous for outside journalists to go. But Farah, as a Gazan stuck in the center of Gaza City, had nowhere to go, and so she remained right in the thick of the action, tweeting endlessly, uncensored and relentless.

Which caused her problems. Many Israelis, Farah claimed, would tweet at her to accuse her of being a "terrorist" or just threaten her: "your GPS is turned off but we will find you anyway," and "if you don't stop we will kill you." She didn't bother replying; she just retweeted the threats so that the world could see what she was being subjected to. Power, she believed, came from her words, not from their threats. And as Israel's military might swept over the tiny Gaza Strip, the greater became the sympathy for Farah and her fellow Gazans. The Palestinian narrative war was in full effect and—internationally, at least—proving a potent force. The IDF was facing a catch-22: the more it won on the physical battlefield, the more it lost on the narrative one. In essence, the more it succeeded at the military dimension of war, the more it failed at the informational one.

Then, Farah says, the pro-Israel tweeters switched tactics and started to report her account to Twitter in an effort to have it taken down. Then the fake Twitter accounts claiming to be her appeared. She wasn't scared, though. For her it was simple: it was war. Gazans were under occupation and would get their land back. Now even she was starting—finally—to understand the narrative conflict in which she was involved, and the effect it could have on the war.

Around two weeks into Protective Edge, Farah was receiving thousands of tweets and direct messages (DMs) every day—so many she couldn't answer them all. Numerous people tweeted their support at her, urging her to continue what she was doing. "Be safe. I pray for you and Palestine," a user named Victoria Barber (@drzendn) tweeted in what was a typical show of solidarity.[19] Many people simply asked questions because they knew so little about Gaza; many people were surprised it had Internet and schools. Many were just shocked that Farah had blue eyes.

Farah's career as a citizen journalist had crescendoed from the first day of the war, but it was July 28 that made her. To this day, Mohamed told me as we sat in Farah's living room, Gazans remember it as the war's worst night. Things had started well enough, comparatively speaking. It was the second day of Eid al-Fitr, the religious holiday that follows the holy month of Ramadan for Muslims. Farah woke up early and immediately checked her Twitter account. By that time she had become so well known that every time she slept or was otherwise away from Twitter for any length of time she would return to it to find a deluge of worried tweets and messages from people around the world fearful for her safety.

Normally, Eid al-Fitr would have been a time of joyous celebration following a month of arduous fasting between sunrise and sunset. Normally, Farah would have bought new clothes for the occasion. But with the war, shopping trips were out of the question. So instead she lounged around the house in her pajamas. By that time, she estimated, the power in Gaza had been cut off for sixteen days, after the Israelis had bombed the main power station. So Gazans got their electricity from personal generators, for just a few hours a day. That day she ate breakfast and stayed in her room, tweeting for hours about the bombs she heard falling all around her. Her day was a cacophony of drones and F-16s.

Just after midnight Farah decided to go to bed. But then the bombs started to fall even more heavily, and she couldn't sleep. She lives opposite Al Shifa hospital, where her father works, and she could hear the shouts and screams of people running from their homes to take refuge there. This wasn't normal. Ambulances, drones, F-16s flying low now—everything around her seemed to be exploding into an indistinguishable blur of anguished, aggressive noise.

Then the flares started. The Israelis used them to light up the area to see their targets more clearly. But they instilled terror in the population—the ferocious explosions that accompanied their burst into flame were accompanied by the perennial fear that they might set homes on fire as they fell to the ground. Farah was now terrified. Lamar was screaming, over and over again, "I don't want to die! I don't want to die!" Farah went out onto the gray stone balcony with its elegant black railings to briefly observe the chaos while her family screamed at her to come back inside. She wanted to record what was happening, but as the night wore on she became more and more scared; she would run out, leave her cell on the balcony to record the scene, and then run back inside until it was time to go out and get the phone again.

Still, she was determined to let the outside world know what was happening and began tweeting again. "They are bombing heavily in my area. This is the worst night in this war. I just want you to know that I might martyr at any moment #Gaza," she tweeted around an hour after midnight; that garnered a sizable 1,362 retweets.[20] She wanted to describe the full details of this terrifying attack, and so she did, updating her followers every few minutes. At 1:07 a.m., for example, she tweeted, "We are sitting in darkness bc th power is off, flares r lightening up th area just like it's midday,we're just hearin bombs,drones,f16s#Gaza." Photos played a vital role. "Flares in the sky allll the time #Gaza #GazaUnderAttack #AJAGAZA #ICC4Israel [International Criminal Court for Israel]" soon followed, along with a photo of a flare bursting into flame.[21] She tweeted everything she could think of and everything she saw: images, sounds, and plaintive cries filled her feed. Her output that night was a powerful and detailed portrait of the besieged and pummeled city of Gaza.

But, once again, it was the description of her own feelings—a narrative of the sheer depth of terror she and her family felt—that, for her audience, far outweighed the mere documentation of the devastation being wrought. "I AM CRYING AND CAN'T STAND BOMBS SOUND! I'M ABOUT TO LOSE SENSE OF HEARING #Gaza #AJAGAZA #GazaUnderAttack #ICC4Israel" is typical of the poignant content she put out that night and was quickly retweeted just under 1,500 times.[22] Farah's tweets had reached across continents. Her feed was explosive. It was a dramatic serialization of firsthand suffering.

Then her mobile's battery began to die, and she asked her father to turn on the generator so she could recharge and keep tweeting, which he did. Despite some initial misgivings because of all the threats she was receiving online, he had come to support her efforts. After yet more bombardment Farah posted a photo of the night sky lit up with Israeli flares beneath her terrified statement: "This is in my area. I can't stop crying. I might die tonight #Gaza #GazaUnder Attack #ICC4Israel #AJAGAZA."[23] It was retweeted 15,547 times. Farah had reached the zenith of her night's narrative.

Farah's output over the course of that night captures Twitter's unique ability as both a visual and written medium that enables its users to react in real time and thereby become the perfect propaganda tool for war, when everything is in chaos and events happen so rapidly that the stream of information is incessant. Twitter may not always be the best medium for receiving a clear and impartial picture of events during a conflict, but it's the perfect way to get your version of events out immediately—something that would prove vital to the Palestinians in their narrative battle against Israel. And Farah was the perfect example of this principle in action. Twitter's qualities had enabled her to use documentary reality to both accompany and bolster her narrative, which had now become a story of immense dramatic power.

The photo coupled with the image Farah painted of herself as a terrified, crying girl who feared it might be her last night on earth was so powerful that the outpouring of sympathy for her was instant and global. Even foreign journalists tweeted their support. "Heartbreaking tweets from 16 yr old," said Róisín O'Hara, whose Twitter bio describes her as a "Media Professional—Broadcast Journalist Dublin based."[24] Meanwhile, others did more than just empathize, even offering to attack the Israelis on her behalf. "#anonymous are going to help you. Somehow. Not sure how. But if genuine. We will," tweeted Mark Bryant, referring to the mysterious hacker group that has launched several cyberattacks against Israel.[25]

Then came the inevitable outpourings of hate for Israel. "The world is behind you @Farah_Gazan. Child murdering genocidal Israel has never been more despised. #FreeGaza," tweeted Will Black (@WillBlackWriter), an "Author, journalist & former clinician," to his 79,400 followers.[26] Farah was reaching people on Twitter with their own huge followings. It was an information cascade.

The narrative war that the Palestinians fought against Israel during Protective Edge had two limbs, both of which featured heavily in Farah's output and the reaction to it. The first was to elicit sympathy for their plight. The second, and perhaps the more important one, was to increase international outrage at Israel's behavior. If this could be raised to sufficient levels, then there was always the possibility it might translate into political action against Jerusalem, whether in the form of a UN resolution or even international sanctions (arguably the preeminent political goal). And so, as Israel rained down bombs on Gaza, millions around the world rained down their wrath on Israel.

Farah continued to tweet. Despite her terror, she was determined to try to keep her younger sister calm, so she took Lamar into her bedroom and told her over and over that they weren't going to die, even though Farah was sure that they were. Eventually they fell asleep, exhausted. Farah woke in the morning to find thousands of messages and tweets from people asking her if she was okay. She assured them she was: "I COULD SURVIVE LAST NIGHT!! I AM ALIVE!! Alhamdulillah [Praise be to God] #Gaza," she tweeted to an anxious world.

Farah's tweets from July 28 and the early hours of July 29 had gone viral, their reach and influence amplified exponentially. The popularity of her story had also become a story in and of itself, and the foreign media duly descended. "Sixteen-year-old Palestinian girl live tweets Gaza missile attacks from her house," screamed the UK's *Daily Mirror* that very same day. The article laid out her most emotional tweets—thus further expanding their reach to millions of the newspaper's readers.[27] "A teenage Palestinian girl has given the world a front row seat to the ongoing Gaza conflict," it claimed. The article went on to detail the civilian loss of life Israel had caused and quoted then UK prime minister David Cameron as saying, "What we're seeing is absolutely heartbreaking in terms of the loss of life, and the pictures that everyone has seen on their television screen are really heart-rending and everyone wants to see this stopped, so an immediate unconditional ceasefire, that is what is required." The article had, in effect, uncritically picked up Farah's narrative and, through use of her tweets, made it its own. Thus had the Palestinian narrative (as opposed to traditional journalistic coverage of the war) now entered the mainstream media.

And it wasn't just in the United Kingdom that Farah was making waves. Over in the United States, NBC News interviewed her soon after she woke up on July 29.[28] On August 1, Al Jazeera America was also on the case. "Sudden Gaza spokesgirl: 'This is my third war . . . but this is the worst one,'" ran the headline.[29] Farah's tweets were again laid out in detail, enabling the article to put a strong emphasis on the suffering the conflict (and by implication Israel) had caused for Gazan children. Articles about Farah appeared across the world, even in generally pro-Israel newspapers like the conservative *Telegraph* in the United Kingdom.[30] Almost all of them included her tweets. She was, in essence, treated as both expert witness and journalist, worthy of presentation without any media filter—crucial to any underdog in a conflict, whose only real chance to compete is at the narrative level. Farah's tweets (and, critically, not merely her photos but her emotive statements) gave her a credibility that she would otherwise have lacked.

This was the most important and highly unusual factor of all. Farah's content upended the traditional structure of the news piece.

While all the articles carried some description of Farah, and some even ran quotes from interviews with her, the majority of articles were based on her tweets and the narrative structured around them. In effect, they treated her Twitter feed like a newswire service; a tweet became comparable to an Associated Press bulletin. In almost all the articles on her it was possible for the online reader to click on featured tweets and be taken directly to Farah's feed. Thus did such articles morph—whether intentionally or not—from traditional articles discussing or analyzing a subject to platforms that inescapably promoted their subject's content. Readers could become one of her followers with just a click on the Follow button of any featured tweet. And they did, by the thousands. According to TwitterCounter.com, on July 23 Farah had 4,934 followers; a little more than two weeks later, on August 11, she had 167,000. Journalists had become, in effect, her PR agents.

Farah's output, like that of so many other thousands of Palestinians tweeting their horrific experiences of the war (she was of course just one node, albeit a highly prominent one, in a much larger network), not only had an effect at the level of media discourse but helped to transform online discourse into action on the ground and in cities across the world. As the *Middle East Eye* noted:

> Even when the power was out, citizen journalists managed to post pictures of dead bodies, destroyed neighbourhoods and injured people to the outside world. Photography has always been a powerful force, but the Gaza conflict was one of the first wars to be photographed mainly by amateurs and social media platforms, allowing those images to spread far and wide at the click of a button, helping the people of Gaza win hearts and minds, and subsequently causing unprecedented outrage against Israel. In demonstrations around the world, such photos were enlarged and carried by demonstrators, demanding that their respective governments take action to halt Israel's onslaught.[31]

The effect that Farah's tweets (and those of the many people like her) and such demonstrations had on Israel's military objectives during the war was almost certainly negligible—and most probably entirely absent. But at the information level of war (which could eventually affect military calculations), they were critical and, as we will see, Israel took them very seriously indeed.[32] Tweets begat retweets, which begat greater audiences, which begat news coverage, which begat demonstrations, which begat yet more news coverage, most of it pro-Gaza. Social media platforms empowered individuals like Farah to become citizen journalists, uncensored by editorial guidelines, institutional policy, or even a need to remain impartial and unbiased. This makes them better able to spread their message and point of view in more direct and visceral ways than ever before. More people took to the streets on their behalf, screamed in solidarity with them online, and damned Israel to hell. While Israel hammered Hamas in Gaza, the pro-Gaza narrative hammered Israel internationally.

Farah had, in her own small way, become a symbol for it all. The information cascade had reached a frenzy. Her tweets, boosted by the Western media, made her personal story go global. She had become that most powerful of things: a brand. And for the Palestinian cause it was the perfect brand: one of childhood suffering. In the great propaganda drama being played out between Israel and Gaza, she was now officially a star.

Farah stands as one example of the apotheosis of *Homo digitalis*. As a young Middle Eastern girl caught in a horrific war, she should have been utterly powerless. Yet when her tweets were networked and amplified, her influence became vast. The question is, why?

Of the many things that are striking about Farah's story, perhaps the most interesting is that she rarely, if ever, took part in explicit political debate. She didn't engage Israelis on Twitter or sloganeer on TV (at least not predominantly). She didn't become popular through political punditry or analysis of the conflict. Rather, she became popular by using social media to tell a story that detailed in depth what she was living through.

But thousands of Gazans tweeted daily about the horrors of the war. Images of dead bodies and destroyed homes filled my Twitter feed daily during those fifty-one days of conflict. But there was only one Farah. Her story was undoubtedly dramatic, but so were the stories of the many other Gazans who tweeted while being pounded from the air and on the ground. Admittedly, she spoke English, which many people in Gaza do not, and this allowed her to reach the non-Arab world. But this ability, though less common, was also not unique to her. Rather, what made Farah unique was Farah. Young, telegenic, deeply vulnerable, fair-skinned, and—perhaps most important of all to a Western audience—blue-eyed, she provided what the most powerful stories need: a dramatic leading lady. A forty-year-old dark-skinned bearded man tweeting an equivalent narrative of suffering would almost certainly never have had the same effect. In a sea of the faceless, Farah was Taylor Swift.

And the public couldn't get enough of this tale of a helpless teenage girl caught up in a war she didn't fully understand, living in perpetual fear of a brutal, violent, and, most of all, possibly imminent death—and all of it serialized in real time. Farah turned her fifty-one-day narrative, by virtue of its regularity, acute tension, and eventual popularity, into something akin to a soap opera: an addictive, dramatic story line—one that Twitter allowed her to play out globally and instantly. And it was a soap opera of the most intense kind, made extraordinarily potent as a tool of information warfare because it was genuinely a matter of life and death.

When I asked her why she thought that she, among so many people tweeting, had become so successful, she answered without pause: "Because I did something different—most of the Palestinians I was following were posting photos of dead people—and I was only sixteen and I wrote in English. And I slept only a few hours a day and I was writing constantly. The videos and photos would get more retweets because the Western media doesn't show this and the Palestinian media just shows the dead people but it doesn't show how those living through the war are affected."

Two months after the war's end, the prestigious American magazine *Foreign Policy* (required reading for much of the diplomatic corps at the US State Department) named Farah as one of its 100 Leading Global Thinkers of 2014, "for cataloguing Operation Protective Edge in 140 characters."[33] Critically, it did not put her in the category of "Agitators" or "Challengers" or "Advocates"; it labeled her a "Chronicler." She was seen not as a resistance figure or activist—even though she was inescapably both—but as a chronicler. That is to say, a storyteller.

It is perhaps unsurprising, then, that even before the *Foreign Policy* list came out, Farah had been likened to one of history's most famous chroniclers, the young Jewish diarist Anne Frank, killed during the Holocaust. In the eyes of many, Farah was the Anne Frank of Gaza.[34] Whether or not the comparison is accurate or just—certainly many Jews and Israelis felt insulted by it, as it implies an equivalence between Israel's actions in Gaza and the Holocaust—the fact is that it took hold. Farah even included it in her Twitter bio for a while after so many people online began making the comparison. "I read some of her book and I felt we were both victims," she told me. "But I was lucky. I survived. She didn't."

In "The Question of Palestine," the literature professor Edward Said makes the point that Palestinian voices never stand for themselves. They're either completely erased or supplemented by other (usually Western) voices, from Western academics studying Palestinian society to European film festivals showing Palestinian films. Historically, both the Israelis and the Palestinian elites have been able to contain ordinary Palestinian voices and, in wartime, control the narrative. The British journalist Jon Snow, who covered Protective Edge from inside Gaza, witnessed firsthand how social media counteracted this trend and empowered ordinary Palestinians. When I asked him what role social media had played in Gaza, he was typically blunt. "It has counterbalanced the power of weaponry with the power of information," he said. "It's certainly changed the dynamic in a big way. And it has given the people that suffer the most a voice."[35] During Protective Edge the people who suffered the most were Palestinians, under siege from Israel's superior military force. This is the democratization of the wartime narrative in action, and it benefited only one side: the Palestinians.

Of course, the democratization of news only goes so far. Farah provided that little bit extra that would prove so vital. Soap operas, public diaries, serializations: all are products designed and packaged for consumers. Farah's soap opera, with her as its star (and her family as the supporting cast), became a hit online, which, crucially, enabled it to be picked up and then packaged by the media into a consumer good delivered into the homes of millions eager for her content. Farah had created the perfect "product," one impossible to ignore. It was this that allowed her to reach the consumer—the most crucial ability for any citizen journalist. And she achieved this through being first embraced by and then ultimately transcending traditional media's most powerful force: the gatekeepers of legacy journalism.

Media scholars Sadaf R. Ali and Shahira Fahmy describe gatekeeping as a "selection process where 'gatekeepers' pick and choose which news articles and/or visual images to run in the media."[36] These gatekeepers—the editors and journalists at legacy news outlets— choose, curate, and filter, selecting the content that best suits their purposes. This has serious consequences for the dissemination (and therefore the potential impact) of citizen journalism. It is because of gatekeepers that the content we see in traditional media "tends to follow organizations' news routines and narratives."[37]

Farah's ability to first seduce the gatekeepers and then, critically, to transcend them is a key aspect of her narrative victory. And for her to achieve this she had to initially provide something special that the gatekeepers would find appealing. At the center of this lies the very idea of what "news" actually is, and how the gatekeepers go beyond merely curating the news and (almost) into creating it. In the words of Matt Sienkiewicz, assistant professor of communication and international studies at Boston College:[38]

> Gatekeepers have for decades crafted ideas of what is newsworthy. For example, privileging people in dramatic situations or privileging attractive or interesting looking people. This system has created norms—things deemed interesting or "newsworthy." So the world has been primed for her [Farah]. She gave the audience what it wanted, but partly what counts as a compelling identity or position is very much steeped in the history of news telling, that is to say the practices of gatekeeping. We have expectations as to the type of story that is interesting, but they don't come out of nowhere, they come out of conventions that the gatekeepers have established.

Farah's narrative—made Technicolor through Twitter—was something the gatekeepers could embrace. And thus did she invert the natural order of traditional media. Only once it was proven that the public liked her did the gatekeepers notice her, which is backward from the general order of things. With Farah, as Sienkiewicz notes, "Twitter was the dog and the news outlets were the tail."[39] Farah was able to use Twitter to become a source of interest to legacy media, but it was only when it picked her up that she became an international star. The monopoly legacy media, once held up as gatekeepers of what is deemed newsworthy, may have receded in importance as citizen journalism has grown, but without the gatekeepers' acceptance, citizen journalism can only get so far. The Telegraph still had to pick up Farah for her to go global. And what's more, she had to be a Palestinian Taylor Swift for them to do so. Gatekeeping practices ensure that, even in wartime, only the messages of a select few will break through, because the "documentary" reality citizen journalists must provide to enter the mainstream still privileges the output of characters who are deemed most appealing to traditional gatekeeping norms.

Not everyone can tweet to the masses—you need a story that speaks to people on an emotional or intellectual level—and it is legacy media that is best positioned to identify and curate these stories. In wartime, when events are at their most dramatic and when the public's desire for news matches legacy media's desire for clicks, the powerful narrative of a figure like Farah can be nearly unstoppable. The media beast needs to be fed, and she provided it with content of the most dramatic kind. In a time of war, Farah is a godsend for legacy media. And because of this, she is also a godsend for the Palestinian narrative war—for the Palestinian cause itself.

A final question remains: can Farah truly be called a citizen journalist, or was she merely a propagandist or activist? This question is key to understanding the role she played in the narrative war because its answer illustrates the severity of the threat facing established hierarchies like the IDF. Farah promulgated a narrative of Palestinian despair and Israeli cruelty that could have come straight from the lips of a Hamas spokesman. But she is a private citizen, a young woman with no stated political agenda. Her narrative was so powerful and credible precisely because she was not a member of Hamas—a designated terrorist organization that readers and viewers would expect to spout propaganda. And this is what makes her so dangerous to Israel. Rather than politicize the Palestinian cause, she *personalized* it, and in so doing helped to increase outrage and anti-Israel sentiment across Europe and the United States.

"Hello, I'm Farah Baker. I live in #Gaza and Hamas is NOT using me as a human shield," she tweeted on July 27, 2014. It was retweeted just under a thousand times, mostly by people in the West.[40] This tweet is particularly instructive when it comes to understanding the difficulty of distinguishing between the propagandist elements of her output and mere reportage.[41] That Farah believed she was not being used as a human shield is credible. She was, she told me, never moved to any military location; she was merely confined to the house she had lived in all her life. Nor did she ever suggest that Hamas militants had used her house as a base from which to target Israelis. The tweet was, from her point of view, most likely truthful. But that Hamas did use human shields and stockpile weaponry in locations like schools is not in doubt. Farah lives just opposite the Al-Shifa hospital, a building that Hamas used for military purposes when it interrogated the journalist Radjaa Abu Dagga there, which he duly reported in the French newspaper *Libération*.[42] Whether she realized it or not, because of her proximity to the hospital, Farah had become a de facto human shield.

Moreover, her tweet was explicitly meant as a direct counter to a major part of Israel's information war against Hamas: namely, the claim that the group hid its militants among the population and deployed human shields as a prominent military tactic.[43] In tweeting what she believed to be a clarification, Farah was implicitly supporting Hamas's story and aiming to discredit Israel's.

Notably, on that same day she tweeted, "Tens of MASSIVE bombs since the early morning. there's no ceasefire #Gaza #AJAGAZA."[44] The implication of the tweet is clear: Israel was violating the cease-fire. But the fact is that Israel had implemented a unilateral twenty-four-hour extension to the cease-fire agreed the day before, an extension that Hamas had rejected. Moreover, Farah told me on several occasions that she was not a supporter of Hamas, yet this claim is contradicted in articles like an *International Business Times* piece from August 11, 2014: "Baker supports Hamas, saying that it defends people. 'People say that Hamas hides behind people but it doesn't—Hamas defends people,' Baker told NBC News. 'I do not want this war to end until we become free, because the blockade is killing us.'"[45] But I have also seen various anti-Hamas statements on Farah's Facebook feed.

It is undeniable that her story had an agenda. The fact she so often employed the hashtag #ICC4Israel (International Criminal Court for Israel), used on Twitter to demand that Israel be referred to the court because of its actions in Gaza, is indicative of that. More than this, she did on occasion directly attack Israel. According to an article on Al Jazeera America's website, "On Twitter, she prays for Hamas rockets to hit their targets in Israel."[46] One of her tweets, depicting Israeli prime minister Benjamin Netanyahu with a Star of David on his forehead and blood dripping from his mouth while he feasts on a dead Palestinian child, clearly plays into long-standing anti-Semitic tropes.[47]

But on balance she can be called a citizen journalist. Journalists are not without agendas or biases; indeed, for columnists those are a requirement. But during Protective Edge she was more than just a journalist; she was an actor. Whether or not she intended it, Farah had enlisted as a soldier in the information war against Israel, and in this realm her power was akin to the most elite special forces unit. Toward the end of our interview I asked Farah if she believed she had played a role in the war. Her answer was unequivocal: "Yes. I don't have the ability to carry a weapon and I would never kill anyone, so my only weapon was to broadcast the truth and to let people know what was happening here. I was more effective than I ever imagined, because of the amount of followers I got and because so many people told me I had changed their minds [about the war] and opened their eyes."

She was right. Farah's story is a triumphant one: she helped strengthen international outrage at Israel's behavior and highlighted Palestinian suffering. But it is important to remember that she was just one among thousands of voices who, tweeting similar output (though lacking the personal qualities that made her go viral), provided the verification needed for her narrative. She was one in an army of citizen soldiers seeking to counter the Israeli narrative of the war, and she performed heroically. Over the course of fifty-one days Farah became more than just a helpless, frightened sixteen-year-old girl; she became a soldier. And her weapon was not a machine gun or a rocket launcher but a smartphone.

Farah's story is more than just the tale of a young girl able to tweet her individual story of suffering; it is more than just a case of *Homo digitalis* gone viral. What Farah's story illustrates on a wider scale is the new challenges individual, networked citizens bring to asymmetric warfare. Farah represents newly enhanced power for smaller, less militarily powerful nations. Her "military" efficacy, her wartime value, lay in her ability to affect war by using social media to amplify a narrative of Palestinian suffering that mobilized international outpourings of rage—often at the political level—against Israel. In so doing she was able to affect the discourse surrounding the conflict. In contemporary conflict, where the boundaries between war and politics have become so blurred that the two are almost indistinguishable, the importance of this cannot be overestimated. Indeed, it threatens the very idea that wars between state and non-state actors are asymmetric. In a world where the battlefield alone is no longer the only important arena of conflict, the power embodied in Farah illustrates an almost entirely new development in warfare: states can win the physical battle on the ground but lose the war.

This is because when war becomes "armed politics" and the Clausewitzian paradigm becomes less relevant, one side can win militarily but lose politically. This idea lies at the center of Farah's power. She cannot shoot, but she can tweet, and the latter is now arguably more important in an asymmetric conflict that the Palestinians can never hope to win militarily. It is this newfound ability to spread narratives via tweets and posts that allows hyperempowered, networked individuals such as Farah to affect the battlefield. Up against Farah's narrative and the role it played in galvanizing anti-Israel opinion worldwide, Israel faced a decision that only decades ago would have been unthinkable: win the military war or the political one?

2

THE SOLDIER:
THE STATE FLOUNDERS,
AND *HOMO DIGITALIS* EMERGES

I n an obdurately dull building in downtown Tel Aviv, Peter Lerner is talking about dead babies. "There is nothing that a government spokesman can tweet or post to combat the image of a dead baby," says Lerner, the head of the Foreign and Social Media branch of the IDF's Spokesperson's Unit, as I sit across from him in his small office. He speaks from experience. During 2014's Operation Protective Edge, both social and legacy media were filled with photos of dead children that had been killed in the cross fire between Israel and Hamas.[1] It brought international condemnation down on Israel and was a major weapon in Hamas's information war against Jerusalem. "And rightly so," he continues. "I can't compete with that, and I don't want to compete with that."[2]

War is central to the creation and evolution of the state as we know it. It was the need to raise money for military campaigns that brought into being the centralized bureaucracies, taxation systems, and eventually professional armies that constitute it. As Michael Howard notes in *War in European History*, "The growing capacity of European governments to control, or at least to tap, the wealth of the community, and from it to create mechanisms—bureaucracies, fiscal systems, armed forces—which enabled them yet further to extend *their control over the community*, is one of the central developments in the historical era which, opening in the latter part of the seventeenth century, has continued to our own time."[3] As Howard further notes, it was only comparatively recently that soldiers went from fighting for honor, feudal obligation, or money to becoming servants of the state who fought for the national interest and had career prospects in the military. The emergence of this shift in conjunction with the emergence of the nation-state is no coincidence—the relationship between the two is symbiotic. As Howard concludes: "It was only with the development of these full-time professionals that it became possible to draw any clear distinction between the 'military' and the 'civilian' elements in society."[4]

Thus was the twentieth-century nation-state eventually born, with its standing armies that centralized the practice of violence and kept it largely as a preserve of the government alongside that other cornerstone of warfare, control of information. But, as Parag Khanna has argued, "much as modern nation-states seem to have lost their monopoly on armed forces"—through not just the rise of terrorism but also the growing presence of private security contractors, which, for example, played a huge role in Iraq after the initial invasion and war—"so too has evaporated their dominance of information flows and narratives."[5] At the crux of this shift is social media, which—especially in wartime, when the state traditionally makes the greatest effort to control the flow of information—has allowed for the emergence of alternative voices like Farah's that can now resonate globally, with a power and reach once reserved for large media institutions or governments. This poses a severe threat to militaries in wartime, most of which are still geared toward twentieth-century conflict. The discourse surrounding war has always been important, and information warfare is as old as physical warfare—during World War II, for example, both the Axis and the Allies launched huge propaganda campaigns directed at the other side. But social media has transformed information war from physical war's attendant to, at the least, its equal.

Any military battle between Israel and Hamas will only ever yield one winner. But during Protective Edge Israel was no longer merely fighting Hamas, the political and military organization. It was fighting Farah and the thousands like her. It was fighting not just armed militants, whose capacity to inflict harm was limited. It was fighting *Homo digitalis*, whose capacity to create narratives was unbridled. And the capacity of these narratives to inflict harm on a global political level is potentially limitless. The IDF had only one choice: to respond with a narrative of its own, to fight fire with fire, and to do so within the same communicative forum: social media. And it was Peter Lerner's responsibility to win this battle.

Lerner's uniform is immaculate: a light blue shirt with studded dark epaulets atop each shoulder complements perfectly pressed dark trousers. LIEUTENANT COLONEL PETER LERNER is splayed across a badge along with the Israeli flag on his right breast. He is courteous and well-disposed, every inch the military media man.

"If you are absent on the social media space," Lerner explains, "you cede that space to the enemy. You have to be there to lead the conversation, especially in wartime. If you're silent on social media, you're not putting anything in your enemy's way that prevents their message from gaining steam; if you're silent on social media, you're not getting your own message across; and if you're silent on social media, you're not giving your supporters ammunition to use. My job is to prevent that from happening."

The IDF's Spokesperson's Unit sits at the end of a quiet, tree-lined street, atypical of Tel Aviv's lively center, not far from the bars and cafés of the city's trendy Rothschild Boulevard, where Israeli youth go to eat, drink, dance, and hang out and be seen. I approach the building's entrance and am buzzed into the reception area, where I am greeted by a familiar sight: young Israelis, in their teens and early twenties, mostly female, who look just like those in the crowds I saw partying away on Rothschild only the night before, but today they are in army uniform. Two or three have M16 assault rifles slung across their back. Automatic weapons and combat fatigues by day, crop tops and high heels by night—only in Israel.

The receptionist calls upstairs to announce my arrival, and a young soldier named Talya Sugarman, who is Lerner's assistant, comes down to fetch me. She beams and greets me in American-accented English. As she leads me up two flights of stairs, I notice that the unit is filled with women. Walking the corridors, working at computer terminals, bunched together in conversation, they are everywhere. All of them are young. A meeting ends and four women exit a room to my right. By my (highly unscientific) reckoning they outnumber the men at least four to one. I sit in a chair in the hallway and wait for Lerner.

He greets me and we enter his office. He works behind an L-shaped desk. Three keyboards and two screens sit to his right. On top of one of the screens is a tiny Israeli flag. Next to it a pile of Lego-like bricks with letters on them are stacked on top of one another: BE WELL AND DO GOOD DEEDS, they spell out. The first question I ask him is why the unit has so many more women than men. "They're just generally much better than guys; they're much more creative—it's unbelievable," he says with a smile.[6]

The IDF takes its Spokesperson's Unit (Dover Tzahal in Hebrew) very seriously indeed. A brigadier general commands it, while a lieutenant colonel heads up the foreign press branch—a single department within it—under which the social media department works.[7] Lerner took up this post in April 2013 when the social media department was already running smoothly. But things had not always been this way. It had begun as nothing more than three people with a MacBook and a desk in a corner office somewhere in the building commanded by an American Israeli soldier called Aliza Landes. Landes created what the unit's social media department has become, and she was three things that characterize it today: young, female, and adept with social media. She was *Homo digitalis* within a state bureaucracy—something that would prove to be her greatest frustration and its greatest fortune. It was the first Gaza war, Operation Cast Lead, which ran from December 27, 2008, to January 18, 2009, that started everything. But it was the Gaza flotilla raid on May 31, 2010, that made the IDF truly understand the immense power of social media.

In the words of Tomer Simon, a researcher who studies the IDF's social media use, "This [incident] was the first alarm bell regarding the effect social media could have on global perceptions of legitimacy."[8] The *Mavi Marmara* was a civilian ship loaded with humanitarian aid, one of six ships in the "Gaza Freedom Flotilla" that were attempting to break the sea blockade of Gaza. Israeli naval commandos intercepted and boarded the ship, and in the ensuing fight they killed nine of those onboard. The protesters instantly relayed their version of events to the world via social media—a tale of innocent civilians murdered in cold blood for trying to bring food and blankets to Palestinians. It was almost twelve hours before the IDF was able to provide conclusive evidence to back up its side of the story—namely, footage from the boat revealing that the protesters had themselves been violent, swarming and beating soldiers, trying to kidnap one

Aliza Landes (far left), Avital Leibovich, Mark Regev, and David Baker (both from the Prime Minister's Office) standing outside the press building in Jerusalem at the height of Operation Cast Lead.

and throwing another overboard. But it was too late. The narrative of Israeli aggression had been fixed in the world's eyes.

The incident's mishandling caused uproar in Israel—crucially among the Israeli media, which meant that people needed to be held to account. The Spokesperson's Unit received huge criticism for failing to release the footage before the flotilla's narrative of Israeli aggression had taken hold and run unchecked for twelve hours. Defense minister Ehud Barak had called a press conference to try to set the matter straight, and multiple officials had also gone on record, but it didn't matter—without irrefutable proof to the contrary, the journalists weren't going to change their minds. Why, the Israeli media demanded, had it taken so long to provide the necessary evidence? As Landes told me, the real impact the flotilla incident had on the Israeli military was after the fact. There was a major report on it, which focused on what the unit could have done differently. One of its major conclusions was that the army needed to be able to respond faster to occurrences of this nature.

For the first time in its history the IDF had come up against the full force of social media's powers to broadcast a message and then amplify it at unprecedented speeds. Critically, the Israelis had jammed communications from the boat soon after their soldiers boarded, but the protesters managed to broadcast enough footage and reports for the international media to seize upon. That the IDF had blocked the boat's communications only made matters worse, as journalists began to report on rumors and would not accept any corrections—at least not from the Spokesperson's Unit. One video from the boat was cut off in mid-broadcast, which of course only made the watching world even more hysterical. The flotilla narrative thus went viral before the Israelis even had a chance to adequately respond. Eschewing social media for conventional messaging processes, they failed to produce the proof needed to bolster their counternarrative fast enough. They were fighting an analog narrative war in a digital age, and they lost.

Soon after the *Mavi Marmara* incident, the IDF Spokesperson's Unit established a visual operations room. It was sorely needed. On the day of the *Mavi Marmara* incident, for example, the top story on the IDF website (which looked like it had been uploaded in 1997 and not been touched since) was about a solider winning the Ms. Israel title; it was especially unfortunate that she was in the navy.

It was remarkable that the unit had any online presence at all, and what little existed was due almost entirely to the efforts of Aliza Landes. Specifically, it was due to her initiative—and to her willingness to battle both the IDF's entrenched bureaucracy and its aversion to change.[9] Landes was working on the unit's North American desk when the first Gaza War, Operation Cast Lead, began in December 2008. Here, the Israeli government made an egregious mistake. It banned international journalists from entering Gaza through Erez Crossing in Israel (which it shut down), telling them to instead enter through Egypt. Journalists who couldn't make it into Egypt were reduced to standing on an Israeli hill overlooking Gaza (which they christened the "Hill of Shame"), and as a result, Landes believes, they unofficially boycotted IDF materials. "We're not doing another story on rockets going into Israel" was the message she kept receiving.

Landes spoke to journalists constantly, and she was repeatedly told that the decision to bar them from entering Gaza was absurd. Off the record, journalists told her that there was a lot of anger over the ban. No matter how many times Landes would patiently point out that Israel did not control the only access into Gaza and they could go in through Egypt, it made no difference. Sometimes the answer would be that the Egyptian border was closed that day, so why couldn't they just enter through Israel?

What made it so frustrating was that Landes believed that the IDF was not using all the tools at its disposal to rebut the Palestinian narrative of the IDF targeting civilians and civilian infrastructure, which went into overdrive as soon as the fighting started. The Spokesperson's Unit had reams of material that she felt showed the exact opposite: video footage from Israeli planes about to target a position and then aborting when civilians came into view, or another video showing secondary and tertiary explosions after a mosque was struck, proving that it was being used for weapons storage. But none of this was showing up in the media's coverage of the war—at great cost to the IDF.

Six months earlier, Landes had written a position paper with another soldier, Aviv Sharon, about the importance of "new media"—blogs and other online platforms—to the changing media landscape. They decided to submit it to a military journal, *Maarachot*. The paper was highly critical of the IDF's lack of engagement with these new information tools, and it was never published. But the concepts of blogs and new media were now at least in the IDF's ecosystem. "It was blogs that set the stage for the social media," Sharon told me.[10] Landes agrees: "In many ways bloggers were the natural avenue for the army to become open to social media," she said, "because they fell under the rubric of 'new media' in its mind, but bloggers, although they were not traditional journalists, were closer to the idea of a journalist [for the top brass] than the amorphous notion of trying to reach the general public through platforms like Facebook, which were regarded as being just for kids."

The staunch bureaucratic resistance to the ideas in the position paper had been a great source of frustration for Landes. She was twenty-five, she understood social media, and she understood just how dismal was the army's online presence. The opening days of Operation Cast Lead were now revealing just how damaging that was. As Israeli planes began their air campaign over Gaza, Landes's mind went back to an apocryphal tale that had become the stuff of legend among her fellow soldiers: that the Spokesperson's Unit had only moved over to email announcements in 2005 (from faxes, no less) when a soldier pointed out that even the Taliban now used them. Landes was never able to verify the truth of the story, but in her eyes it encapsulated just how badly the unit dealt with new information technology.

The IDF, she believed, cared about the message but had little concern for the medium. In Landes's early days the IDF had just about managed to deal with the introduction of the twenty-four-hour news cycle, but it still had virtually no Web presence. "When you see legacy media broadcasting breaking news now, they incorporate tweets from citizens and journalists on the ground," she told me. "It used to be that journalists would have to call up the unit and get briefed by a solider, who more often than not would need fifteen minutes to come back to them with the relevant information. In this day and age, fifteen minutes and it's over." In the months leading up to Operation Cast Lead, Landes's goal was simple: to bring the unit into the twenty-first century.

But with every step she took, she ran into opposition. Memos went unanswered, suggestions remained stuck in the chain of command. The wheels of bureaucracy ground so achingly slowly, and the concerns of her superiors were so distant, that it just seemed hopeless. Now, in the opening days of the war, the cost of this was plain to see. She was getting a lot of requests from independent bloggers for video clips of Israeli media with subtitles (which the international media weren't interested in, as they were boycotting IDF output). Typically it would be American bloggers who lived in Israel, who would see on Israeli news some IDF footage that clearly delivered the IDF point of view. They would check to see if they could find it on any English-language medium, and when they couldn't, they'd ask her for an English-subtitled version to publish on their blogs.

Landes knew that with the unofficial foreign media boycott in place, blogs were a more important resource than ever for getting the message across, so she began sending out clips herself. These sorts of activities were well beyond her remit. During peacetime she was a noncommissioned officer on the North American desk, dealing with media requests from mainstream North American media outlets. But now that war had broken out, the foreign media branch was in emergency mode, and she essentially took on the role of personal assistant to the head of the Spokesperson's Unit foreign press branch, Avital Leibovich, scheduling her twenty-odd daily interviews and accompanying her everywhere.

But Landes was determined to try to bypass mainstream journalism in order to fight back in the narrative war that the IDF was losing so badly in the war's opening days. On December 28, for example, just one day into the operation, she sent an email to her father, the historian Richard Landes, who also ran a prominent blog on Middle East affairs, with the subject line "Video link of Hamas shooting from civilian area." The email contained a simple injunction: "Link it." Landes's father was extremely active in the blogosphere, and because she was in the unit, he would tell bloggers to contact her. In a country as small as Israel, personal contacts are critical, and that meant young soldiers like Landes could take some initiative. "No institution can plan for any eventuality," she told me, "but the IDF has enough flexibility, and proximity between officers and lower ranks, that improvement can come from the bottom up."

Landes did everything she could think of—even cold-contacting bloggers to see if they might be interested in disseminating IDF materials. On December 29, for example, she wrote to a group of bloggers she calculated might be favorable to her overtures. The email carried the subject line "IDF Footage and Information," and her message was direct as could be:

Hello,

XXXXXX gave me all your contact information, some of you I have met, some I have not. My name is Aliza Landes, and I currently serve in the IDF Spokesperson's Unit on the North American Desk.

Given current events unfolding in Gaza, I am trying to reach out more to bloggers (like yourselves). Should you be interested, please just respond to this email and I will start sending you information, photographs, footage, etc. from our IDF email account. I realize that bloggers like links rather than files, and I will be working on having a place to post in the next couple of days.

In the meantime, here is a link to some footage that we released several hours ago, which was posted to YouTube by solomonia. It is IAF [Israeli Air Force] footage of one of our planes destroying tunnels, a launch site and a weapons depot: http://www.youtube.com /watch?v=yxKwfXVK5IA&eurl=http://www.solomonia.com/blog/

Additionally, should you have questions or specific information requests, feel free to contact me and I will try to get you comprehensive answers within a reasonable timeframe (no promises though, the army works a bit slowly). You can also call the office.[11]

It was a remarkable state of affairs. With the mainstream media alienated, and with no official social media platform to use, Landes was, in effect, now acting as a mini Spokesperson's Unit within the unit, focusing on the new media she wanted so desperately to reach.

Sending out such large video files regularly was simply not practical, however. Landes couldn't email files of such large size to too many people, and certainly not all at once. She decided to call her direct commander at the time, the head of the North American desk, who was out in the field handling journalists, to ask him for permission to set up a YouTube channel. He told her to ask Leibovich, and, moreover, to make the URL end in /nadesk (North American desk), so if it worked, the desk would get the credit.[12] This was, Landes told me, typical of the "old army mentality," one that inhibited swift innovation. "On the one hand, he [her direct commander] couldn't take the risk of giving me approval, and felt he had to pass it up the chain of command to Avital [Leibovich]; simultaneously he wanted to make sure that if the project was successful his desk would receive credit for the initiative. Had we not been in emergency mode, Avital would also have gone for approvals at a higher level. Wartime provided a small window of opportunity with the temporary removal of our bureaucratic shackles."

Landes duly asked Leibovich's permission to put the relevant materials online. As the IDF's spokesperson to all international media, Leibovich was the face of the Israeli military to around eight hundred foreign reporters, most of whom were stationed in Jerusalem, and she was doing as many as fifteen TV interviews a day, plus radio and print. She had a thousand others things to be thinking about. Knowing this, Landes phrased her request casually one day: "Do you mind if I just upload these videos to YouTube?" That way she could frame the question as being merely about a means of distribution, a way to disseminate information to bloggers and journalists.

Leibovich remembers the moment well. "One of my female soldiers, Aliza, came over and suggested we open a YouTube channel, and the other soldiers urged me to do it as well," she told me over coffee in Tel Aviv.[13] "The rationale behind it was that we needed to engage with the many aerial attacks [the IDF was carrying out]. The planes had footage of those attacks and through those videos we were able to show that Hamas was using civilians as human shields." Leibovich assessed all the factors and decided it was worth it.

The impetus for the YouTube channel had come from Landes, but as the unit's head, it was down to Leibovich to give it the green light. Without her decision to let Landes proceed, the IDF never would have made the move to social media during Operation Cast Lead. As Leibovich put it: "The social media revolution [within the IDF] began with the opening of the YouTube level. We understood that we were on to something revolutionary—the ability [to disseminate information] without any editor's touch or a middleman."

The emergence of the IDF's social media presence rested on a serendipitous convergence of three factors. The first was Landes, with her youth, dynamism, and sheer drive.[14] The second was Leibovich's willingness to listen to her subordinates. As the *Atlantic* reported, "Leibovich also takes pains to credit the youth of her staff . . . she sees this as an asset, and a source of guidance. 'One of the advantages that I have maybe compared to others,' she explained, 'is the fact that I have 18-year-olds. . . . When [we recruit] the soldiers they're 18 . . . the age of someone who was almost born into social networks.'"[15]

The third and most important factor was the retreat of bureaucracy during wartime. As Leibovich told me, "We were working around the clock until two, three a.m. The US news programs generally started at midnight Israeli time, so there was no time for bureaucracy—I was given a lot of independence in my work."

As Sharon so aptly put it:

It is vital to remember that it was not the high brass but the enlisted soldiers, who made no more than 1,000 shekels per month, that were the driving force behind the change to social media. Eventually the higher brass followed and they needed a particular set of conditions to do it—and these conditions were essentially the flexibility that allowed Avital to say yes to Aliza because the bureaucratic norms had retreated during a time of war.

Leibovich's willingness to listen would only increase as Landes pushed harder and harder to expand the IDF's online presence in the months and years to come. But all that was still a long way off. For the moment, Landes now had the okay from her boss, so together with two other soldiers, Noam Nadler and Lee Hiromoto, Landes set up a system where during their regular shifts they would also work unofficially on their pet project, tagging videos, subtitling them, and then finally uploading them to YouTube.

Then came the greatest gift to the entire enterprise—and probably the biggest stroke of luck in the history of the IDF's Spokesperson's Unit's social media arm: YouTube removed their videos. Landes couldn't be sure, but she guessed that Palestinian supporters had reported the channel for some reason (if large numbers of people red-flag a video, YouTube will automatically remove it and then undertake a long review process, which usually takes months). She had read YouTube's guidelines carefully and knew there was nothing in the videos' content that violated the site's terms and conditions. She didn't know anyone at YouTube, so instead she called up her friend Noah Pollak, who wrote for the US magazine *Commentary*, and he wrote an article about what happened entitled "What YouTube Doesn't Want You to See."[16] It was a hit.

The operation had started on December 27; the YouTube channel had opened three days into the war, on the twenty-ninth, and was taken down the following day, with the *Commentary* piece appearing a few hours later. Twenty-four hours after that, the story went viral. It was now five days into Operation Cast Lead, and the IDF was just about to send in ground troops; the international press was filled with article after article about Israel pounding Gaza from the sky. Then along came the *Commentary* piece, using some of the footage that Landes and her team had so painstakingly put together. It was different—it was both a technology story and a war story—and both CNN and the BBC, as well as many other outlets, covered it. Ironically, *Commentary* wasn't using the footage for its original purpose, to get the IDF narrative out, but because the piece was about censorship, the material made it past the unofficial foreign media boycott and found the global audience Landes was aiming for.

As a result of the coverage, the Israeli government finally began to take an interest in the project. The Foreign Ministry even called to ask if the unit needed them to intervene to help get the channel back up. But twenty-four hours after the article appeared, YouTube reinstated all of the videos. Leibovich recalls the satisfaction that her superiors, notably Brigadier General Avi Benayahu, the overall head of the Spokesperson's Unit, now felt at the IDF's first foray into the world of social media. "Not only did he understand what the unit was trying to achieve," she told me, "but when he attended the daily war meeting headed by the IDF's chief of staff he proudly mentioned the fact that the YouTube channel had received so many views." The new IDF social media presence was now being promoted within the army itself.

Landes saw her chance and set up a Twitter account. She was instructed to tweet out IDF material verbatim in endless numbered tweets, which was ridiculous. But she knew she had a limited window of time to do something different before the normal bureaucracy kicked back in. She also created a blog to get around the IDF's appalling website, paying for the domain name on her own credit card.[17] Everything she did was designed to create "facts on the ground." "Social media," she told me, "was seen as something for kids, not as a means of disseminating information. My job was basically to nag my superiors endlessly." She likened her work to that of the original pioneers in modern Israel during the British Mandate period, who knew that the British administrators in Palestine had to adhere to an old Ottoman law specifying that if a structure went up overnight it couldn't be taken down. Just as the settlers would roll out new Jewish outposts overnight that the British couldn't legally tear down, so Landes took advantage of the chaos of wartime to open as many social media platforms as she possibly could. She would have to fight for two years to set up an IDF Facebook page. "Had I not opened a Twitter account and a blog during Cast Lead, I would most likely have been forced to fight for two years to establish those as well," she told me.

It was a basic social media presence, but it was there, and the unit now had something to build on, a means of getting content out in a timely fashion. The *Commentary* article plus the resulting publicity meant that by the end of Operation Cast Lead the YouTube channel had received several million views. And the IDF got kudos, especially from the Israeli media, for being the first military to put out constantly updated footage. And as Landes knew, recognition from the Israeli media was what mattered most.

It is both odd and instructive that it took a soldier instead of a diplomat to greatly expand Israel's public diplomacy and propaganda machine. According to Tomer Simon, this happened for two reasons: economics and demographics. "For the government to have thirty 19- or 20-year-old soldiers working on these initiatives costs them nothing," he told me. "It's far better than hiring thirty PR professionals. The young have zero cost to the army. And the young are the most in tune with social media. It's the way they communicate." This is why it took an ordinary soldier like Landes to start what was a bottom-up initiative. As Simon put it: "The young have already done their basic training on social media before they join the army."[18]

By the summer of 2009 the IDF bureaucracy had returned with a vengeance. Senior officials realized that shutting down the platforms

Landes had created would involve a loss of face, and that social media could no longer be ignored, but they weren't about to go all in, either. After a meeting, the head of the Spokesperson's Unit, Brigadier General Avi Benayahu, agreed to set up an official new media operation, headed by Landes. And the extent of this new operation? It would, Benayahu said in Hebrew, consist merely of "Aliza, delet ve shelet"— Aliza, a door, and a sign.

Operation Cast Lead (and, of course, the *Mavi Marmara* flotilla incident in 2010) laid bare the inability of any military, no matter how powerful, to adequately fight a twenty-first-century war without social media. Of course, on the battlefield Israel would only ever be the winner. But the fact that Israel was fighting an asymmetric conflict in which it had the overwhelmingly superior firepower only served to strengthen a Palestinian narrative of war that centered on victimhood. As the war and the flotilla incident showed, without social media's ability to broadcast messages—and therefore promulgate its own narrative—almost instantly, and then have those messages amplified across the world, the IDF could not compete, even with just several hundred passengers on a few ships. An entire unit within the military, arguably the most powerful institution in Israel, was utterly outmatched by *Homo digitalis*. And it was only with the emergence of the same phenomenon within its own ranks that things in the IDF eventually began to change.

But change it did. The IDF has come a long way since then. The current unit head, Lerner, now has a staff of around fifty, half of whom are involved with social media. The team's defining characteristics are its youth (the average age is around twenty-one or twenty-two) and its language capabilities, the most important of which are English, French, Spanish, and of course Arabic. For Lerner, the goal is to bridge the distance, both psychological and physical, between the IDF and its global audience. The unit's structure is simple: the social media desk runs the English, French, and Spanish desks, and the

Arabic desk runs the Arab social media side of things (because of its uniqueness), but the desks work closely together.

When Landes started the IDF YouTube channel, it was essentially just to distribute materials to Israeli-based and foreign journalists. But over time it became clear to senior staff (with relentless prodding from below) that traditional lines of communication were changing and the IDF would have to adjust its methods of disseminating information. Traditional media remains the most important information conduit, but eight years down the line, social media is so deeply integrated into its young soldiers' lives—as well as among global opinion makers—that it cannot help but play a crucial role in the creation and dissemination of information. Lerner's philosophy is that the unit exists, above all else, as a source of information on the Israeli military.

Today, social and traditional media work in tandem for the military, and as regards the foreign media, it's all under Lerner's purview. Every time the unit puts together a package for traditional media, it needs to be supported on social media to help facilitate its distribution to both traditional journalists and "consumers" alike. Social media's amplification effects are vital to this process. "It's a challenge," admits Lerner, "because maintaining platforms is a constant feeding-the-beast scenario—you always have to have information going up, you always have to be looking for stories because we need continuous content. We have journalists constantly calling us up telling us they'd like to do a story on something they saw on our website.

"Everything today breaks on social media," he continues. "It's [a question of] being on top of things so you can raise a red flag and say, 'This is something foreign journalists will be looking into,' or, on the other hand, suggesting they do a story on a particular issue." The shifting media space has fundamentally changed the nature of reporting. And the unit has more tools than ever to influence an audience or journalist. This has its pluses and minuses. But everything returns to its social media arm, which is built to create interest around the IDF so that more people will like its Facebook page or Twitter account, even—or especially—when nothing is going on.

That way, it can build a following for which it will become the go-to resource for information when crises do happen. And when it comes to Israel and Hamas, as Farah Baker would learn so well, crises are never far away: in 2012, the two sides fought a brief, one-week war known as Operation Pillar of Defense.

In 2014, almost five years after the IDF's first foray into social media, Israel would go to war with Hamas again, this time for fifty-one days—the longest war in the country's history. In this conflict, however, it would be better equipped than at any other time in its history to battle not just on the military front but on the narrative plain as well. Operation Protective Edge would see the fully evolved *Homo digitalis* face off against a state army finally able to harness the full power of social media. Operation Cast Lead was Israel's last twentieth-century war; Operation Protective Edge would be its first full-fledged twenty-first-century one. And it would highlight the degree to which war will never be the same again.

3

THE OFFICER:
MILITIA DIGITALIS TAKES TO THE
"BATTLEFIELD"

The extent of the power that *Homo digitalis* now wields is clear from the fact that, as Operation Cast Lead showed, to wage twenty-first-century war effectively the IDF cannot function without its Spokesperson Unit's social media arm, any more than it can function without tanks. As we have seen, social media has flattened the space between institutions and individuals. Asymmetric conflict is not so asymmetric anymore. The IDF would have to meet Hamas not just on the battlefield but in cyberspace. War would have to be fought at the narrative as well as the physical level.

For Farah and the many Gazans like her, this was self-evident. Hopelessly outgunned, their side could never hope to win militarily. The narrative war was the only one in which they could compete, and the best they could do was to show the world the damage being done to them and hope the world would act. Israel, however, wanted the world *not* to act—to leave Israel be while it completed its military objectives. At one time this would have been relatively easy to achieve. Now, however, the strength of the Palestinian narrative war (which

Farah had demonstrated) was such that, despite its huge military advantage, Israel needed to win, or at least compete, at the narrative level, too. This is because it is from the narrative level—or more correctly the discursive level, which, as will be shown, the narrative dimension of war is almost solely designed to affect—that Israel derives the legitimacy it needs to use force. Lose this legitimacy and the IDF, and by extension Israel, faces a threat of grave proportions.

With the kidnapping of the three Israeli teenagers and Hamas's subsequent barrage of rockets, Peter Lerner's unit was already on high alert during those early days of July 2014. Everyone in Israel knew serious conflict was now a possibility, and they were proved right when, on July 8, the unit officially tweeted that Israel was at war with Hamas. "The IDF has Commenced Operation Protective Edge to Defend Israel's Civilians Against Hamas Terrorism" was the tagline, accompanied by an image of an air force pilot, his black visor pulled down, white oxygen mask emerging from underneath it, as he saluted patriotically into the camera.[1]

Lerner knew a social media war strategy would have to be mapped out, and fast. But that wasn't a problem. The unit was always prepared for the eventuality of conflict. Preprepared materials all lay in the virtual drawer: packages on senior Hamas figures, on Hamas tactics involving the use of human shields and nonmilitary infrastructure, and on IDF military techniques designed to avoid human casualties. All were ready to be broadcast across various social media platforms. Key information about the IDF in wartime was ready for use when the time was right. The graphic designers, video team, editors, and writers were all on standby. As ever, the plan was twofold: deal with the Israeli audience first, and then address the international one.

Responsibility for the international audience would fall to Daniel Rubenstein. A corporal in the reserves, his job description on the social media desk (he never had an official title) was "managing editor

Lieutenant Colonel Peter Lerner, head of the IDF's Spokesperson's Unit Foreign and Social Media branch 2013–2017. (Courtesy of the IDF Spokesperson's Unit)

of the IDF social media platforms in English." He would oversee all the English-language social media content the Spokesperson's Unit produced.

On July 7, 2014, the day before the start of the war, the situation in Gaza escalated perilously. Hamas fired eighty rockets, and overnight into July 8, the IDF declared the start of Operation Protective Edge. In the morning, just before he got on the bus to go to his civilian job at the Jerusalem Center for Public Affairs, Rubenstein checked with Sacha Dratwa, an officer at the Spokesperson's Unit (who reported directly to Lerner), to see if he was needed for any IDF work. He was told that he wasn't, and so he got on the bus.

Later on that day, however, Dratwa called. His tone was now more serious, which to Rubenstein indicated that the IDF might be at the beginning of a significant operation. Dratwa told Rubenstein that it was now time to come in. Having already arrived in Jerusalem, Rubenstein wasn't available immediately, but he told Dratwa that he would check in later—and he did, after work, when he gave Dratwa feedback about what direction he thought things should take. Soon after he arrived at the unit, an officer from the reservist liaison office came to him with papers, and Rubenstein signed on the dotted line: he was on active duty once more. He would report to Dratwa, who in turn would report to Lerner. He didn't even have a proper uniform until a friend found one for him. On July 9, he sent an email to his coworkers at the Jerusalem Center for Public Affairs. "I'm officially in *miluim*," read the subject line—a confirmation that he had been officially called up for reservist duty. The email itself was terse: "I'm working out of the IDF Spokesperson's office in Tel Aviv until further notice."

And that was the case for the next fifty-one days.

With his team now in place, Lerner had to implement his war strategy. The content creation process was already well established and consisted of five steps. First, evaluate the newsworthiness of an event. Did it merit the creation of content? Was it relevant at this time? Second, liaise with the creative team in the office to brainstorm possible ideas. Third, speak to the Spokesperson's Unit's representatives embedded within army divisions in the field, to make sure the unit had the most up-to-date information. Fourth, create the content, which involved taking the chosen message or news event and turning it into something attractive to different audiences. Graphics, tweets, images, and videos all went through editing processes and translation into multiple languages (the unit preferred original-language narration rather than subtitles). The fifth and final step was to send the content to Lerner for approval, to fit into an editorial plan for the next twenty-four hours.

Rubenstein was in charge of multiple platforms, but the main ones as far as he was concerned were Facebook, Twitter, and YouTube.

He was also responsible for the IDF blog, which was vital for promulgating the IDF's message in greater depth, though it was subject to cyberattacks and went down repeatedly. But above all he wanted to be in charge of Twitter because that was where the important people "lived." He had a list of influential journalists reporting from Gaza, and updated it depending on who entered and left. He wanted to be aware at all times of what journalists on the ground were saying, and he shared the list with his colleagues in the unit as well as with the foreign press branch, which used it to monitor the journalists they communicated with regularly.

Facebook always carried the potential for content to go viral, but since people had to like the IDF page in order to follow it, Rubenstein felt that he was primarily dealing with people who were already fans. Twitter allowed him to reach a wider audience that included not only Israel supporters but many of the "undecideds" who might be brought around to the Israeli point of view, so it came first. He also knew that Twitter had the most impact in wartime. Sometimes he

Daniel Rubenstein, during his service in Operation Protective Edge.

would look at a directive from the military or receive from another department an SMS in stilted English, in which case he'd put it into accessible language and tweet it. He understood that what starts on Twitter doesn't stay on Twitter. Often he'd check, say, the *New York Times* website and realize that most of its information on Israeli military activity was coming from the Spokesperson's Unit. Just as had happened with Farah, sometimes the article would actually embed the tweet on the page.

Rubenstein was on the day shift, which ran roughly from 9:00 a.m. to 9:00 p.m., though often he'd stay until two in the morning. The unit worked in two 12-hour shifts, with a day team and a night team, ensuring that enough content was always pre-produced to feed the twenty-four-hour news cycle and that if something came in from the field they could get it ready for distribution. As day shift leader, Rubenstein needed to work in sync with the night shift leader so that both knew what to expect for the following twelve hours. Each morning he would come into the office and ask his team how things stood, what had been done overnight, if there was video or script that needed looking at. Then he checked what journalists were saying on Twitter. Some of the day was invariably spent waiting: reports would come in from the field about Iron Dome interceptions or rocket sirens in Tel Aviv, for example, and the team would have to react on the fly to get the news out. But the biggest challenge was to keep things newsworthy over the fifty-one-day duration of the war. By the end of the operation the night team didn't know what daylight looked like.

There were, Rubenstein knew, two schools of thought on social media within Israel. The first was that the international mainstream media hated Israel, so Israeli institutions should use social media to circumvent it and speak directly to a global audience. But Lerner and Rubenstein both had proof that when the unit sent out clear and compelling content, legacy media picked it up and used it. Accordingly, they subscribed to the other school of thought, which held that the unit should focus on shaping the way the media told its stories about the war, not just tweet stuff at people. Rubenstein's goal, in line with Lerner's strategy, was to try to reach journalists and influential opinion-makers, especially in the United States.

Past experience had taught Lerner that there were several conversational themes, or narratives, that the unit had to participate in, and try to lead if at all possible, if they wanted to have any hope of swaying public opinion. So over those fifty-one days, Lerner instructed his team that there were three main messages that had to be pushed at all cost. First was the rocket threat that Israeli civilians were being subjected to; second was the tunnel threat, with Hamas burrowing deep underground and across the border into Israel, again to threaten civilian lives; third, and most important, was Hamas's use of human shields as a military tactic. And the key to getting these narratives out on social media in the most forceful way was visuals.

Regarding the first narrative, the IDF was adamant that the war had begun with Hamas repeatedly firing rockets at towns and villages in southern Israel. Recently it had expanded its rocket fire to Tel Aviv, Jerusalem, and even Haifa, in the north of the country. The team needed to quickly get the message out that Hamas was the aggressor—and central to that was highlighting the threat that rockets posed to Israeli civilians.

In order to push the narrative of civilians under rocket fire, the team had to hammer home the message that almost the whole country was now under threat from Hamas's rockets. Rubenstein knew from his experience during the 2012 Pillar of Defense conflict that on social media you needed to give people a "hit"—they needed to be able to see everything you wanted to show them almost instantly. The unit's audience was people scrolling through their smartphones, and only something eye-catching would make them stop and take notice. A tweet saying "Click on the link to see everything the IDF is doing" would be largely ignored. He needed everything to fit into 140 characters or a short Facebook post. And graphics, he believed, were much easier for the brain to absorb.

Rubenstein sat down and worked with a graphic designer to make things happen. He would prepare each sentence, making sure, for example, to start it with a verb (to ensure that each sentence in the tweet paralleled the others, which made them much more memorable). Then he'd create the title and subtitle, and after that he'd see what a graphic design wizard could do with the copy. And more often than not, together they would create a work of art—a poster.

The team made multiple videos illustrating just how little time Israeli civilians had in order to run for cover in different areas. One memorable video opened with the text "The world's fastest man can run 200 meters in 20 seconds." The video then switched to the Olympic 200 meters final, set to the sound of an air raid siren. Viewers saw images of Usain Bolt sprinting to victory interspersed with footage of terrified Israeli civilians running toward bomb shelters. At the race's end a simple message came up: "During a rocket attack, Israelis living near Gaza only have 15 seconds to reach a bomb shelter."[2]

Such creativity was prioritized at all times. Statistics and facts had to be packaged into something that people would retweet, post, or click on; content had to be something that appealed to the audience, or perhaps more accurately, the "consumer." Lerner was adamant that the unit wouldn't resort to clickbait; in wartime it would have to step up, not down. He knew that the most successful things on social media are either funny or have good music. But in this case humor was out of the question, and music could support the message but never *be* the message. The unit's content had to speak for itself: to be powerful yet simple enough to reach an audience and make it gasp. As I sat in his office that April afternoon he scrolled through the timeline on the IDF Facebook page, stopping when he got to Protective Edge. "You see, everything is graphics and videos," he told me. "Everything is visual. And as you see, each video reached about three million people."

The second narrative the unit put out that summer was the threat that the Hamas tunnels posed to Israel. It highlighted how

Hamas was diverting to its tunnel construction internationally donated funds that could have been used for humanitarian purposes. One infographic that was eventually produced carried the heading "The Price of Hamas' Tunnels." Underneath that it read, "1 Hamas tunnel = 350 truckloads of building supplies. With those materials Hamas could have built 86 homes, 7 mosques, 6 schools, 19 medical clinics. Each tunnel costs $3 million. So far the IDF has found 30 tunnels. That's $90 million that Hamas could have invested in the welfare of its people."[3] The graphic was clear, it was easy to understand, and it could fit into a single tweet. Perfect.

It also focused on the threat the tunnels posed to Israeli citizens. Again a graphic was used to give color to the content: "Hamas uses its vast tunnel network in Gaza for infiltrating Israel; firing rockets; smuggling; storing weapons; command centers." Each point was illustrated (for example, a masked militant with an RPG on his shoulder was drawn popping out of a tunnel opening), with a map of an underground tunnel for further emphasis.[4]

The final narrative—and it was unquestionably the most prominent of the three—was Hamas's use of human shields. Given that social media had enabled images of almost every Gazan civilian death—especially of children—to be broadcast in real time and in the most visceral way, it was crucial that the IDF put out a strong counternarrative. Israel's killing of civilians (which the IDF argued was accidental) was the most strident line of attack against it throughout the war, and pressure came not just from the Twittersphere and people like Farah but from journalists, NGOs, and even the UN and government officials.

Part of the problem was the sheer density of Gaza; air strikes could not help but inflict collateral damage. The people simply had nowhere to run. But the main problem, as far as the IDF was concerned, was Hamas's use of human shields, whereby the group surrounded military targets with innocent civilians in an attempt to prevent Israeli attacks. Evidence of this practice would ideally come first from independent journalists (thus supplying what the unit called third-party verification—verification from non-IDF or non-pro-Israel sources), which the unit would then seize upon and tweet and post.[5] But Lerner's unit couldn't rely solely on others. It had to get this counternarrative out proactively. Again its approach centered on images and graphics, often using Hamas's own video footage against it. "Hamas spokesperson Sami Abu Zuhri advocates using civilians as a human shield: Hamas Official Channel, Al Aqsa TV" ran the headline to one video, in which Abu Zuhri praised Gazans for being "willing to sacrifice themselves against Israeli warplanes . . . and we, Hamas, call on our people to adopt this practice."[6]

Here, the Spokesperson's Unit's proximity to the war on the ground—its field coordination—was vital. Not only did the unit have members embedded with regiments in the Southern Command in Gaza who would relay relevant material, but it also had a strong working relationship with IDF intelligence, including one branch that dealt only with open-source information: its soldiers listened to Hamas radio and watched Hamas TV, and put their findings into reports that often went nowhere. But a number of years earlier someone from the Spokesperson's Unit had asked the branch to pass across anything useful that they could upload onto social media. Now it had a wealth of satellite imagery, Hamas handbooks, and maps discovered in Gaza, in addition to recordings of Hamas broadcasts telling their people to ignore IDF warnings to evacuate.

Another video opened with footage of Hamas rockets being fired, accompanied by dramatic music and an accompanying voiceover: "Hamas uses civilian areas in order to protect its terrorists and infrastructure in Gaza. Concealed rocket launchers, weapons storage facilities, and command centers are located in civilian neighborhoods. Some of them are even located inside of houses," the voiceover said to footage of the purported weapons. The video went on to illustrate, with the use of graphics, original Hamas texts urging civilians to remain in areas the IDF had told them to evacuate.[7]

The key was to give perspective. Lerner and all those working under him understood that both the media and the general public are human-interest-focused: they would always focus on the individual affected by the conflict (which is why, for example, Farah's narrative became such a hit) and not necessarily the reason *why* she or he was suffering. If, say, the IDF fired on the courtyard of a mosque, the key was not to talk about the mosque courtyard but to show the rocket launcher inside it. From there you could, for example, draw lines emanating from it to show the civilian buildings in its immediate vicinity, whether those were houses or schools or UN facilities.

Lerner understood that social media, Twitter especially, is one thing above all else: effect without cause. At all times the IDF had to work to lead social media users to the cause, or at least to the context. For example, the IDF was endlessly accused of targeting houses, which in fact it did. Rubenstein worked with lawyers as well as designers to produce a poster that conceded the IDF's targeting of houses while explaining why it did so. He came up with the slogan "When is a house a home? And when does it become a legitimate military target?" It was catchy, he thought. The graphic designer then created a infographic to go with the text, showing a house with a normal bedroom next to an operations room, and then a living room alongside a weapons storage room.[8] A Facebook post used the same image but made the message even clearer with additional text: "When houses are used for military purposes, they may become legitimate military targets under international law," it read.[9]

As far as Lerner was concerned, there was a constant need to show and voice the realities of today's battlefield, preeminent among which is the challenge of asymmetric warfare. From Iraq to Syria to Gaza, government militaries are forced to fight adversaries who place themselves within the civilian arena. Moreover, Lerner told me, regular militaries have laws to which they must they adhere, while "terrorist organizations use those laws to enable them to attack you." It was this concept that underpinned much of the IDF's output during Protective Edge.

Lerner says that the IDF's humanitarian response to Hamas's use of human shields actually put its own soldiers at risk. One of the first things he learned as a cadet in his officer-training course, he told me, was the importance of the element of surprise. And as far as he was concerned, during Protective Edge the IDF ceded that advantage: it dropped leaflets, sent texts, and made radio announcements to tell people on what day and at what hour they should vacate the area.[10] In essence, the IDF set itself up for ambush because Hamas knew when and where they would be arriving. He ensured that the unit's content reflected this fact as well by tweeting and posting visuals of leaflets being dropped from the sky and graphics of warning text messages sent to Gazans translated into English, French, Spanish, and Arabic.[11]

This was coupled with footage of the IDF's own attempts to avoid harming civilians. "The IDF Works to Prevent Civilian Casualties in Gaza" was the headline of a video produced on July 9, 2014, just a day after the war had begun.[12] Footage from an IDF plane's camera scoured the area as the pilot discussed potential targets with his controller back at base over the crackling radio. "The entire area is full of civilians," he said. "There are a lot of children. Right now there are about 15 people within 10–15 meters range from the structure," came the reply. "I see, moving on to another target," came the pilot's response.[13] Whether the pilot was motivated by genuine concern for human life or the possibility of another PR disaster, the Spokesperson's Unit used it to full effect. While Hamas worked to disseminate images of destruction and dead children, the IDF worked equally hard to put them all in context.

Rubenstein had used social media during 2012's Operation Pillar of Defense, in which the IDF had declared war in a tweet (the first army in history to begin a war this way).[14] In fact, Rubenstein had been the one to do it. "There was never a plan to declare war on Twitter," he told me. "The general in charge of the unit gave a briefing to Israeli military reporters. My officer [Dratwa's deputy at the time] listened to the call and brought me her notes and said, 'Here, you can tweet this.' I made the official statement on Twitter before reporters had a chance to publish what they had just been briefed on."

But that had been an eight-day conflict. Protective Edge would last almost two months. And it was a period of twenty-four hours between July 28 and 29 that made Rubenstein truly understand the power of social media to achieve his unit's objectives. This was both in terms of projecting its own narrative (in this case a counternarrative against misinformation) and in influencing and shaping press coverage of the war, which in turn shaped the conversation about the war at the most important level: the political one.

The late afternoon of July 28 seemed like an ordinary day. Rubenstein was sitting at his desk monitoring Twitter. As usual, he was focused on what journalists inside Gaza were tweeting. Scrolling through his feed, he came to an abrupt stop when he saw a tweet from NBC News's Ayman Mohyeldin: "Israeli airstrike has hit the outpatient clinic at Shifa Hospital. Local Palestinian media is reporting several children among dead #gaza."[15] This wasn't good. Nor did Rubenstein think it was likely to be true. But when he saw the tweet he immediately understood the unit was facing a crisis: a well-known reporter with almost 150,000 Twitter followers was publicly accusing Israel of targeting Gaza's most important hospital. There had been rumors that Hamas had been operating out of the hospital's basement; there was also a constant media presence there throughout the war. The situation was, as ever, confused. Nonetheless, he instantly alerted his superior, Dratwa, and asked him to make some phone calls to establish what had happened. It was out of his hands for the moment. But he had raised a red flag. It was 5:24 p.m.

Nine minutes later Mohyeldin tweeted again. "TWO (2) STRIKES in #Gaza in last 45 minutes: 1) at the outpatient clinic at Shifa Hospital AND 2) at Al Shati Refugee camp."[16] Israel was not mentioned in the tweet, but it was clear to Rubenstein, given that the tweet was a follow-on from Mohyeldin's previous one, that Mohyeldin was now accusing Israel of striking not one but two significant civilian targets in the space of forty-five minutes. The problem had just gotten worse. It was 5:33 p.m.

And Mohyeldin was just hitting his stride: "Israeli strike on Shati Camp: victims rushed to shifa in civilian cars, on motorbikes, in ambulances. more than 30 casualties brought so far."[17] There was no doubt that the unit now had a grave crisis on its hands. This was the worst position for Rubenstein to be in, because he didn't want to be responding to a crisis; he wanted to be leading the conversation. Most of all, he wanted the IDF to achieve its goals without needlessly harming civilians. It was a battlefield problem that threatened to become a political problem. He was tired, he was stressed; he was on Excedrin. It was 5:47 p.m.

But Dratwa's phone calls had had an effect. The Spokesperson's Unit got answers from the relevant military units, and it was able to send the IDF's initial response to all reporters on its list via SMS. Mohyeldin copied and then tweeted their statement: "IDF: Palestinians killed in Gaza at Shati refugee and strike at Shifa hospital were result of Hamas rockets that landed in Gaza."[18] It was 6:46 p.m., an hour and twenty minutes after the first tweet had gone out. The response time might be seen as slow, but in reality Rubenstein was happy: for wartime, it was a job well done. The unit needed time to find out what had happened—you obviously couldn't just call up the pilot and ask if he'd dropped a bomb on a hospital. But eventually the information came in: vital details, most important being that the IDF was definitely not launching anything in this area, and also that the attack had happened at around 4:58 p.m. Armed with the relevant information, the IDF had now made an official response.

The reasons for sending out an SMS first, instead of tweeting an official response or posting it on Facebook, both of which would have reached a larger audience, were simple: first, it ensured that reporters wouldn't miss it, and second, it enabled them to tweet it first—it was in essence a form of third-party amplification. Many times Ruben-stein would compose an SMS and see reporters tweet it verbatim after a phrase such as "IDF sources say . . . "—exactly as Mohyeldin had done. Soon after the SMS was sent, Rubenstein did tweet an official IDF response: "A short while ago, terrorists in Gaza fired rockets at Israel. 1 of them hit Al-Shifa Hospital in Gaza. The other hit Al-Shati refugee camp."[19] Now the whole world would see the IDF response. The counternarrative had publicly begun. It was 6:56 p.m.

The response was almost immediate. Mohyeldin had already written an article on the strike, which was published shortly after his tweets. NBC was now forced to update and alter the story by in-cluding a short paragraph detailing the IDF's denial of his initial re-ports.[20] More than that, the *Daily Dot* picked up the story and ran its own article, headlined "NBC News Deletes Journalist's Claim of an Israeli Airstrike on Gaza." The article reported that "after an attack on the Al-Shati refugee camp in northern Gaza that reportedly left at least 10 people dead, an NBC News report initially assigned blame to the Israeli Defense Force. But shortly after the article was posted on its website, the words 'Israeli strike' were removed."[21] The updated ar-ticle had become its own story, which only bolstered the IDF's claims. The counternarrative had escaped social media and had made its way into the mainstream.

Later in the evening the unit received information from ra-dar able to track rocket fire, which enabled Rubenstein to produce a simple graphic that drew four red lines from the origin points of the rockets—all of which were in Gaza. One clearly went to the Shifa hos-pital and one to the Shati refugee camp. Of the other two rockets, one went into the sea and the other was intercepted by Israel's Iron Dome anti-missile system. Of course, skeptics or Hamas could say it was fab-ricated, but the unit now had evidence to back up its counternarrative. It was a strong and clear claim that could not be misunderstood, and Rubenstein tweeted the image and accompanying text accordingly: "Gaza terrorists fired rockets today, hoping to kill Israelis. Instead, they hit a hospital & a refugee camp in Gaza."[22] It was 2:28 a.m.

It had been roughly nine hours between Mohyeldin's original tweet and the IDF's evidence-based public rebuttal. Rubenstein was especially pleased when, scrolling through his Twitter feed that night, he came across a tweet from an Italian journalist, Gabriele Barbati, a neutral source—a relatively obscure guy with comparatively few followers: "Out of #Gaza far from #Hamas retaliation: misfired rocket killed children yday in Shati. Witness: militants rushed and cleared debris."[23] Rubenstein was excited: here was a journalist confirming the official line that it wasn't the IDF but Hamas that was responsible. He immediately retweeted it, making Barbati's tweet visible to everyone who followed the IDF's Twitter account. For the military it was the holy grail of information warfare: third-party verification. For Barbati it meant a day of being a mini-celebrity. It was July 29, 5:46 p.m.

Rubenstein assumed that someone in the Israeli Ministry of Foreign Affairs monitored the unit's work and used it where relevant, but the process was generally slow. In this instance, however, he was fortunate: one of his good friends was the assistant to the Israeli ambassador to the United States, Ron Dermer. As soon as Rubenstein published the infographic, he sent it to his friend via WhatsApp. As it happened, Dermer was scheduled to go on MSNBC in the United States that evening, and his assistant called the show several hours in advance to tell them that the ambassador would use the infographic to clear up the confusion. Dermer went live on MSNBC carrying a printed-out version of Rubenstein's graphic, which he held up; it was also put up on the screen for a number of seconds, showing millions of Americans the IDF's official response.[24] Here again, the strength of visuals was clear to see. It gave the TV network something to put on the screen beside photos of dead children. The images could never be equal, but it was the best Israel could do, and it had been done by a couple of guys in a small office in Tel Aviv less than twenty-four hours earlier.

To Rubenstein it was the perfect example of how social media could shape the war. In this instance, however, the unit went one step further than the battle of competing narratives: it provided a senior official, who had the ability to say things the Spokesperson's Unit could not, with the tools to take the counternarrative to the political level and make Israel's case in diplomatic forums. Dermer could now take the IDF's evidence to the US president or secretary of state; it could even be presented at the UN if need be. To Rubenstein, the power of social war in wartime had never been clearer.

The IDF's performance on social media during those fifty-one days clearly shows that it had learned from the failures of Operation Cast Lead. But the question remains: who won the 2014 war? Ten years ago, that question would have been easy to answer. At first glance, the answer still seems easy. By the end of Operation Protective Edge, the UN estimated, at least 2,104 Palestinians had died, including 1,462 civilians, of whom 495 were children and 253 were women. Israel claimed that around 1,000 of the total killed were Hamas fighters. Meanwhile, 66 Israeli army personnel died in combat, as well as 6 Israeli civilians and a Thai national who were killed by rockets and mortars fired from Gaza.[25] The IDF had also destroyed at least 34 known tunnels and forced Hamas to expend almost two-thirds of its 10,000-strong rocket arsenal.[26] Jerusalem also refused to lift the siege on Gaza. In purely operational terms, it was an unquestionable success for Israel.

The IDF had also learned other lessons from Operation Cast Lead, during which the government had banned journalists from entering Gaza, telling them to use the crossing from Egypt instead. This lack of transparency was one of the reasons for the UN's December 2008 Goldstone Report, which assessed the IDF's actions in Gaza and initially accused it of war crimes. Crucially, the report also addressed Israel's media policy, as the South African former judge who chaired the inquiry, Richard Goldstone, declared that "the media ban, coupled with the comments made by the Director of the Government's Press Office have raised concerns, aired in the media, that the ban was aimed at controlling the narrative of the conflict."[27] In 2014, by contrast, journalists were allowed into Gaza, which, together with the IDF's far greater transparency—amply displayed on social media—ensured that there would be no UN cease-fire resolution, as there had been with Cast Lead. And, crucially, there was no Goldstone Report. The army's adept use of social media had enabled Israel to influence the political conversation by bypassing traditional media. The IDF had become the first state military in history to fully harness the power of *Homo digitalis* within its own ranks during wartime. *Militia digitalis* had been born.

The story of the Spokesperson's Unit during Operation Protective Edge thus makes clear how profoundly the IDF came to understand the importance of the narrative dimension of the war, which through social media technologies had been empowered to degrees previously unthinkable. The extent to which the IDF worked to get its counternarrative into the social media space attests unequivocally to this fact. In this sense, the story of the IDF's evolution from a social media–averse institution to one that came to embrace new information technology as a key component of its military doctrine is the story of the IDF's evolution from a twentieth-century army into a twenty-first-century one. It is a military that understands that the physical battlefield is no longer the single most important arena of conflict. For a country that has fought so regularly over the last seventy years and that regards the concept of military might as key to its existence, this change in mind-set has been drastic. Social media has unleashed forces that the IDF has had no choice but to embrace.

Implicit within this is the understanding that, especially in what is arguably the most politicized conflict of the last half century, politics can no longer be separated from war. Israel is a small nation that needs the backing of more powerful ones, notably the United States. Just how critical this is to its thinking was seen in the furor in Israel that greeted Washington's December 2016 decision to abstain (and therefore refrain from using its veto) on a UN Security

Council Resolution condemning the expansion of Israeli settlements in the West Bank. In 2014, accordingly, the IDF's efforts were almost as much a political exercise as a military one. Its military operations had several critical goals—for example, reducing (if not eliminating) the tunnel threat—but key among them was the need to support information operations.

Wars are now fought in multiple dimensions. First is the physical dimension: soldiers fire on soldiers, tanks fire on tanks, and planes drop bombs from the air. The second is the information or narrative dimension, which is the battle the IDF Spokesperson's Unit engaged in against Farah and her fellow Palestinian tweeters. But there is a third dimension in which wars are fought, especially when they involve small countries such as Israel. This is what the narrative war is designed to affect above all else, and it is best described as the discursive dimension. Put simply, the narrative war frames the raw data emanating from war zones. It is *designed* to get that raw data (even if it's dishonest data) out of the battlefield and into the information sphere. The watching world then processes the data to make up its mind about a conflict. From this, it then decides where its sympathies lie, which translates to either support or opposition at both the popular level and, more important, the political level. Every tweet or post of a graphic that the unit shared in its narrative war was designed to affect the war at this discursive level—to ensure that political support for Israel did not falter or wane.

The public rarely views unprocessed information, especially in wartime. Rather, it views that information through whatever filters its members trust. Whether it's the BBC and other legacy media or newer forms of media, all information goes through a filtering process. An Israeli strike or Hamas terror attack is the raw material around which a narrative is shaped; framing is put around the facts and figures. The purpose of this narrative is almost always to have an emotional impact on the reader or viewer and, in so doing, affect the war at the discursive level. As Matt Sienkiewicz, assistant professor of communication and international studies at Boston College, points out: "The average citizen is not a data chewer; logic really plays little part, so she sorts out her views with her emotions."[28]

What allows smaller nations to fight wars *is* the discursive level. Israel is a small nation, and while it is a world leader in producing weaponry (and indeed exporting it), it receives significant military aid from the United States. Most smaller states buy weapons from larger ones, which means that if they wish to keep receiving this weaponry, they have to justify their use of it. For a country like Israel, it is crucial that the United States continue to stand behind it: it must win the discursive war in Washington, DC. Lose that, and there might be less aid forthcoming; enemies might start to get ideas.

The success of Israel's global discursive war is mixed. It loses the war in the Arab world as well as parts of South America and Europe. But, crucially, it wins it in Washington, as well as among the governments of the major European powers: France, Germany, and the United Kingdom. The battle is not even, of course. Government opinion on Israel matters less in Athens and Bogota than it does in Washington or London. And with Washington behind it, Israel has mostly been able to act as it wishes in wartime.[29]

According to Sienkiewicz, before the rise of citizen journalism, the discursive pattern in the United States was predictable. First the government and media would foreground the threat to Israel, then they would focus on the necessity of Israel's decision to go to war; eventually there would be some analysis of the destruction, then a discussion of the cease-fire. In previous wars, such as the 1990 US-led Gulf War or Israel's 1973 Yom Kippur War, an American woman watching TV in her home in West Virginia might see images of a destroyed hospital, accidentally hit by coalition or Israeli forces, but it would take an act of imaginative extrapolation to imagine the dead and mangled bodies of children and babies that undoubtedly lay inside.

Israel's wartime narrative is based on a specific set of principles: the right to self-defense, the right to respond, the right to defend

Jewish life at virtually any cost. And that narrative is a powerful one, especially to a German or American audience. As long as things remain at this discursive level, the Israeli government can trust that the Palestinian narrative of victimization will be overpowered. Certainly the Palestinian discourse has great appeal across the world, but it is not sufficient to make the major powers stop Israel from fighting when it feels it needs to. And—crucially—the woman watching TV in West Virginia continues to support Israel.

But with the advent of social media, it may no longer be sufficient to fight a discursive war—at both the political and popular levels—based on principles. For the woman in West Virginia, an Israeli war is now no longer solely about Israel's right to defend itself; it is about the images of dead children that she sees every time she logs onto Facebook or Twitter, images that resonate on a personal level in a way that political argument cannot. And it's not just the images: it's their volume. In Protective Edge, for example, the extent of the destruction being wrought on Gaza caused global outcry. It's the visuals that were new, and which—as the IDF Spokesperson's Unit knows—really matter.

"IDF's forces are broadly critiqued but still supported by top US officials," says Sienkiewicz. "Some outliers criticize, but in Washington the IDF is still seen as credible and justified in its actions. The fact that this plausibly might change shows the impact of citizen journalism. This idea previously seemed impossible to me. It no longer does."

Lacking the capability to inflict serious harm on Israel's soldiers, Hamas cannot force Israel to stop fighting wars in Gaza. If it could inflict sufficient Israeli casualties to make fighting Hamas unacceptable to the Israeli public, it would. But it cannot, so it does not. Instead of inflicting intolerable losses on the enemy, it allows its citizens to broadcast their own losses on social media, in order to make those losses intolerable to a global audience. The outrage must be international. This is what Gabi Siboni, former chief of staff of the Golani Brigade, one of the IDF's most highly decorated infantry units, describes as the goal of Hamas's use of the "victim doctrine," which aims to damage Israel's status in the international arena by drawing out the operation as much as possible to maximize Israeli-inflicted injury to Gaza's civilian population.[30] And once more, the key is to get out a narrative. As Hamas spokesman Ihab al-Ghussain said during Protective Edge: "It's not just about taking pictures of dead people. . . . We're now telling [the story of] this family, and how they were eating breakfast when they were killed."[31]

Social media has given Hamas the tools with which to do this job more effectively than at any previous point in the history of warfare. Two years on from Protective Edge, Israel still wins the discursive battle where it matters. But social media may well mean the IDF is given far less leeway in its next Gaza operation. Israel maintains its right to self-defense and has shown time and again that it will strike when it feels threatened, even in the face of US condemnation.[32] But the media landscape that surrounds war and shapes its discursive battles has changed irretrievably. In any war, Israel has goals it needs to fulfill, and it has shown that it will fulfill them. Beyond that, it's a question of how much the world will tolerate—in a media environment more antithetical to established institutions like the IDF than at any other time in modern history.

In a seminal 1978 article entitled "The News Net," sociologist Gaye Tuchman set out to explore how news was created and how it was consumed.[33] In so doing she advanced the idea of the "news net," which she defined as the "pattern of staff deployment used by news organizations," which "imposes order on social reality." She observed that the general public has a sense of the news as being whatever happens in life, when in reality it is merely what happens within the areas that journalists are assigned to cover and, within those areas, only events that are deemed big enough to not slip through the net.

The news net is the principle that has governed news for over a century, and at its heart lies the process of centralization. As Tuchman explains:

In the 1830s, when the modern American newspaper was invented, increased competition for advertising attained by building circulation led newspapers to develop centralized sources of information. These were comparable to umbilical cords, connecting the newsroom to its sources of sustenance. . . . Faced with intense competition . . . ten men, representing the six most important New York newspapers, sat around a table in the office of the *Sun* one day early in May, 1848. . . . For their own mutual advantage, they founded the first cooperative news service, the Associated Press.[34]

The goal was to get out as much information as possible for the minimum investment. Together, these wire services eventually became a worldwide net "capturing occurrences in their mesh." But it was always a selective net, loose and filled with holes. The Associated Press and United Press International, for example, kept "day books" listing what would be happening in the city that day, ostensibly to inform the media about events they might wish to cover. PR firms would strive to ensure their clients' events made it into the book. The *New Yorker* magazine "noted a high correlation between events listed in the UPI New York Day Book and local New York media coverage."[35] Essentially: if it wasn't in the book, it wasn't worth covering—it wasn't a "strip of life" that would make it into the public domain.

The result is that "the news net not only excludes some occurrences from consideration . . . but also orders priorities by which sort of employee or service produced an item, whether reporter or stringer, staff or wire-service reporter. . . . The editors make news together."[36] The explosion of citizen journalism drastically threatens this model of news gathering and dissemination. Where the basis of legacy media is centralization, the basis of citizen journalism is decentralization. Where legacy media is designed to capture the big fish, citizen journalism captures the innumerable small fish. This is where the greatest challenge to the IDF came during the war. Previously, Lerner could have relied on the news net's blind spots; now that everyone and every place is a potential source of news, he no longer can.

Social media has greatly expanded the news net. The mistake is to believe that it has been expanded infinitely. There are still blind spots. For example, Twitter cannot see North Korea or great swaths of Africa, places where a lack of technological advancement or other factors mean the population cannot access it. And while journalism has become increasingly decentralized, there are still centralized clusters from which news emanates. Just as Einstein's gravitational field dips at the point of the planets, journalism still has various centers of gravity. London and New York, the BBC and the *New York Times*, are always going to remain major nodes or hubs within the net. Social media has introduced new nodes (the Twitter trending list or Facebook's "What's Trending" box, to name just two), but when you click on the relevant link, more often than not it sends you back to legacy media.

Nonetheless, if something happens anywhere across most of the world, it can be filmed or photographed by someone with a smartphone. The New York police killing of Eric Garner in 2014, for example, was caught on a smartphone, which transformed the story from a "man dies in police custody" headline (most likely buried on the inside pages of the *New York Times*) into the onscreen capturing of someone's life slipping away, and it became a national scandal. As Sienkiewicz says: "Social media has not yet transformed the news process, but you cannot undersell its importance to Eric Garner's story"—or to Farah's.[37]

Farah's story caught on because the news net caught it. But, crucially, it could not have done so in isolation. It could never have happened if she had been the only Gazan tweeting, even though her story took such a hold that she became, in essence, an international face for Palestinian suffering. Social media enabled Farah to go from voiceless to voiced, nationally and then globally. But she was in many ways an accidental hero, one of an army of tweeters. Those thousands of faceless Palestinians who tweeted constantly but remained essentially anonymous gave credence to her narrative; they provided corroborating facts and helped to create the information cascade that so challenged the IDF.

The importance of Farah, and the army of Gazan tweeters and Facebookers behind her, cannot be underestimated, because wartime is traditionally when the news net is at its weakest. To have a successful news business during wartime, legacy media needs a constant flow of up-to-date information. In previous wars, media outlets were forced to set up their news gathering in ways that were acceptable to war's gatekeepers, whether state militaries or groups like Hamas. Limitations, from restrictions on the number of journalists allowed into a war zone to controlling access to certain sites and even the distribution of journalistic credentials, were all ways in which gaping holes could be left in the net. Farah and her army have simultaneously tightened the news net and expanded it. In the words of Sienkiewicz: "The news net has become like a really nicely knit blanket that your grandma made. It's not impervious like a canvas blanket—smartphones and Internet access are not ubiquitous—but not much gets through now."[38]

As well as empowering the individual, citizen journalism has simultaneously disempowered, to a certain degree, institutions like the IDF. Once the power of the gatekeepers is weakened, the narrative of a war becomes more unpredictable. As Sienkiewicz points out, the Israeli government can, to a degree, predict how the *New York Times* is likely to cover an incident, and it can plan accordingly. When the gatekeepers are safely in place, Israel has some idea of how the world will come to understand its actions, because it can look to the past and see how legacy media covered similar incidents previously. The unit also knows the important journalists and the types of stories they will likely write. Legacy media offers a predictable set of norms for consumption that the Israelis could bank on. But now that social media has empowered Farah to the point where she can get her largely unfiltered narrative out, the raw material that can influence world opinion becomes harder to predict. No longer can the Spokesperson's Unit or the Israeli Ministry of Foreign Affairs rely on the inbuilt blind spots that the legacy media has carried with it for over a century. And for a small country like Israel, the potential ramifications of this are grave indeed.

As the news net has expanded to capture almost every detail, the biggest challenge the IDF faces in any war with the Palestinians—the question of proportionality—has been brought into sharper focus than ever before. The issue of proportionality is so dangerous because it provides the catalyst for another challenge the unit has to deal with: emotion. The IDF Spokesperson's Unit is geared, above all, toward dealing with facts—to give context to destruction, to combat images of suffering with images of causation. It has to fight sentiment with logic, which is an almost impossible task. As Tomer Simon points out, during Protective Edge the IDF used social media extremely well, ensuring that its message was heard. But a fundamental problem remained: the gulf between the message and the visuals coming out of Gaza. The IDF could reveal that Hamas was firing from hospitals and using its citizens as human shields, but the world also knew that Israel had Iron Dome, which protected its civilians from Hamas's rocket attacks. And so the question naturally arose: if the threat to Israeli civilians was almost nonexistent, why the need to flatten Gaza?

As Lerner told me: "Because of our technology, people don't necessarily acknowledge the fact that there is a rocket threat, which is a big problem. I would say that the threat needs to be made clearer." Proportionality, he told me, would always be Israel's Achilles' heel, because no professional or legal standard exists that delineates what is proportionate and what is not. Indeed, he continued, "Even if you accept some of the Palestinian figures, then you have about 2,200 killed—and about half of those from our analysis are terrorists, so that is a ratio of 1:1. The ratios of NATO forces in Afghanistan and Iraq were anything from between 1:4 to 1:10. We have been criticized by military professionals for setting the bar too high."

Nonetheless, if the IDF feels all other avenues have been exhausted and that its civilians are living under an unacceptable level of threat, international public opinion won't stop it from taking military action. As far as Lerner is concerned, the IDF is first and foremost answerable to the civilians of Israel; above all, it has to secure their existence. But, equally, he accepted that when it came back to the issue of proportionality in Operation Protective Edge, the media zoomed in on the Palestinians, because legacy media privileges human interest stories and Gazans' use of social media enabled them to provide such stories in abundance. Conversely, because the Iron Dome system was so successful, there were comparatively few Israeli victims. But the IDF was not going to stop using its missile defense so that it could compete by posting images of its own dead. It all came back, once more, to trying to give context to the situation: to explain why Gazans were dying.

The unit could produce images of Israelis in distress; civilians fleeing to shelters; hospitals, schools, and day cares shut down; towns and villages vacated or rendered unlivable by mortars. But even that could not compete with the images coming out of Gaza. As one bureau chief told Lerner: "Peter, it's the old rule: if it bleeds, it leads." The Israelis weren't bleeding, so they weren't leading. But as Lerner told me in no uncertain terms: "We don't want to bleed." In the narrative war, Israel was in a lose-lose situation: if it struck Hamas targets embedded in civilian areas, it received international condemnation, but if Hamas succeeded in kidnapping or killing any of its soldiers, Hamas won again.

Israel's greatest disadvantage is arguably that it is the underdog online. Its supporters are far outweighed by its enemies. This fact was clear during Protective Edge, when the pro-Palestinian hashtag #gazaunderattack was tweeted around 2.6 million times, according to Topsy, a social media analytics firm, while the pro-Israel hashtag #israelunderfire was tweeted a mere 283,050 times.[39] But because of its vastly superior military and established institutions, Israel is still regarded as the bully. It has all the disadvantages of being the underdog without any of the advantages.

So, to get back to the question I posed earlier: In the end, who won the 2014 Israeli-Palestinian conflict? As Lerner pointed out, the media did not stop the war. The relentless images and media coverage did not translate into diplomatic pressure on Israel to disengage. There was little outcry from leaders, who understood it to be a more complex issue than Israel bullying poor Palestinians again. Lerner was disarmingly honest in his answer to the question. "I wouldn't say we won," he told me. "But I definitely wouldn't say we lost. The conflict went on for fifty-one days despite the images. I would say that the reality and the underlying messages that we wanted to convey—that our enemy was literally hiding behind its civilians so it could shoot ours, and was investing in this huge, expensive network of tunnels only for bad things, to infiltrate into Israel, to breach our sovereignty, kill our civilians—those messages were accepted and received and understood."

Among the public, however, it was a different story. As Lerner conceded, "The court of public opinion reflects very much what happens on Twitter; and on Twitter there were two groups talking to themselves and shouting at one another. And the Palestinian side had bigger numbers; they had more people on Twitter and more people out on the streets, which translated into greater successes." Domestically, Israel never lost the support of its population during what was the longest war in its history. Domestically, it unquestionably won the information war. Globally, it unquestionably lost.

In a world that mistrusts institutions and privileges narratives—particularly ones deemed "sincere"—scarcity of resources can become a virtue, abundance a liability. This is the advantage that a Farah has over an institution like the IDF: an inherent authenticity that is almost impossible to emulate. (Indeed, had she employed the services of a PR firm, it's unlikely her story would have been so successful.) Ultimately, Lerner could never escape the fact that he worked for what was, in the eyes of many, a tainted institution. He could never escape that "original sin." And because he worked for a democratic state—for Jerusalem, not for Moscow—he could not pump out falsehoods and manufacture Israeli casualties where none existed. Israel lost the global information war because it did not "bleed" enough, and as long as it maintains its military advantage, it never will.

4

THE FACEBOOK WARRIOR 1:
THE VIRTUAL STATE

Social media contains two preeminent abilities: to amplify messages and to mobilize people. The importance of these processes in wartime or during times of civil strife cannot be overestimated. In Gaza, Farah was able to successfully use Twitter to amplify a message of suffering that formed the central pillar of the Palestinians' narrative war against Israel.

The 2011 Arab Spring brought into sharp focus social media's second preeminent ability: mobilizing people. Having seen and read social media footage and reports of the Tunisian people toppling their longtime dictator Zine El Abidine Ben Ali, crowds turned out on the streets of Cairo hoping to overthrow their own tyrant, Hosni Mubarak. A total of around two million people protested at Cairo's central Tahrir Square throughout the revolution—a large percentage of them mobilized through social media. Facebook in particular was a powerful tool, as individuals set up pages devoted to those who had died at the hands of government forces; these pages then became online rallying cries for the masses. Others set up pages with the sole purpose of helping people to coordinate meetings and demonstrations. So seriously did the government take this threat that it attempted—with some success—to cut the country's Internet access.[1]

Thus did *Homo digitalis* begin to emerge—and to emerge in the most effective and diffuse of ways. The Arab Spring revealed the power of social media to affect civil conflict to an extreme degree: it helped to mobilize enough people to force a dictator who had ruled for over thirty years to step down. Its use in war was only ever a matter of time. So it has proved in Ukraine, where one woman, Anna Sandalova, was able to use the exact same abilities—to amplify messages and then, more crucially, to organize and mobilize, albeit on a much smaller scale—to do her bit for her country. Social media, this time Facebook rather than Twitter, enabled a civilian far removed from war to affect even the *physical* battlefield. And, critically, Facebook's networking capabilities allowed her to do this in ways, and at speeds, that the weak Ukrainian nation-state could not. Anna's story reveals that as the state fails, *Homo digitalis* rises to take its place.

Dawn breaks in Kyiv. The city center is bathed in grayish amber light; a skyscraper puffs out tendrils of smoke into the morning air. In the distance a statue of a winged figure holding a spear sits atop a domed roof, watching over the broad roads beneath. It's December 2014, and it's cold. The war in Ukraine is now almost eight months old, and the soldiers fighting on the front lines in the country's east are doing so in temperatures of −4°F. It's been almost a year since Russian soldiers—dressed in green uniforms without any insignias or identifying marks—marched into Crimea in late February, just days after the Euromaidan protests overthrew the Kremlin-backed former Ukrainian president Viktor Yanukovych, and hoisted the Russian flag over municipal buildings in the region's capital, Simferopol. After a "referendum" held on March 18, 2014, which Ukraine and most of the international community, including the United States, deemed illegal, Crimea was formally annexed to Russia.[2]

Russian president Vladimir Putin was badly shaken by the Euro-maidan revolution next door, which began in November 2013 when at the last minute Yanukovych backtracked on a pledge to sign the EU Association Agreement, which would have strengthened political and economic ties between the European Union and Ukraine. Fearing that Ukraine, which it considers to be firmly within its sphere of influence, would draw closer to Europe, Moscow exerted pressure on Yanukovych to instead join Russia's own Customs Union. It worked. The consequences, however, were far greater and more damaging than either Yanukovych or Moscow could have foreseen. Outraged, a Ukrainian journalist, Mustafa Nayyem, wrote a Facebook post urging people to gather in Maidan Nezalezhnosti (Independence Square) in protest. And they did. First just a few hundred came, then more, and more—mostly students and young people. They stood in the square during the daytime; many slept there overnight, refusing to leave. They wanted their government to hear them.

It heard. And on November 30, 2013, it made what would prove to be a fatal error, ordering its riot police, the Berkut, to use violence to disperse the protesters. Many were badly beaten—but they weren't cowed. Over the following weeks and months the number of protesters grew to hundreds of thousands, who now called for Yanukovych's removal as well as the signing of the EU Association Agreement. The army moved in, and snipers placed on the roof of the Hotel Ukraine, which overlooks the square, killed dozens of demonstrators. The streets of Kyiv ran with blood. By late February 2014 the government had killed more than a hundred protesters and injured almost two thousand. Politically, it was too much: on February 21, Yanukovych fled Kyiv, and by February 25 he was in Moscow. The revolution had succeeded; the people had won.

They had done so, however, at what would prove to be a significant cost. Moscow simply could not allow any government that replaced Yanukovych's to cede to the people's wishes and draw closer to the European Union, which in its eyes meant drawing away from Russia. Putin needed to destabilize Ukraine, and the best way to do that, he knew, was to focus on the eastern part of the country. Living so close to its border, eastern Ukrainians have always had more affinity with Russia than with many in the country's west or even those living in Kyiv. Russian is almost exclusively spoken in the region, and former president Yanukovych came from its heart, the Donetsk Oblast. Many eastern Ukrainians had watched the Euromaidan protests with unease, especially when, on February 23, Ukraine's parliament adopted a bill that repealed the law supporting minority languages. Russian suddenly lost its "regional language" status, which had allowed for its use in courts, schools, and other government institutions under certain circumstances. The new bill in effect made Ukrainian the sole state language. The country's acting president, Oleksandr Turchynov, swiftly vetoed the bill, but the damage had been done.[3]

In the weeks after Euromaidan, protests and demonstrations against the revolution broke out across the country's east as its citizens—fed a daily diet of Russian TV—feared that the new government intended to destroy their way of life. Calls for a referendum and pleas for Russia to annex the eastern part of the country, as it had done with Crimea on March 18, 2014, emerged from a small but vocal minority in various eastern cities. Then, in April, Moscow made its move: the "little green men" (as the media had christened them) that had first appeared in Crimea now reappeared in eastern Ukraine. I was there in late April, traveling across the east as pro-Russia separatists took hold of government buildings in the major cities, notably Donetsk and Luhansk. As the weeks passed, the protesters, who started out wearing civilian clothes and arming themselves with bats and clubs, morphed into uniformed quasi-soldiers, carrying automatic weapons and operating under chains of command. In Luhansk, on assignment for *Foreign Policy* magazine, I sat inside the city's security services office forty-eight hours after its takeover. Masked, armed men were posted throughout the building. Valery Bolotov, a gruff former paratrooper in the Soviet army, announced the creation of the Autonomous People's Republic of Luhansk (LNR).[4] Meanwhile, in Donetsk, journalists would soon need press accreditation to report in the People's Republic of Donetsk (DNR), which was being propped up by a steady flow of Russian arms and logistical support crossing the border. Putin was trying to break Ukraine apart, and the new Ukrainian government seemed powerless to stop him.

On a cold morning in mid-January 2014 Anna Sandalova decided that enough was enough. She had watched Yanukovych's thugs first beat up and then fire on protesters as she helped out each day on Independence Square, making tea, clearing garbage, and doing shifts at the makeshift medical centers set up there. A former PR executive with fifteen years' experience in the industry, she had taken a break from her career to spend more time with her husband and two young children: she was the definition of an ordinary, everyday citizen.

As the Euromaidan protests wore on, Anna found that her friends separated into two distinct groups: those who participated in events and those who did not. Facebook made clear which of her friends' profiles were filled with talk of the revolution, requests for supplies, arrangements to meet on the square to man barricades, and various other activities. Then there were those who were silent. Anna was already one of the "doers," and many of her Facebook friends had become real-life friends. This made her think: What might be possible if she used Facebook to help with revolution? She decided to set up a private Facebook group—for around forty people only—dedicated to raising money to provide medicine and warm clothes for the protesters camped out on Independence Square. It was made private because she feared that a public group might come to the attention of government security forces. It was a success: over the course of a few weeks she raised about $3,000 (including around a third of that within a single twenty-four-hour period) to buy shoes and warm jackets for the protesters. Anna was beginning to understand how social media could enhance her small role in the revolution. Then in February 2014 Russian troops marched unopposed into Crimea, and she

Anna Sandalova, the Facebook Warrior, in eastern Ukraine. (Credit: Maia Mikhaluk)

watched as Ukraine's army, devastated by two decades of government corruption, stood by, helpless to stop them.

I met Anna in mid-May, soon after I returned from my first trip to the east, in a restaurant on Khreshchatyk, Kyiv's main street, which runs off Independence Square.[5] "Crimea showed us that the situation was worse than we had imagined," she told me. "We cried. The army was in such a bad state: it didn't have equipment, it didn't have enough vehicles, it didn't even have food. We saw that in the General Command and Military of Defense there were a lot of stupid and unpatriotic people."

The Ukrainian army is the state in miniature. It emerged, like the country, from the USSR in 1992—huge but bloated and rotting inside. Corruption, Ukraine's disease, has atrophied military development since independence.[6] In April 2014, when war broke out, Ukraine's military budget stood at just under $2 billion per year, or 1.1 percent of GDP (Britain's military spending, by contrast, was $62.3 billion, 2.3 percent), and much of it disappeared into the pockets of corrupt officials.[7] Progression through the ranks was dependent not on ability but on bribery, and military officials were trained not in the art of war but of theft. Parts, weapons, and even uniforms were all up for sale. "Corruption is inevitable," an advisor at the National Security and Defense Council of Ukraine told me in a coffee shop a few weeks before I met Anna. "A private earns $110 a month; imagine if he has a family to support." Then there was the problem of equipment. "It's outdated," he continued. "Many of our tanks and helicopters don't work and we can't afford to fix them."[8] Little surprise, then, that the Security Council made the decision not to confront Russian forces in February.

The state couldn't cope, and Anna was convinced she could help fill the governmental void. As a former PR executive, she is typical of the "Maidan generation" of activists: educated and professional. And in this sense they are nothing new. From Cromwell to Jefferson to Gandhi to Lenin, revolutionaries have always come largely from the middle classes, the intelligentsia, and even the upper echelons of society. It is no coincidence that Facebook, a largely English-language American product used only by a minority of Ukrainians (most of whom, especially in the poorer east, favor its Russian equivalent, VKontakte), is the activists' social media platform of choice.

Mustafa Nayyem began the Euromaidan revolution with a Facebook post. A young Ukrainian journalist of Afghan descent, he is a rare example of multiculturalism in Ukraine, certainly in anything approaching public life. When I met Nayyem in the offices of Hromadske TV, on the thirteenth floor of a huge Soviet building looking out over Kyiv's Dnieper River, even he seemed surprised at the power social media had unleashed. "At around 4:00 p.m. on November 21 Yanukovych announced he wasn't going to sign the EU Association Agreement," he told me. "There was a lot of anger on Facebook, so

I wrote that if enough people showed their support on my wall we would go to protest in Independence Square. I never thought so many would come."[9]

Anna honed her social media crowdfunding skills during the Euromaidan protests, developing a reputation as someone who got things done. On March 2, 2014, she woke up to find that one of her old school friends had made her an administrator for the Facebook group EuroMaydanArmy (which would later become Support the Army of Ukraine), a group dedicated to raising funds to provide supplies for soldiers fighting pro-Russia separatists in the east. Anna wanted to help, but she had no links whatsoever to the military or political establishment. "What do I know about the army?" she asked her friend. "You'll be fine," he replied. And she was. At the time, she was also involved with a group that worked to house people from Crimea who wanted to leave the region after its annexation, which meant first getting them out (and all the logistics that entailed) and then finding families in Kyiv and other Ukrainian cities willing to host them. Now the army became her responsibility, too. Buying everything from body armor and radios to helmets and underwear, she and her fellow volunteers personally drove the goods to the front lines. Via social media they created online networks of helpers in the occupied cities, and through those people they obtained access to places government forces could never go.

In the process they blurred the boundaries between the state and its citizens. Anna began to regularly liaise with senior military commanders and the top brass of the army establishment. "As bad as some elements of the army are," she told me, "there are guys there that share our aims: to win, to rebuild our army and update it as much as we can. And we need to support these generals and colonels, the good people among the higher echelons of the army. As volunteers, we have learned to tell the good guys from the bad guys. So we try to support them as much as we can and also to help to improve the image of the Ukrainian army. We need to unify around our armed forces."

Many of those who faced Yanukovych's riot police on the front lines at Independence Square now fought on the front lines against Russia. But what struck me was how many, just like Anna, used new media to fight—and fight effectively—away from the front lines. Online groups sprang up across Ukraine, doing everything from disseminating information on the crisis to housing refugees to raising money to repairing planes to buying trucks on which the army mounted rocket launchers. All used social media to circumvent the lumbering government bureaucracy, create networks to raise money, and mobilize and inform the populace. They did what their government couldn't do. Empowered by social media, they became, in effect, a virtual state.

Dozens of these groups appeared as the fighting intensified, their virtual roots spreading throughout Ukraine. "It's all about networks," said Anna as we chatted. "And social media is designed to create networks. Facebook is the main tool I use because there is an entire community on there who can find solutions. People always know other people who can provide what we need."[10] Facebook, she explained, provides a reach that the government simply doesn't have. Anna is based in Kyiv, but most of her work is geared toward the occupied east. "It allows us to make contact with all parts of the country. I post a request on Facebook for help in a target city and we soon have a network among the local population there. In every occupied city in the east we now have teams of volunteers that help us out on the ground there."

The day before, there had been heavy fighting in the separatist-controlled town of Sloviansk, and Anna was on a drive to deliver medical help to wounded soldiers there. "We can react to things as they happen—that is critical," she said. One of the first things the group did, in late March, was to evacuate an entire division of two hundred soldiers from Crimea, arranging everything from buying train tickets to sending cars to collect the soldiers.[11] The Ministry of Defense, she explained, was legally powerless to act, as Russia had officially closed the border. Then there was the problem of logistics.

Organizing the evacuation through official channels would have required obtaining a series of permissions, which would have taken time that simply wasn't available. "But we are not a government department facing endless bureaucracy; we just don't have these problems."

By way of example, Anna's colleague Andriy (whom I met a few days later) highlighted the group's work with Crimea SOS, a Facebook group that at the time provided information on the ongoing crisis. "[A few] month[s] back, Crimea SOS wanted to protest against the inadequate equipping of our troops, so some of their activists collected a bunch of toy guns and placed them around the Ministry of Defense [MOD] building. We liaise regularly with the MOD—they need us and they know it. We were inside having a meeting to discuss how we could help them overcome these very problems," he explained mischievously. "The disturbance outside made them nervous and more open to our suggestions. Basically, we played 'good cop, bad cop.'"

The MOD was clearly a subject close to Andriy's heart. "Twenty to 30 percent of its staff should be fired immediately; they are useless," he said. He reserved a special loathing for the ministry's financial chief, Lt. Gen. Yvan Marko. "Marko's been there since 1995, I think. Twenty years in the same job has allowed him to develop his own corrupt networks. He sums up the problems of the Ukrainian state perfectly."

There are thousands of Markos across Ukraine, embedded in its government and institutions, officials who have spent years embezzling money in a vertiginous kleptocracy that reached its nadir with Yanukovych. The catalyst for the Euromaidan Revolution may have been his failure to sign the EU Association Agreement, but its root cause was popular disgust at two decades of ubiquitous corruption. In 2004 Transparency International's Corruption Perceptions Index rated Ukraine 122nd in the world, alongside Niger and Bolivia. By 2015, it was 130th, below Sierra Leone, Gambia, and Kyrgyzstan.[12]

One cold but sunny afternoon I met with Vitali Klitschko, a former world heavyweight boxing champion turned Ukrainian

politician, in the offices of his party, UDAR, on a quiet street of period buildings in central Kyiv. The offices were small; narrow corridors led into compact rooms. At six foot seven, Klitschko seemed
boxed in by the space and consumed with nervous energy. He was
running for mayor of Kyiv and, like all post-Maidan politicians, keen
to display his disgust for the former regime. "The system was totally
corrupt," he told me, leaning across the narrow desk and jabbing a
colossal finger at me for emphasis.

"Maidan showed the strength of Ukrainian society. The people
said that they had had enough of living without rules; enough of living with corruption; enough of living without a future." He paused to
glare at me, a habit of his. "And it set a precedent. If someone comes
to power now and they don't listen to the people, the same thing can
happen again."[13]

On Independence Square, where I met Anna, the truth of his
words was plain to see. A hard-core group of protesters remained
camped out in dozens of tents that littered the square, refusing to
return home until the parliamentary elections scheduled for September. People washed clothes in buckets and chopped firewood while
humorless Cossack militiamen lifted weights. A stall selling toilet paper bearing Yanukovych's image blocked the entrance to an international bank. The square's inversion echoed that of the state itself: the
people were proudly on display; officialdom, for the time being, was
in retreat.[14]

December 1, 2014. It's been almost eight months since I first met
Anna. I'm with the Emmy Award–winning director Andrew Smith,
who is accompanying me to make a short film on Anna's work, and
we are going to take a trip east with her and her fellow Facebook warriors to witness firsthand the extent to which social media can now
affect the battlefield.[15] Anna's office is on Vasylkivska Street, just a few
metro stations from Independence Square. The building entrance is
a bland glass door, beyond which lies a small reception area. Inside

are several floors of offices. It's a basic operation. Company signs are taped to doors that lie off bleak corridors—as I peer through the odd opened one on my way up to see Anna on the second floor, it seems that some of the offices are little more than glorified storage units. On the door of Anna's office is her group's logo: a blue inner circle displaying a white dove of peace, with SUPPORT OF THE ARMY OF UKRAINE written in Ukrainian in a surrounding yellow band. (Blue and yellow are the colors of the Ukrainian flag.) Below is the group's Web address: UkrArmy.org.

The office is its own war zone of boxes, military uniforms, cartons, plastic bags, and, in the corner, a mound of more than a hundred pieces of body armor. A stack of boxes with HELLO FROM KYIV stamped across them forms an uneven tower just left of the entrance. Opposite it hangs a Ukrainian flag alongside half a dozen framed certificates. Putin may fear a Ukraine that draws closer to NATO, but this hasn't stopped Anna. "This is a certificate that Anna SANDALOVA (CIV) has participated in NATO CIMIC Training. 24–28 November 2014. Kiev, Ukraine," reads one. Anna has become something of a celebrity in Ukraine, and one of the certificates testifies to her newfound status as one of the country's "100 Most Powerful Women." Lying on a table is an issue of the magazine that drew up the power list. Anna now shares its pages with former Ukrainian prime minister Yulia Tymoshenko.

Inside, Anna is rustling through bags filled with supplies. She sips from a white plastic coffee cup. Dressed in a purple shirt and casual trousers, she looks just like the civilian she is. She checks Facebook almost pathologically. It has been a stressful twenty-four hours. The previous night she realized she lacked the money to buy all the goods needed for the trip, and so she posted a heartfelt request on Facebook. "You all know me," she wrote. "I honestly used all the money we have amassed so far to buy lighting for the checkpoints [in the east] and I need money urgently for this trip—for more supplies, for gas, for many things." It worked. The post was shared more than a hundred times in one hour, and the donations flooded in—at a rough estimate, Anna raised around $1,500 in the first few hours alone. The trip would go ahead.

But, before that, the first task of the day is to supply a group of soldiers with uniforms. They are setting off to the east and need clothing to protect them from the cold. At around 10:45 (forty-five minutes late), they arrive in three minivans; Anna comes out into the building's parking lot to greet them. A bald soldier in his early thirties introduces himself as Sasha, and Anna tells him she has the uniforms she has crowdsourced for them. In the background, dressed in full military fatigues, with the majority sporting thick beanie hats, their automatic weapons slung casually over their shoulders, the rest of the soldiers mill around the parking lot, smoking, talking, and occasionally blowing into their hands against the cold.

The soldiers are divided into three groups of seven to ten men, each with its own group leader, to make it easier for them to go up to the office and select their gear. It soon becomes apparent why people like Anna are so sorely needed. As she stands in the cold talking to Sasha and another group leader, Maxim, it emerges that the third group leader has disappeared. Eventually he reappears in the distance. "Ah, there he is," Maxim says. He turns to Anna and shrugs sheepishly. "He hasn't been group leader very long," he says by way of explanation.

Anna sets out how things will work. The soldiers will come into the office one group at a time. They will then try on clothes from packages that have already been opened, and once they know their size, they can pick up a sealed pack to take with them. Each soldier is to be allotted trousers, a jacket, and underclothing.

We head back inside, and Anna turns to see the thicket of soldiers that has now invaded the office. "Hmmm . . . this is more than ten people," she says resignedly. "Why don't some of you from group B go to the canteen area and have a coffee? It's self-service!"

She is now surrounded by curious soldiers, poking, prodding, and examining: a small purple dot among a sea of camouflage. Her helpers—all women—are doing their best to assist, steering soldiers to the correct boxes, helping them to try on jackets. But there is a further problem. The uniforms have been sourced from Germany and are all in German sizes, which are different from Ukrainian sizes. Worse than that, some of the soldiers—despite being in the army—don't appear to know what size they are. A black-haired woman in a yellow Ukraine army T-shirt gets a soldier to bend over so she can look at the label inside his jacket collar.

Everywhere I look, soldiers are trying on and taking off jackets. One has found the kettle and is taking Anna's advice and making coffee while he and some friends wait. Down on one knee, Anna hands out pants to the soldiers, but they have suddenly become coy—reluctant to disrobe in front of Anna and her female helpers, plus a watching journalist and filmmaker. "Come on, guys, you need to try them on to make sure they're the right size," says a helper encouragingly. Anna calls out after her: "Don't forget to take the German flags off the uniforms!" She turns to me. "They really like the German uniforms," she says. "They're really high quality." Anna has volunteers based abroad—found through Facebook—who visit warehouses in Poland and Germany where they buy the latest military gear and then ship it back to Ukraine in a process that, again, is all coordinated through Facebook. "If you compare these uniforms with the latest Ukrainian ones, it's no contest, the guys much prefer the NATO German versions." Each set, she says, costs $50. So to equip just the twenty-seven soldiers who have come today costs $1,350—a significant amount in Ukraine, and all of it either crowdfunded or donated.

In total, Anna has found through Facebook about fifty volunteers who come from time to time to help out. The office has to be manned constantly to ensure that someone is around to receive donations, to receive and pack supplies, and to hand them out when necessary. She has a further hundred volunteers, again all found through Facebook, who perform another vital task for the group. Giving up their time, they stand outside supermarkets and major shopping malls in their yellow SUPPORT THE ARMY OF UKRAINE T-shirts, handing lists of needed goods to people going inside. If they feel like it, the shoppers can buy items on the list and hand them to the volunteers on their way out. On a good weekend the volunteers can fill two minivans or a truck with supplies this way. Despite everything, Anna doesn't find her job difficult. She has two children and says that is much harder work. She gets frustrated only when she receives requests for specialized equipment that she cannot always fulfill immediately due to paperwork bureaucracy and, occasionally, expense.

Returning to business, Anna tells all soldiers who now have a complete set of clothing to check their names off against the list. Only a few seem to have reached that stage. The shambles continues, and eventually Anna puts a stop to it. There's been a change of plan, she tells them: only group A will try the clothes on. The rest of the soldiers will get their clothes from the boxes, and if there are any problems, she will sort it out later on. The office is a cacophony of queries, grunts, and noises of frustration. Her cell phone rings—it's an officer from the eastern (Ukrainian-held) city of Kramatorsk. He needs supplies and has heard about Anna. She asks him for his name and details, telling him to be specific, as she already deals with many regiments in the area. She tells him we're setting off to the east today but that she'll be back on Friday and will speak to him then.

A few of the soldiers are drawn to the pile of body armor in the corner, picking up the vests almost wistfully and talking quietly among themselves. The whole affair is an odd sight—not least, I realize, because I am watching a group of soldiers who are fighting a war to protect the sovereignty of the Ukrainian state against Russian aggression, and every single one of them is speaking Russian, not Ukrainian.

The soldiers start loading boxes onto their vans. They are part of a new rotation that is being sent to the front today. "We'll probably see a lot of them when we are in the east," Anna says. One of the vans is filled with diapers—for orphaned children in the east, Anna says proudly. Her phone rings, and it's bad news; the ambulance that Anna's Facebook group bought through online donations won't be ready until Wednesday. It's a blow. The ambulance is badly needed

in the anti-terror-operation (ATO) zone, the conflict area of eastern Ukraine where the Ukrainian army is in control, and Anna had
rushed through all the paperwork to get it ready to come as part of
today's convoy to the east. She puffs on a cigarette in the cold parking
lot, clearly disappointed, though she remains cool, level headed, and
as charming as ever. The soldiers, now loaded down with supplies,
honk their horns in farewell as, one by one, the vans drive out of the
parking lot. Anna waves and smiles as they turn right onto the main
road and disappear off to the east, into an uncertain future.

Back inside, it's now time for us to start planning our trip to the east.
The problem, Anna explains, is always judging how many vehicles
to take. Often they budget for two cars but find out once they are
filled up with goods that a third is required at the last minute. Now,
without the ambulance, we are a vehicle short. Support the Army of
Ukraine's Facebook page is filled with people offering their services
in general, but with a journey to the east—and at the last minute, to
boot—Anna needs someone she knows she can trust, someone who
has a large vehicle and will be available at 7:00 p.m., seven hours from
now. A few calls later, the situation is resolved. "It's better," she says.
"This car will be more comfortable."

At all times, Anna monitors the group's Facebook feed. A message comes in from a potential donor wanting to help out but, reasonably enough, wanting to know what they may be funding. It's then up
to Anna to come up with, as she puts it, a "concrete project" to convince them to donate. Two students from the Psychology Department
of Kyiv University, who come once or twice a week to volunteer their
time, are loading supplies into boxes. Not all the supplies are logistical necessities; along with the food and clothes are several posters
with images of models wearing skimpy clothing and combat gear. In
one image a buxom redheaded woman wearing only a bra sits cross-
legged on a box, the finger of her right hand poised seductively at
her lips while she holds a sniper rifle in her left hand. The Ukrainian

trident is tattooed on her bare midriff. FATAL RENDEZVOUS, reads the caption. Anna tells me these posters cheer the men up no end.

The group also receives care packages for the soldiers, donated from Facebook followers, boxes that include chocolate, socks, coats, and drawings from schoolchildren in Kyiv showing their support and appreciation. "Slava Ukraine" (glory to Ukraine) and "A big thank-you" reads the childish scrawl across a drawing of a woman with a handbag and several hearts. The students work hard, packing each box (all of which feature a sticker with the Facebook group's logo) individually, then checking all items are in place before sealing the boxes with tape (also with the group's logo on it) and stacking them into a pile, ready to be loaded into the cars due to arrive in the early evening.

Anna checks Facebook again and finds more good news—someone in possession of a gas pump has offered them coupons for as much gas as they need for the trip. Also, someone else has offered Anna a ton of mandarin oranges. The power of social networks yields everything from petroleum to fruit, it seems. It becomes plain just how much Anna has to organize at the last minute. That she gets so much done is a testament to both her perseverance and her organizational abilities. Today's trip, which will last a total of three days, will involve seven drop-offs at various points in the ATO zone. Our first stop will be the soldiers of the 28th Mechanized Guards Brigade, which is situated near the occupied city of Donetsk and has checkpoints surrounding the area. They need uniforms, sleeping bags, and boots, but above all they need night-vision goggles. Supplies will also be delivered to the 84th Division and the 1st Tank Brigade.

Anna proudly shows me photos sent by soldiers on the front lines of them holding her boxes, standing by armored vehicles near Donetsk and Debaltseve, close to the heart of the fighting. Posting such photos to the group page is vital to her operation, she says. People need to see where their money is going; they need to see the tangible results of their donations. People who donate goods directly are always keen to view her posts to see if they can spot "their" hat or pair of gloves. Watches are of particular interest. Anna asks people to donate old analog watches because the soldiers are not allowed to use their smartphones to check the time, as the enemy can use the phone's signal to locate them. People are always looking out for their old watches on the wrists of soldiers in photos. This is why Maia—a professional photographer who will accompany us on the trip and take photos of the entire process, which Anna will then post to Facebook—is so vital to the work Anna does.

The idea of crowdsourcing funds, and even more generally of donating and volunteering, is not embedded into Ukrainian society, Anna explains. And in a society so ridden with corruption, people are especially suspicious of giving money. Anna needs to prove that she uses the money she receives for the purposes she claims. Also, she continues, the medium is new; the way the group now uses Facebook to communicate with thousands of people is so novel that everyone is learning a new set of rules. "We need to gain people's trust," she says. "And it's easy to lose that trust." She posts the group's accounts to Facebook, detailing the money received and what it has been spent on. She forces herself to post about the group's activities at least once a day, though two or three times is better—enough that there is a steady stream of information for her thousands of followers. The group's Facebook page is filled with photos of smiling soldiers receiving goods and of Anna, dressed in body armor and a helmet, handing them out. People want to see the numbers, but more important, they need to see exactly where their money is going and how grateful the soldiers are; that is what will get them to keep on giving. As well as seeking general donations, Anna also uses the page to crowdfund for particular projects. She will post a request for donations for anything, from badly needed sets of body armor to high-tech equipment, stating how much she needs to raise. Once the equipment has been purchased and delivered, she always posts the relevant photos so that people can see the results their donations have produced. The main group page has around 8,700 followers and Anna has, on her personal page, around 2,500 friends. The typical donation is between

$20 and $40. The largest donation she ever received was just under $58,000. Since she joined the group in March it has raised around $1.3 million. Some comes from the Ukrainian diaspora abroad, but most still comes from Ukrainians at home. It's a staggering sum for such a poor country in a state of war.

Another call comes in. It's friends from the army asking if Anna can deliver some packages to them. Now she has to rethink the size of the extra vehicle needed—she'll have to find a minivan. She makes more calls, discussing the size of vehicles on offer. As ever, things are changing at the last minute, and it falls into the hands of an ordinary mother of two, whom senior personnel from the armed forces are now relying on for help.

Almost as important as the delivery of physical goods is the psychological aspect, Anna explains in between phone calls. When you bring body armor, bought by funds donated from Ukrainians across the country, and drive it yourself to the soldiers on the front, they feel that they are appreciated, and it raises their morale. The letters and drawings they get from children are especially popular. "It all makes them feel that we're not just carrying on with our lives," she continues, "going to bars to drink beers and thinking about where to go on vacation. It's our war, and we all share a common aim. We are not soldiers, but we share their goals and have to change our lives accordingly, spend less money on the stupid stuff. And if the whole country does the same, I'm sure we'll win quickly."

She scrolls through the organization's Web banking page. The list of donations seems to go on forever. Since her heartfelt post for immediate funds yesterday evening, they've now raised around $7,000, and the donations are still coming in. "When you write something from the heart on social media, it really works," she explains. "Facebook allows you to communicate directly with thousands of people—and to communicate in your own words. And I can be as emotional as I want because they can see it's coming from me, an individual person with a human face on a profile page." Scrolling through her banking page again, she estimates that since last night 730 payments have come in—a record. Anna's husband, Dmitry, chimes in: "Most likely someone famous shared the post," he says. Her phone rings again; a politician, who wants to remain anonymous, has donated around $1,000, and his driver will bring the money now. Speed, as this post demonstrates so well, is everything. Funds received through the organization sometimes take days to process because of the bureaucracy involved, so Anna included her personal credit card details so people could donate directly to that. It's all aboveboard, as the bank is aware that funds donated to her personal account are used for the purchase of equipment, as are the various politicians she liaises with.

Evening sets in, and it's time to load up for the trip. The convoy will consist of two vehicles this time. Anna has sourced a white van and, along with her brother, Dmytro, and friends Maxim, Volodymyr, and Oleksandr, loads supplies into it as well as into Dmytro's car. The various mounds of bags and boxes stand almost six feet high.

The Yanukovych family, notably the president and his son, Oleksandr, became rich through effective manipulation of the various branches of the state, in particular using the judiciary and the public prosecutor's office (appointments that Ukraine's president constitutionally controls) to target profitable businesses. Those that refused to pay were hit with tax investigations and other forms of government harassment—all legal. The state became their personal fiefdom. In a report on Ukrainian corruption by the Legatum Institute, *Looting Ukraine: How East and West Teamed Up to Steal a Country*, the journalist and analyst Oliver Bullough estimates that about $15 billion was stolen annually from Ukraine's $50 billion state procurement budget alone.[16] The state was rotten to its core.

In Ukraine, new media is allowing people like Anna to replace the state. Social media is tailor-made for the post-Soviet space, where institutions have atrophied from years of pervasive corruption; all you need is a laptop and a Facebook account and you can take action. People like Anna are virtual government ministers. They decide which army divisions receive what equipment and when.

Ask a Ukrainian where to find the most reliable source of military news and she'll point you not to the *Kyiv Post* or the MOD website but to *Information Resistance,* a widely read, Facebook-based analytical review. Want to know what tenders the government is taking bids on? Easy—check out the Facebook page of the civil society group Reanimation Package of Reforms.[17] These different Facebook groups, each with their own quasi-governmental functions, have allied with each other to increase their cumulative influence, almost organically. They have formed what I recognize to be an emerging virtual state in Ukraine, with *Homo digitalis* at its heart.

5

THE FACEBOOK WARRIOR 2:
HOMO DIGITALIS ON THE BATTLEFIELD

When Mustafa Nayyem wrote a Facebook post that drew Ukrainians to Maidan to demonstrate, he was merely following in a tradition established by his predecessors across the Arab world. He was a Generation I social media revolutionary. Like the Egyptian protesters during the Arab Spring just over two years earlier, he used Facebook to get people onto the streets. Anna is Generation II. She is a Facebook warrior, a social media jihadi. For the first time in history, social networks and smartphone apps are being used as tools of war. *Homo digitalis* does not just affect the discourse of war; he (or in this case she) can directly affect the physical battlefield. The degree of this impact would become abundantly clear as I journeyed into the heart of Ukraine's battlefields with Anna and her crew.

It's 10:00 p.m., and the sky is black apart from a sliver of moonlight that casts a pale glow on the frozen ground beneath us. We are on our way to the anti-terrorist-operation zone (ATO) in eastern Ukraine. Having changed into appropriate clothing at Anna's house—thermal underwear and camouflage pants underneath ski pants and two sweaters—we set out, the white minivan backing cautiously out of Anna's ice-covered driveway. We will travel through the night to arrive in the ATO zone early next morning. There we will first meet with soldiers from the army's Civil-Military Cooperation (CIMIC) section, which helps Anna coordinate her activities with the military. We will then journey throughout the Ukraine-held part of the war zone, distributing supplies to various brigades in need.

It's cramped in the van among the boxes. Dmytro will take the first driving shift. Anna sits in the back with me and Andrew, explaining that the meeting with CIMIC is vital to planning our route through the ATO zone—we don't want to end up straying into separatist territory or, worse, the middle of a firefight. On a recent trip Anna had tried to deliver supplies to the front lines, but the fighting was so heavy that in the end it wasn't possible. The biggest dangers, she tells us, are snipers and the possibility of an ambush by separatists emerging from the forests that dot eastern Ukraine.

After about forty-five minutes, just outside of Kyiv, we pull up to the gas pump to fill up using the coupons promised to us hours earlier by a donor. Anna continues her briefing: we need to be on the lookout for suspicious-looking people, cars parked in odd places, she tells us. We are staying overnight at the CIMIC camp, and she outlines the rules we must observe there at all times. Under no circumstances can we leave its confines unattended, as the area around it is heavily mined. At any camp or checkpoint, she continues, we also need to immediately apprise ourselves of the whereabouts of its bunker—often little more than a hole in the ground—in which we will take refuge if our position starts being shelled. If we are traveling and shelling starts, the first thing to do is exit the van and lie down on the road. Body armor and helmets must be worn at all times.

Anna reminisces about her first trip east as a Facebook warrior. She arrived near the army camp at 4:00 a.m., but because of high winds and intense rain the convoy couldn't make it through.

So the CIMIC soldiers they were with found a nearby field in which the group slept while the heavily armed soldiers formed a perimeter, standing in a circle around them, fingers resting on their triggers. "That," says Anna, "was an experience."

Apart from a few trucks, the route is almost deserted as we speed along. Kyiv is far behind us now, and my view consists of nothing but concrete road and the seemingly endless string of lights that bisects the freeway. Anna communicates with the other car via radio. Eventually the road starts to roughen and on either side of us trees replace buildings. I doze for a while and wake to the sun rising, a golden dot on the windshield as the sky turns a pale purple. We drive through a village of low houses with sloping roofs covered with snow and eventually pull up at a gas station to stretch our legs and use the toilet. "We have to pay to use it," says Anna. "And try the hot dogs, they're great."

We are now at the first checkpoint in the area, just around forty minutes from where we will meet our CIMIC liaison. The checkpoint is manned by Pravy Sektor (Right Sector), the far-right militia group that played a leading role during Euromaidan. The group was at the heart of the fierce fighting with government forces on Independence Square and subsequently became a primary (and convenient) enemy in Russian propaganda. In particular, its leader, Dmytro Yarosh, was throughout 2014 the embodiment of the "fascist junta" that Russian TV claimed (and still claims) now rules Ukraine (in fact he held no government position and received just 0.7 percent of the vote in Ukraine's May 25, 2014, presidential election). Yarosh is a deeply distasteful figure, undoubtedly sympathetic to neo-Nazi politics. But the vitriol against him emanating from both pro-Russia eastern Ukrainians and Russian state TV was almost entirely manufactured—vitriol that social media made all the more potent through the circulation of endless memes featuring him across multiple online platforms.

It's winter and daylight hours are short; we need to move fast. Enlivened by hot dogs, we pile back into the minivan and drive on. As we enter the ATO zone we stop to change into our body armor and don our helmets. We soon hit the Pravy Sektor checkpoint, near the occupied city of Donetsk, its black and red flag fluttering in the wind beneath the Ukrainian one. A pile of sandbags covered with snow is positioned outside a metal guard hut. After about ten minutes our CIMIC representatives, Natalia and Sasha, arrive in a beat-up old car. Natalia will act as translator, while Sasha is responsible for logistics. It's clear we are now in the war zone. "Now you will feel like a man," Sasha says to Anna with a smile, "a real man." Anna nods to Natalia, remarking on her gun, and then adds with a smile, "We have our own gun with us, too," much to Natalia's mirth. The two CIMIC soldiers will guide us to their camp on the outskirts of Donetsk; the road, Sasha tells us, has been badly damaged by the war, so we will have to drive slowly.

After a cautious journey of around an hour we arrive in the middle of a thick forest. Trees coated with snow, snapshots of beauty among a vista of military hardware, surround a clearing in which the army has made its camp. Several olive-green canvas tents dot the area. Wooden crates stacked carelessly on top of one another sit by a tree stump; a couple of spades rest against them. Someone has stuck a Ukrainian flag on a tree. In the camp's corner is a broken-down truck covered in snow, a white elephant on its knees. As per Anna's instructions, we locate the bunker: it's nothing more than a rectangular hole dug deep in the snowy ground, padded on each side by frozen sandbags. Peering inside reveals nothing but darkness. We enter the camp's main tent to discuss arrangements for our "mission."

Inside, the area is lined with beds; a makeshift clothesline filled with drying laundry is strung across its center, while a small wooden table serves as a dining spot. The floor is a collection of wooden planks and sawdust. A central pole holds up the tent, next to which is a wood-fired boiler that keeps the soldiers warm. An ax embedded in a small log lies ready to feed it with more fuel; a blue neon light enables us to see. It's clear that the men here live under the most basic of conditions. We meet Misha, a senior figure at CIMIC: red-faced with cropped dark hair and a dark, manicured beard, he brims with personality, hugging Anna and greeting me and Andrew with gregarious informality.

Several soldiers are looking at a map and arguing over the best route to take for our drop-offs throughout the ATO zone. One soldier suggests going via a small town nearby, but this idea is dismissed by a colleague who says there have been four GRAD attacks there recently.[1] Anna looks over the map with Sasha, discussing the best place to meet with representatives from the tank brigade. "The tanks can go wherever they want!" he jokes. First, however, we have to meet with the 28th Mechanized Guards Brigade. Their unit has taken heavy fire today, so we cannot go to them—we'll instead have to rendezvous somewhere safer. While we make plans, Anna mentions to Misha that she has the night-vision goggles he requested. Anna wants to give out the thirty care packages people have sent, but Misha tells her it's better that we just drop them off at each checkpoint we pass, given that we'll go through so many.

In the background, Maia snaps away, recording everything so that Anna can post it to Facebook once the trip is done. The clicking of her camera will be the soundtrack of our trip. Anna hands out cigarettes and sweets to the soldiers as supplies for the camp are unloaded from the van. In the background, a soldier is brushing his teeth in the open air. We start to put colored tape on our helmets and body armor, across the back and on each shoulder—red, to signify which area of the ATO zone we will be traveling through. The ground is a sea of white, the tree branches are lined with snow, and once again I think how beautiful it is and how it could be a scene from a postcard—until a heavily armed soldier walks into view.

We set off to meet with the first group of soldiers from the 28th Mechanized Guards Brigade. Originally based in Odessa, they are now spread throughout the ATO zone. It's so cold that my iPhone has switched off; Anna is having similar problems and tucks her cell into her sleeve to warm it up. Anna has been in phone contact with members of the brigade, and they are coming from the front to meet us, fresh from heavy fighting just an hour or so ago. To my surprise, Anna tells us they have taken taxis to the agreed location. We pull into a gas station, where Anna agreed to meet Maxim, a soldier from the 28th. He is a handsome man in his mid-twenties, with piercing blue eyes. They embrace, and he kisses her hand before introducing his colleague Oleksandr, a squat man with a light brown beard. Both men are heavily armed. The fighting earlier on was intense, they tell us. Maxim has a British flag on his uniform—evidence of yet more foreign-sourced materials for the badly undersupplied army. Anna asks him if he minds the presence of journalists here, and he says it's fine. He did, he tells us, have one bad experience a while back, when, during an interview, his face was shown on TV, and someone called his family telling them that he should leave the front and go home or else they would be hurt. But nothing is going to stop him from fighting for Ukraine.

Maxim tells us that pro-Russia separatists from the DNR-occupied areas shell his camp with GRADs and artillery every day. It's remorseless, he says. The weather makes things even harder; the field conditions are bad, and the soldiers are regularly forced to fight in below-zero temperatures. The group unloads the goods for Maxim's division: shoes, uniforms, some optics, coffee and tea. Warm clothing is especially needed, given the temperatures; nothing shows the dire state of the Ukrainian army more than the fact that it cannot equip its soldiers with the barest of necessities for winter.

Anna also hands Maxim some analog watches; he had requested a special bag used for carrying medical supplies, but Anna was unable to procure it. She makes him sign a paper to say he has received the goods and then gives him cash to pay for the taxis he and Oleksandr have hired to come and collect them. Sasha, our CIMIC liaison, says Anna's help is vital, as the goods she has handed out are of high quality. Echoing what Anna told me earlier, he says it's also important for the soldiers, on a psychological level, to know that the people are supporting them. It means a lot, he says. "Anna is a true patriot," he concludes. "Everything we are doing is to secure the future for our children—it's vital work."

We set off again in the minivan, and Anna remarks on how the local villages have emptied—there is little smoke rising from the chimneys of the houses, and few people are visible on the streets. Many people have left the east as the war has taken its toll. Those remaining are mainly elderly people who cannot move, but it seems some families have also chosen to stay. As we move through several villages, remaining vigilant at all times, Anna points to a small child on the sidewalk of a central street we pass through. "I don't understand how you can remain here if you have a child," she says.

At our next drop-off we were supposed to meet the commander of the 1st Tank Brigade, fighting the separatists at Donetsk airport—a vital strategic point that was a major battlefield in the war in the east—but he was recently wounded, so we are going to liaise with some of his men instead. Eventually we stop outside a mini-mart on the road to Donetsk. Nearby a yellow-and-blue sign advertises the services of a twenty-four-hour garage. The snow on the ground is an almost unsullied pure white. "Argh, it's cold!" says Anna.

The soldiers arrive, and Anna hands out more goods: heaters and a mobile kitchen as well as parcels with clothing to keep them warm. Anna wants to move fast—in an hour darkness will set in, and being near the airport, where fierce fighting is raging, is not safe.

Another soldier from the 1st Tank Brigade arrives in a large truck. Wearing a black beanie, he smiles broadly. Posing for a photo with both thumbs up, he tells us not to worry. "Everything will be fine," he says. "Everything is great. Morale is high. We will win!" On the truck's dashboard is a Minion doll (a small creature from a Disney animated film, *Minions*), yellow with blue overalls, like the colors of the Ukrainian flag. A blue-and-yellow Ukraine banner is affixed to the truck's grille. Just below the windshield he has written the name of his home town, Negin, close to Kyiv, in white paint. He poses for more pictures, laughing and joking. It's a rare burst of positivity amid

the general gloom. "We will show the world how tough we Ukrainians are!" he says with yet another broad grin.

He climbs on the back of his truck and puts on some pop music. He gets out a Ukrainian flag and starts waving it around. "Let
the world know who we are!" he says. I spy two chairs in the back
of the truck, and he sits down on one and puts his feet on the other,
posing for more photos. He calls out to Anna to come and dance;
after some initial reluctance she takes off her coat and he helps her
onto the truck. Hands joined and outstretched, they begin to waltz
around in circles; he twirls Anna, who is dressed in full body armor,
and they laugh. It's an incongruous sight. He gets her to wave the
Ukrainian flag and passes his phone over to a member of the group
to take a photo of the two of them. "Grazie!" he says when it's done.
Anna asks him if he will get into trouble for this sort of behavior.
"From who?" he replies. "Even in Soviet times during World War II
they had concerts!"

"Let the world know who we are!" The soldier's words stick in my
mind. Everything he did was for show: the dancing that he knew
would be photographed and shared on social media, his insistence
that Ukraine would triumph, his repeated assertions that morale
among the troops was high. It all pointed to a deeper truth that I only
later understood. The impact that Anna's use of social media has on
the battlefields is not just a question of her giving out badly needed
supplies; it is in fact a two-way process. In eastern Ukraine Anna isn't
merely reaping the rewards of social media's ability to mobilize people (in this case moving them to donate). She is also using its amplification abilities to give soldiers a voice. She is allowing them to
tell their stories, to get *their* narratives out. It is instructive that at
almost every military installation we visit, soldiers are keen to have
their photos taken and to express their gratitude, via Anna, to those
who donated. Her efforts both help to keep them warm and, equally
important, help to humanize them.

Anna is pleased at how the trip is going, and she makes sure Maia shoots enough footage of goods being handed out to the soldiers at each stop. The media aspect of the trip is always there—Facebook must be fed constantly with new material to keep things going. "You feel good here," she says. "In a way, even more so than in Kyiv. When I'm back home I am always worrying about the soldiers. Here when I see them laughing and joking I feel more relaxed." With the dancing done, the back of the army truck reverts from a disco to its traditional purpose, as the volunteers start to fill it up with boxes of supplies. Darkness is now setting in, and Anna says we need to move or it will become too dangerous. "These guys have been here for nine months, which is probably why they are so calm—and can dance on a truck!" she says by way of explaining the surreal experience she has just enjoyed.

A tank rolls past. "Come on," she says, "let's go."

The next stop is Kramatorsk, and the central army command center for the ATO zone. It's safe, and Anna feels comfortable visiting during darkness. She recently funded a housing unit for around six or seven soldiers there and wants to see how good a job the builders have done. After a minor misunderstanding at the guard post involving Anna's friend Maxim's personal firearm, we are waved through. Then it's time to head back to the camp.

There Anna introduces us to Yaroslav, who, with a group of volunteers, has been granted access to separatist-held territory to retrieve the bodies of fallen Ukrainian soldiers that lie buried in shallow graves. It's a grim tale he has to tell. Retrieving Ukrainian bodies is, it seems, his occupation: he still searches for the bodies of those who were killed fighting for the Red Army during World War II.

After he tells me his story, it's time to relax. I visit the camp's "toilet," a metal grate placed over a hole dug into the dirty snow. I return to the tent, where food and, more important, alcohol, appears on a table brought into the hut especially for the occasion. Ukrainian cognac and vodka are poured into plastic glasses. We all toast to better times. More food is served and more alcohol is drunk. Misha becomes even more red-faced, making us do a couple more toasts. Then, with almost religious reverence, he brings out the *spyrt*, a special Ukrainian drink that is 90 percent alcohol. He only allows me one small measure of it. Then he raises his glass again. "On the third toast," he booms, "it is traditional to toast to women. But in these times, we toast our fallen comrades instead." We drink, and for a moment the atmosphere thickens as the soldiers around us, heads briefly lowered, remember friends who have died in the conflict. In the background, the distant noise of artillery can be heard, almost serene in its monotonous regularity.

The next day, 7:00 a.m. It's been a cold night tucked into sleeping bags on flat iron beds in the tent. But I am awake. I want an answer to what I believe to be a critical question: Just how much impact does Anna's Facebook group have on the army? How much effect does it have on Ukrainian soldiers—and therefore the course of the war? Slowly I don my body armor and helmet, and go out to find a CIMIC liaison officer to speak to about all this. "Anna's work is very important," he tells me. "She is providing the army with what it needs." I ask him if Anna is, in her ability to influence events on the battlefield, perhaps a new kind of soldier. "Of course the work Anna does has great effects," he replies. "She is not a traditional solider in that she doesn't carry a gun, but just as we have traditionally had civilian doctors entering the battlefield to help the army and making a difference that way, Anna is in the same mold. It's just that, [thanks to social media], she is a new type of civilian able to influence the battlefield in new ways. So in the sense that she is here and that she is helping the war effort, she can be considered a soldier, yes."

What effect, I continue, does he think social media is having on modern warfare? "It's having a huge effect," he replies. "Social networks mean that, for example, civilians back home can access a lot more information about what is happening on the front lines far more easily than in the past. And of course social networks are what enable Anna to provide for the needs of our soldiers." He then reaffirms what Anna told me back in her office: in a country as corrupt as Ukraine, institutions are not trusted. "People just trust volunteers more than official organizations," he says with a shrug. "A final point," he concludes, "is that when we travel to cities with civilian volunteers it makes the locals less fearful of us when they see we are traveling with ordinary civilians just like them. This is extremely useful in a war zone, especially for a unit like CIMIC."

It's now so cold that the minivan has trouble starting and has to be jump-started using the other car in our convoy. Anna points to the two vehicles now linked together by jumper cables and jokes, "They are saying good morning to each other." We're setting out for the city of Artyomovsk (now called Bakhmut) to deliver goods. It will be a three-hour drive, and we need to get moving. Anna packs body bags and spades into the van to deliver to another group, similar to Yaroslav's, that retrieves the bodies of dead Ukrainian soldiers from separatist-held areas.

A group of six CIMIC soldiers, fully armed, is milling around nearby. They will travel with us in their own van, providing a military escort in case things get dangerous. We get going once more. The road and skies both seem completely white; even the sun is little more than a sharp white sphere. Only the bare, dark trees provide relief from the blank canvas that stretches out on all sides. About twenty minutes into our journey Anna receives a phone call. She listens intently, hangs up, and then bursts into tears. She explains that she has just been informed that Ivan, a soldier she has known for a long time, was killed in action the previous day. She last saw him just two or three weeks before in Kyiv when she supplied his unit with goods; he brought her flowers and mugs with his division's logo on them. What makes it worse is that Anna estimates that he probably died in a town just a few miles away at the very same time that she was laughing and dancing on the truck with the soldier from the 1st Tank Brigade.

As we head toward Artyomovsk, a militia vehicle joins us, following behind to provide protection if the need arises. We stop at a checkpoint outside the town of Kostiantynivka, where Anna hands out some care packages. There has been a change of plan: instead of Artyomovsk, we will go to the outskirts of Debaltseve, a city on the eastern edge of Donetsk Oblast, right on the front lines and surrounded by separatist forces. "There is fighting there every day," Anna explains, "so now we need to be really careful." A soldier from CIMIC comes over to us to explain the procedure. "The first thing you do when we get there is find the bunker in case we get shelled," he emphasizes. "The second is to listen out for the sound of a GRAD. With a GRAD the sound comes thirty or forty seconds before it lands, so there is time to flee to the bunker.

"Mortars," he continues, rather worryingly, "you simply don't hear until the last second, but when you do, just lie down on the floor immediately. And hope."

The area around Debaltseve is a different world. We pull into a checkpoint near our destination: the base of the 54th Reconnaissance Battalion. The first thing I see is a tank by the side of the road, covered in snow, with a Ukrainian flag hanging limply from it. The snow-covered sandbags that I have come to recognize as a feature of the ATO zone are everywhere. As we approach the front lines Andrew is not allowed to film the soldiers in case he gives away their numbers and the weaponry they possess. The checkpoint stands by an old, ruined brick building around which the soldiers have formed a cordon. A mounted machine gun points ominously in the direction of the front. It's a sharp contrast to the children's drawings the soldiers have taped over the checkpoint's entrance. The group delivers more boxes of supplies. The van has emptied considerably since the beginning of our trip, and is now far more comfortable to sit in, if nothing else.

We move on yet again and arrive at the 54th Reconnaissance Battalion's camp, just a few miles from the front. Set on a slope, it's larger than the CIMIC camp and is filled with soldiers. Tents and armored vehicles are everywhere. At its center is a tent containing a large metal unit with a pole extending upward. This, we discover, is the camp's kitchen stove. Again, it's as basic as can be; the metal is dented and scratched and the entire unit slopes to the right. Dinner tonight for these soldiers will be rice soup and beef puree. A dog wanders among the detritus. The first thing Anna does is drop off some mobile showers—essentially a metal bucket with a plastic water container and hose attached along with a metal tube. In full media mode, Anna has her photo taken handing boxes of supplies to soldiers that she will post to Facebook when we return to Kyiv. She takes particular care to have Maia get a shot of her handing a box containing night-vision goggles—a specific project for which she had crowd-sourced funding—to a soldier from the battalion. Anna asks which of the soldiers is single. A young man in his early twenties is pushed forward, and Anna gives him a kiss while another soldier takes a photo. The young soldier blushes with embarrassment while his comrades roar with laughter. "I'm passing on kisses from those back in the peaceful territories," Anna explains with a laugh. "I want a kiss, too," says another soldier. "Are you single?" Anna replies. "No!" he says with a laugh. More photos are taken; once again, it's clear that this is as much a media exercise as a delivery. Anna needs to keep her Facebook followers fully apprised of everything their money is achieving to ensure that funds keep coming in.

Anna then gets a soldier to sign a Ukrainian flag. "Thank you for your support!! Slava Ukraine! Soldiers of the 54th Reconnaissance Battalion," he writes before signing his name. Camera flashes go off all around me. When the publicity is done we exit the camp. As we drive we notice a bombed-out car on the roadside, just by some trees from the forest that sits either side of us, the victim of a separatist ambush. "We need to drive fast now," says Anna. "We've done everything we came here to do. It's time to go home."

Anna's story is fascinating for a variety of reasons, perhaps most obviously because it highlights unequivocally the transfer of power from traditional hierarchies and institutions (in this instance primarily Ukraine's Ministry of Defense) to individuals and networks of individuals, like Anna and her band of volunteers, that social media has created. This is the phenomenon that Alec Ross, former senior advisor for innovation to Hillary Clinton, outlined to me in such depth in Maryland.

More specifically, it centers on new media's ability to do two things, as outlined in Chapter 4, more effectively and more rapidly than ever before: amplify messages and mobilize people. In 2009, following the fraudulent reelection of Iranian president Mahmoud Ahmadinejad, thousands of Iranians took to the streets in protest, coalescing around the real winner, Mir-Hossein Mousavi. The so-called Green Movement, as this uprising came to be known, was the first in which ordinary Iranian citizens began to distribute content to the international press and general public via social media.[2]

This culminated in the video of a young female protester, Neda Agha-Soltan, being shot in the street by government forces. The footage spread immediately via social media, and Neda became the embodiment of the Green Movement's uprising. Iranians uploaded the video through Current.com, and it was picked up by major US news networks such as CNN, ABC, NBC, and CBS. Its power was so great that eventually US president Barack Obama, who had previously tried to refrain from meddling in the situation for fear of jeopardizing the ongoing talks over Iran's nuclear program, was forced to publicly condemn the violence.

Neda's murder in 2009 proved that social media was able to bypass strict Iranian censorship. Iranians could get their message out by posting to Current.com as well as YouTube, and their posts were in turn tweeted by thousands of Twitter users abroad in a matter of minutes. It was not until social media became involved that individual voices—or in this case images—of Iranian dissent were heard. The 2009 uprising is often described as the "Twitter Revolution." This is wrong. The protesters did not use social media to organize and rally; rather, it was Mousavi's supporters who fulfilled this role. In actual fact, the main role Iranian social media played was to create awareness of the situation among foreign social media users, mostly on Twitter: it amplified a message that started on the streets of Tehran and, thanks mainly to Americans tweeting at one another, went global.

Social media's ability to amplify messages became clear to Anna during the Euromaidan revolution when Ukrainians took to the streets a little over four years after their fellow protesters in Iran. Without Facebook's ability to disseminate her message, the work Anna does would be almost impossible. At the turn of the century, she would have had to rely on putting an advertisement in a national newspaper (both prohibitively expensive and ephemeral, appearing in only one or two issues) and perhaps the odd TV interview. Even if she had the means to hire a PR firm, it is unlikely in the extreme that she would have achieved the same reach that Facebook has given her. And it is highly unlikely that she would have been anywhere near as successful. Anna's strength, as her heartfelt posts show, is that she uses social media to make her messages personal. They come from a single individual, not with a corporate logo. In an age in which the premium placed on "authenticity" is so great that outliers such as Donald Trump can be elected and the British Labour Party's Jeremy Corbyn can win his party's leadership because they come across as "sincere," the value of this is plain to see.

Now all Anna needs is a Facebook page, which can be accessed at any time from anywhere in the world at no cost whatsoever. And the reach and "authenticity" she has, with absolutely no investment in advertising, are transnational. Monetary donations come in from around the world as well as around Ukraine, but people abroad often see her requests and buy the needed supplies in their own country before shipping them to Anna in Kyiv. Equally important—and what is most new about what she does—is the speed of the message: she is able to react to problems on the battlefield as they occur in real time.

This would, once again, be unthinkable without the platform Facebook has given her to spread her message almost instantly. Her example exists on an obviously far smaller scale than the 2009 Iranian protests, but the principle is identical.

The second critical factor is social media's ability to mobilize people. Here, as also previously discussed, the classic example comes from the Egyptian protests in Tahrir Square in central Cairo during the Arab Spring of 2011. Shortly after demonstrations against Egypt's ruler, Hosni Mubarak, began, a young Egyptian named Khaled Said was beaten to death in an Internet café by Egyptian policeman. While visiting his body at the morgue, his brother used his smartphone to take photos of Said's disfigured corpse, which he posted on social media and which subsequently went viral, creating national outrage. A few days later, from his computer in Dubai, an Egyptian Google marketing executive, Wael Ghonim, saw the photo and created a Facebook page called "We Are All Khaled Said." According to the *New York Times*, "It became . . . the biggest dissident Facebook page in Egypt, with more than 473,000 users, and . . . helped spread the word about the demonstrations in Egypt."[3] The article then quoted Ahmed Zidan, an online political activist who joined the protest in Egypt's Tahrir Square, as saying, "There were many catalysts of the uprising. . . . The first was the brutal murder of Khalid," before concluding that "Facebook and YouTube . . . offered a way for the discontented to organize and mobilize—and allowed secular-minded young people to seize the momentum from Egypt's relatively neutered, organized opposition." Again the speed of diffusion is critical. As Navid Hassanpour, associate professor at the National Research University Higher School of Economics in Moscow, points out: "If 150,000 people show up in two hours, it's much harder to control than if they turn up in batches of thousands."[4] And, mobilized by a Facebook page, hundreds of thousands of people did pour onto the streets, eventually toppling a dictator.

Again, while on a vastly smaller scale, Anna's story rests on an identical power to mobilize. Apart from a couple of friends and her immediate family, notably her brother, Dmytro, almost all the volunteers who work at Support the Army of Ukraine were found through Facebook. They are concerned citizens who want to do their bit for the war effort and can find a way to contribute merely by sending Anna a Facebook message or offering their services on her Facebook wall. In Iran and Egypt, social media's ability to amplify and mobilize allowed people to confront the state; in Ukraine, it enabled them to compete with it. With a GDP per capita of $3,900 in 2013, Ukraine is now officially one of the most poverty-stricken countries in Europe. But it has a middle class with at least some money to give, and a vested interest in using it to defend their country. Social media aggregates power; it multiplies influence. And in a state where power and influence are singularly lacking, it endows citizens with the ability and the means to act in dynamic ways their government cannot.

The ability of civilians to circumvent the state in wartime is not new. In the run-up to the 1948 Israeli War of Independence, for example, the Jewish Agency—a civilian organization—was able to mobilize its members to illicitly procure arms for the Haganah, the underground Jewish army that eventually became the Israel Defense Forces, despite an arms embargo on the region. It bypassed official institutions and channels and sourced enough weaponry for the Israelis to win the 1948 war.

But what Anna, her fellow Facebook warriors, and a host of other online organizations do is new both in its scope and, critically, in its speed. Mobilization can be almost instant, information is spread at the click of a mouse, and the ability to create networks both national and transnational is of an order never previously witnessed in the history of warfare. What it may have taken the Jewish agency months to do, Anna can do in days—and she can do it with international assistance that can be procured in minutes. Many Annas have emerged across Ukraine, each specializing in a particular area—from providing information to housing refugees—to help the war effort. In Ukraine, the virtual state now increasingly supplies the societal cohesion that the "real" state cannot. And like a funhouse mirror, it reflects back onto the state its own nature through grotesque inversion. Where the state steals money, the people donate it; where it is slow and flabby, they are quick and lean. And where the state is filled with the old and reactionary, the people are young and revolutionary.

On the last day of our trip east, after we had finished our final deliveries to the brigade near Debaltseve, Andrew turned to Anna, while she stood drinking coffee and stamping her feet for warmth, and asked her quite simply: "Why do you do this?" She gave him a quizzical look. "Why?" she answered. "I can't *not* do this, is why. I now have the tools to make a difference—to raise money, and to help my country in a time of war. I can't just sit back and do nothing."

6

THE TROLL:
THE EMPIRE STRIKES BACK

Marilyn Manson and Winnie the Pooh—it's quite the combination. The singer's dark locks, heavily made-up eyes, and pouting mouth are tattooed across Vitaly Bespalov's left arm. Winnie's cute eyes and button nose adorn his left leg. I'm in Tyumen in northern Siberia, and it's surprisingly warm for early April. Tyumen is one of Siberia's major cities. It's oil-rich and jobs are plentiful, but cosmopolitan it is not. To set out from Moscow to Tyumen is to cross both space and time. In Moscow, I sipped Bourbon Smashes in hipster bars and wandered through the GUM shopping center near the Kremlin, marveling at the row of BMWs that lines its central hall. Gucci, Louis Vuitton, Moschino, Cartier—almost every designer imaginable is available to the capital's metropolitan elite, high on autocratic capitalism and consumer goods.

Tyumen, on the other hand, sits beneath a gunmetal sky. The light is flat and gray, drained of luminance as it bounces off hulking Soviet buildings and the brutalist architecture that dots the city center. City hall, a squat block of concrete and glass, seems to encapsulate the spirit of the place. Blunt and efficient, and in the eyes of some,

Vitaly Bespalov, the Troll.

a throwback to better days. In a park nearby stands a huge statue of Lenin, his left arm stretching downward while his right rests comfortably in his pocket. Vitaly says he thinks it might be the biggest statue of Lenin in Russia, though he admits he can't be sure. At its base someone has laid roses.

We arrive at the apartment of Vitaly's friend Rashid, where the interview takes place. It's a basic setup, compact but with all the necessities. I am offered beer or wine but decline and instead opt for some Coca-Cola bought a local mini-market. Outside in the street a woman, drunk or high on drugs, hollers and screams. Another friend arrives to translate, and our interview begins.

After several hours, evening sets in and Vitaly, Rashid, and I head out to the Ticket to Dublin, an Irish pub just off a central square in the city. It's like every other Irish pub I have been to outside of Ireland: dark wooden seating clashes with various shades of surrounding deep green. Shamrocks dot the wall. This place is something I never expected to find in Siberia. As we start to drink lager and Guinness, Vitaly remembers a few more vital bits of information about what remains one of the most traumatic periods of his life.[1]

It has become a cliché to say that we live in a post-truth age. Journalists write articles and academics study the phenomenon. It has become ubiquitous in the intellectual sphere. Nonetheless, the term retains an aphoristic value that is plain to see. Users flood Twitter with hoaxes and doctored images; Facebook is awash with detailed conspiracies blaming world crises on the Illuminati or a secret world order. The serpent of anti-Semitism has risen again, this time spitting its venom into cyberspace.

Social media has enabled a light to be shined on the powerless and voiceless. It has enabled the telling of stories that should be told. But through its ability to circumvent media's traditional gatekeepers, it has also contributed to the spread of misleading and outright fake news that is able to reach wide audiences to a degree unprecedented in modern history. The rise of social media has both coincided with and exacerbated a crisis of faith in the West and its institutions. From the 2003 Iraq War to the 2008 global financial crisis to the Snowden NSA spying revelations, politics, finance, the intelligence services, and most of all the media have been systematically discredited.

This is a fact the Kremlin understands perfectly and which lies at the heart of its propaganda. Just as Anna took to social media to fight Kremlin aggression on the battlefields, so the Kremlin will inevitably fight back both to justify its actions and to shroud them in a bewildering array of narratives designed to distort truth and confuse its enemies. In a world where conspiracy theory is turbocharged by social media, this type of obfuscation has found its perfect platforms. "Question More": the slogan of Moscow's most prominent international propaganda arm, the TV channel RT, perhaps best articulates the Russian strategy. In 2016, RT received around $250 million from the Russian state, and it broadcasts in English, Arabic, and Spanish, as well as having a presence in Russian, French, and German; it is reportedly the most popular television news network on YouTube.[2] It strictly hews to the government line, and its goals are clear: RT seeks not to gain global approval for the Kremlin and its policies but to sow discord among Moscow's perceived enemies. In the postmodern Western world, where academics decry the notion of an "objective truth," where the lack of trust in institutions is lower than at any other time in living memory, this type of information finds a receptive audience. "Question More" becomes in effect "Trust Less."

Central to achieving this goal is social media. We return to Evgeny Morozov's argument that the West has seemingly developed an almost messianic belief in the democratizing power of the Internet. This amounts to something he describes as "cyber-utopianism": give people in a dictatorship access to the Internet and it will set them free.[3] To a degree, and for a while, it may. But this belief, as Morozov understood, is ultimately misguided. The Internet will inevitably come to benefit the oppressor as well as the oppressed; it may help the people battle the authoritarian state, but in the end the state will always use the same tools to fight back.

And encapsulated in that fightback—for a brief time and just as a minor player—was Vitaly.

It was early August 2014 in the Russian city of St. Petersburg, and Vitaly Bespalov was stuck. He'd always dreamed of being a journalist, especially in a great metropolis like St. Petersburg—the locus of his dreams. After high school, though, he had been too scared to leave Siberia for the big city, and he'd ended up studying journalism in Tyumen. It was a fruitful time. He made some journalistic contacts in St. Petersburg and began freelancing for a couple of the city's websites. By the time he graduated he had managed to secure a job with an online publication there devoted to politics. The small-town boy had made it.

Vitaly was good. And he was successful; in time, he became the website's managing editor, with a wide brief to write about his passion: politics, both in St. Petersburg and in Russia at large. Then came the Ukraine war and with it, for Vitaly, disaster. As retribution for EU sanctions against Russia in response to its illegal annexation of Crimea from Ukraine, the Russian government instituted sanctions of its own, mainly on food imported from the EU. Vitaly's website was partly funded by an EU-based company, which cut its financial support. Things were no longer tenable, and the website was shut down.

Now Vitaly was unemployed in an expensive city, and he had bills to pay. The next few weeks were spent in a frenzy: he sent out his résumé to every publication he could think of, and he responded to every newspaper and online advertisement that had even a vague connection to journalism or writing. After a month of no success he was desperate. Then he got a call. Could he come for an interview the following day? It was like the first drop of rain after a drought. Over the phone, the lady told him the address of the office, but not the name of the company. He had sent so many résumés out that he didn't even know which application the interview was for. But he didn't care. It was a chance.

The following day he made sure to arrive in good time and, announcing himself, took a seat in the reception area. Though it was nothing more than a small hall with turnstiles, the security was bizarrely high. Several guards dressed in military-like uniforms patrolled the reception area; Vitaly thought they would look good with machine guns. He noticed that only people with a special pass could enter the building, which struck him as unusual, and certainly not typical for anything media-related. While he was waiting he saw a woman, about thirty-five or forty years old, dressed formally and wearing glasses, storm out toward the exit. She was shouting and swearing because it appeared that whoever had interviewed her had asked for her passport information—something she clearly thought was unacceptable. "I am not going to work for you; delete my passport information!" she screamed at security. "I would never work as a lawyer in this *shrashkina kontora* [swindler's outfit]."

"Christ," Vitaly thought, "she's brave."

After about half an hour he was called in to be interviewed by a woman of about thirty named Anna. After some initial small talk, she asked to see his portfolio of articles and gave him a form to fill out. He had to include his address, his passport information, telephone number, previous places of work, parents' names and address, and his brothers' names and addresses—"for security reasons," she told him. He was surprised at the detail required, but he needed a job, so he filled it out anyway. Then Anna set him a test: she asked him to find any news about Ukraine on the Internet and to rewrite it so that the text looked unique—or at least sufficiently different from the original—but stuck to the facts. She left the room to let him get on with it, which he did. He selected an article from RIA Novosti, one of Russia's foremost media outlets. As a journalist, he found the task easy.

When he finished, Anna came back in and read what he had written. While she was out of the room she had read his portfolio, which was filled with liberal-leaning articles on the opposition leader Alexei Navalny and the anti-Putin protest pop group Pussy Riot. She told him that this work would be different. But, she said, it was clear he was capable of doing it. His job, she elaborated, would be to rewrite the news about Ukraine. "Will it be propaganda?" he asked. "No," she replied, "it will be neutral, and it will pay 45,000 rubles [then around $900] per month"—far higher, as Vitaly knew, than the average wage for that sort of work. If the company's security service approved his application, she concluded, he would get the job. The interview was over.

The next day, which was a Friday, he got a call telling him that he could start work on Monday. He had doubts, but his friend told him straight out, "You need the money. Take the job." The number of security guards at reception, the angry lawyer—it all stuck in his mind and made him apprehensive. Also, after the interview he had searched the office address, 55 Savushkina Street, on 2gis (an app like Google Maps), and the building came up as being "under construction." To make matters worse, he looked through all the résumés he had sent out, but he couldn't figure out which application had led to the interview.

Later on, after it was all over, Vitaly would speak to people who also went to interviews there and turned down the job because everything from the appearance of the building to the security to the fact that the computers were arranged in such a way that everyone could see what you were writing spooked them. But Vitaly needed a job so badly at the time, he would have gladly worked in a basement.

That Monday, Vitaly arrived at the office on 55 Savushkina Street, a drab building, all gray concrete slabs and nondescript glass windows, and entered. The receptionist called Anna, who came down and promptly led him upstairs into a long corridor that reminded Vitaly of a hospital: bleak and gloomy, with doors at regular intervals on each side. Eventually the two entered an open-plan room consisting of rows of desks with computers. It looked like an IT room at a Russian school. The walls were bare; it was clear that whoever owned the space hadn't cared enough to spend much money on décor or furnishings. Anna told him he would be working on a project called Ukraine 2, writing articles for the website worldukraine.com.ua. The .ua URL was meant to make the website look like it was based in Ukraine and not St. Petersburg. It was all rather slapdash. No one even bothered to explain to him how being an administrator on a website worked, but he'd learned how to do it at his previous job. New arrivals would often need help, though, and Vitaly would have to talk them through the process.

Anna told him what was expected of him for the Ukraine 2 project: he needed to rewrite twenty articles a day, averaging eight hundred words each. Vitaly asked, once again, if he would have to write anti-Ukrainian propaganda of the type he was seeing all over the Russian media. Anna once again said no. But still, he remained suspicious. Forty-five thousand rubles per month for a job that even a student could do? It made no sense. Nonetheless, he got to work, and it was, as he had been told, simple. The goal was to rewrite articles that could get to the top of Google and Yandex (the Russian version of Google), so the website needed to contain unique text. Social media was vital to the job, as the articles had to be promoted on platforms where they could gain the most traffic: primarily VKontakte, Russia's version of Facebook. He followed the guidelines Anna had laid out at the interview: the facts and central themes of the article would remain unchanged with just key chunks of text rewritten. The website was not openly anti-Ukrainian and had few visitors. Mostly the articles came from Russian websites with a few Ukrainian ones thrown in as well, some written in Russian and some in Ukrainian.

The intended audience was Russian speakers in Ukraine. Vitaly speaks some Ukrainian, and Google Translate is excellent at translating from Ukrainian to Russian, as the grammar is essentially the same, so writing articles of sufficient quality proved to be easy. The changes weren't, he thought, significant. He needed to change words like "terrorist" and "separatist" into "militia" and instead of "Ukrainian army" write "national guard" or "volunteer battalions," which had (often deserved) bad reputations for containing thuggish and far-right elements. Also, to convince Ukrainians that the site was genuine, he would use stylistic tricks, rewriting text to make it friendlier to Ukrainian eyes. He always made sure to use the preposition *v* instead of *na* when talking about Ukraine. Most Russians still use the Soviet "na Ukraine" (on the border), rather than "v Ukraine" (in Ukraine)—the former suggesting Ukraine is not a full-fledged country, but something merely along Russia's border. Also, he could never refer to the cities of Donetsk or Luhansk—it always had to be the People's Republic of Donetsk (DNR) and People's Republic of Luhansk (LNR), the official separatist names for the cities they had occupied. When translating news from Ukrainian media he also had to say it came from mainstream Ukrainian sources when it was actually often from DNR or LNR sources. Above all, he was prohibited from criticizing Russia or the separatists in any way. The job wasn't perfect, but it certainly wasn't an all-out propaganda war of the type he had feared. For the time being, at least, Vitaly could pocket his 45,000 rubles per month with a reasonably clear conscience.

Especially since the job was so easy. Each day, he would arrive at 9:00 a.m., and use his ID card to get through security. Here was one area that the higher-ups did take seriously: when you swiped in, your time was logged, and if you were late, even by a minute, you would pay a fine. Be late by an hour, and you were told to simply go home; the day was lost and you went unpaid. He then sat down in front of his computer and bashed out seventeen or eighteen news articles until lunch at 1:00 p.m. After lunch he'd write the final two or three articles, which would take him up until around 2:00 p.m. The working day ended at 5:30 p.m., so from 2:00 to 5:30 he did his own thing.

He made a friend, Evgenia. Together they would take regular smoke breaks (he'd previously given up smoking, but with the unease he felt over the job had taken it up again) and complain about their jobs, exchanging gossip and badmouthing disliked colleagues. Evgenia worked on Ukraine 1, which centered on the website www .nahnews.org, which was supposed to be a news outlet based in the east Ukrainian city of Kharkiv, but was in reality based out of the room next door to Vitaly's.

Ukraine 1—and therefore nahnews.com—was far more stridently pro-Russia than his own website. It was also far more popular, with more than 100,000 visitors per day, in contrast to the 100 or fewer per day at worldukraine.com.ua (and he suspected that most of those were his friends with whom he shared links). He was public about his feelings on his work. "Look at the nonsense I am doing," he'd tweet with a link to the relevant article. Tweeting and posting were encouraged at all times—the goal was to make articles as widely spread as possible, ideally to go viral—for which social media was obviously vital.

As he grew closer to Evgenia, the two would have lunch together, which was a strict thirty minutes. Evgenia told him that over on Ukraine 1 things were much more tightly controlled. While he got barely any supervision, the nahnews.com editors scrutinized everything the Ukraine 1 team did: she was constantly given feedback on her articles' content. Everything they wrote had to describe the Donbas militia in a positive light and to undermine the Ukrainian army. If, for example, the Ukrainian army claimed they had taken control of an area, nahnews.com would say it was a lie. The team also needed to give the impression that the population of southeastern Ukraine fully supported the separatists and hated the Ukrainian government.

As time passed he learned more from Evgenia. It became clear to him that he was a player (albeit a small one) in an all-out information war against Ukraine. He began to suspect that the reasonably neutral worldukraine.ua was a test, a probationary period, because he was a newcomer, and a liberal to boot. He didn't like the idea. But Evgenia didn't mind. She wasn't political—to her it was just a paycheck, and a pretty good one at that. If, he said to me in the flat in Tyumen that day, she knew he was doing an interview with a foreign journalist, she'd most likely just laugh and say, "Tell him Putin's doing a good job!" On smoking and lunch breaks, however, he found out from other people that "true believers" also worked there, people who fanatically supported the Kremlin's war on Ukraine and enjoyed the work they did.

Picking up snippets about the company from wherever he could, Vitaly was beginning to realize that he worked for what the press would later call a "troll factory" or "troll farm." He felt like he was in a reality show, controlled by external powers that tested just how long people could tolerate senseless work. He was also reminded of George Orwell's *1984*. He had read the book a while back, and whenever he pictured the company's building on Savushkina Street, he could not help but think of the book's "Ministry of Information." He was never told why he was doing what he was doing; he was never given any information, period. When he asked Anna, his boss, she wouldn't give him proper answers. Even worse, Vitaly had the impression that it was because she didn't know, either.

Even when he explicitly tried to find out more about the operation, he found it almost impossible. People on different floors barely talked to each other, let alone had any clue who was behind the troll farm. At one point Vitaly found out through friends that there was another, similar company called Concord, where people wrote articles promoting the Russian army. Vitaly had actually interviewed at Concord before taking this job but had been rejected, he found out later, because he didn't have the appropriate appearance—he didn't look masculine enough. Later, after he left the troll farm, Vitaly would find out that the owner was Yevgeny Prigozhin, who also owns Concord and several restaurants in St. Petersburg.[4]

The troll farm, Vitaly gradually learned, had a clear structure. The first floor, where he worked, was the so-called media holdings department, which consisted of people working on about ten or twelve Russian and fake Ukrainian websites. Those working on the Russian websites were considered more privileged as they would sometimes get to go to other Russian cities on work trips. There were around eight to ten people working on Ukraine 1, and around sixty people in the news department. He estimated that there were around 150 people on all the other floors, though he couldn't be sure. Most of the employees were young and female; Vitaly reckoned that around 90 percent of them were between the ages of twenty-five and thirty. There was no dress code: many people had piercings, trendy haircuts, and tattoos.

On the second floor was the social media department. Here people were responsible for creating cartoons and memes to spread around social media in support of Kremlin policy on Ukraine. About eight people worked there. On the third floor were the bloggers writing fake blogs, pretending to be Ukrainians writing about how desperate their situation was—saying that children in Kyiv kindergartens didn't have enough food, or that parts of the city had no central heating or electricity. They would also blog in English, pretending to be Americans criticizing Obama over his Russia policy. They would create entirely fake American blogs or take information from pro-Russia English-language websites and present those views as representative of the English-speaking world. These blogs would then become "sources" for the fake articles, which was a cause of great amusement for those who wrote them, as they knew the "Ukrainian blogger from Kyiv" was most likely sitting just two floors above them. It was a merry-go-round of lies.

The fourth floor, as well as the dining area, contained the people whose job it was to post comments on social media, including Facebook, VKontakte, Twitter, and YouTube—any social media platform where news was discussed. There was little contact between floors; in fact, there was mutual dislike. The people who posted comments and the bloggers were tight with each other, but the news department, where Vitaly spent his first month, looked down on all the other departments. Generally those on the first floor had, by virtue of the skills needed to perform their job, a higher level of education and literacy. They tended to be journalists who needed the money. "We may be trolls, but you are uneducated trolls" was the general feeling.

After a couple of weeks it was clear that worldukraine.com.ua was not working, and Vitaly's team was disbanded. Some were sent to work on Ukraine 1, but Anna, who knew of Vitaly's liberal views, decided he wouldn't like it there. But she liked the quality of his work, so she instead took him with her to work on a new project under Ukraine 2. Anna started working for a Russian propaganda website, Narodne Novosti, concerned with news about Russia, Ukraine, and the wider world. Vitaly's job, meanwhile, was to get as much traffic as possible for the recently established www.nation-news.ru. It was also propaganda, but for a different, far less well-educated audience. It dedicated around 20 percent of its content to Ukraine, another 20 percent to negative news about the United States, and the rest to Russia and show business. By now it was clear to Vitaly what the purpose of both his job and the company was: to encourage ill will toward Ukraine and the United States and to enrage people. Once united in anger, they would find it easier to support Putin's increasingly aggressive nationalism.

Work was a struggle. Vitaly, in addition to working on nation -news.ru, also was asked to create fake Ukrainian websites. He created one called Livov News (he used the Russian spelling instead of the traditional Ukrainian spelling of the western city of Lviv), for which he would find news on real Lviv websites and translate them into Russian; he didn't even need to rewrite the text, he just used Google Translate. It was strange; in this instance it wasn't even real propaganda, and he thought that maybe the company was trying to create fake websites that would get a lot of traffic, which they could eventually sell.

But the websites weren't successful and eventually, a month into Vitaly's time at the farm, Ukraine 2 was shut down.[5] He was sent to the second floor to join the cartoon and meme-makers. As he expected, it was the worst possible move. He'd heard that everyone hated the people from the second floor—they were rude, considered to be *bydlo* (rednecks). And Vitaly didn't like the people there, either: they were uneducated, having mostly only attended elementary school. They swore a lot and seemed to talk only about how drunk they got on weekends. Their work was equally primitive: they posted links anywhere they could, which meant that their websites often got blocked because of their stupid spamming efforts. After three days, he couldn't stand it any longer and asked to be moved back to the first floor, where he continued working on social media, but at least sat among people he found more tolerable.

The work, though, was mind-numbing. His previous post had at least required a modicum of skill. Now his only job was to promote the farm's fake websites on social media. LiveJournal, VKontakte, Facebook, Odnoklassniki (a Russian version of Friends Reunited), and Twitter were the main outlets. His boss gave him loads of different SIM cards in order to register multiple VKontakte accounts. They were invariably female profiles, as it was assumed that fellow social network users would perceive female accounts as more trustworthy than male ones.

Often his fake profiles would get banned because he was also forced to spam other people's home pages or group pages with links to the fake websites. But that wasn't a problem. His boss would just give him a new SIM card and off he'd go again. The farm seemed to have an inexhaustible supply. The work was tiresome; there wasn't even any logic to it. Many of his colleagues would post articles about Ukrainian fascists in Donbas to groups that had nothing to do with politics.

A key element in the information war had started before Vitaly joined the farm. On July 17, 2014, pro-Russia separatists shot down the Malaysia Airlines passenger flight MH17 over eastern Ukraine, killing all 283 passengers and 15 crew members on board with a rocket obtained from a Russian army unit. The outrage was global. Russia ramped up its information war, spreading various counter-narratives blaming anyone except Moscow for shooting down the plane. MH17 was a big theme for the troll farm, and people would post links to articles saying that the Ukrainians had shot it down, putting the links everywhere—even, in one instance, on the page of a group devoted to meeting for sex in the city of Chelyabinsk, near the Ural Mountains. The goal was twofold. The first was to shore up the Kremlin's own constituency by giving them a narrative to hold on to and subsequently disseminate. The second, more bemusing to him, was to simply sow as much confusion as possible: to counteract the realities on the ground with counternarratives made forceful not by the strength of their content, which was blatantly false, but by their sheer volume. It was surreal.

Critical to this effort was capturing users' attention. You couldn't, Vitaly was told, just post a link and expect people to click on it. He was instructed to create memes and to use funny cartoons whenever possible, especially ones about prominent figures perceived as being hostile to Russia's campaign against Ukraine: then–US president Barack

Obama, German chancellor Angela Merkel, and leading Ukrainian politicians were all targets. Mocking Putin in any way was banned. Vitaly was evaluated by the number of visitors the websites received; if he posted a link that got a lot of traffic, it was a job well done.

Since most people, he was told, don't actually read the text or follow the link, the meme or cartoon had to be a way of leaving the message in itself. So Vitaly and his social media colleagues spent endless hours creating memes about Ukrainian fascists, the greatness of Putin, and the perniciousness of Obama. A central narrative theme was that Obama and Merkel were responsible for the situation in Ukraine. In the articles, quotes were willfully taken out of context: if, for example, Obama or Merkel said Ukraine should be a united country and the war stopped, it was presented as if they had said Ukraine should be united through war. In one meme that Vitaly posted to VKontakte, the text "I want to start a war but none of my friends will join me" accompanied a photo of Obama looking almost tearful.[6] A particularly popular meme came out soon after the United States put sanctions on Russia: it featured Putin knocking Obama out in a boxing ring.[7] Vitaly got a particularly good response from a two-panel meme he posted: in the first photo an angry-looking Obama said, "We don't talk to terrorists!" and in the second he was shown smiling with the caption "We just sponsor them."[8] He also created an image of Obama, his face spattered with blood, biting a chunk out of a map of Ukraine.[9] It was basic stuff but effective.

Sometimes they took foreign media articles that criticized Ukraine and presented them as global opinion. The article would claim to represent "foreign mass media" when the content in reality came from just one publication, the name of which was buried deep in the text. Then they pushed the narrative that many Ukrainian cities wanted to become Russian—the farm created endless articles saying that the city of Kharkiv wanted to become a part of Novorossiya (a czarist term to describe parts of southeastern Ukraine). Still, though, the fake websites weren't appearing high enough up the search engines, so Vitaly set up a page on VKontakte and Facebook dedicated to the fake news site nation-news.ru and filled that with content. He also found groups dedicated to supporting the separatists and to glorifying the Russian state and posted the memes there. The people in those groups devoured that sort of material, which meant more traffic. When he posted there, most people clicked on the links, leaving comments like: "Yes, I have ALWAYS KNOWN THAT THE DAMN FASCISTS ARE KILLING OUR PEOPLE IN THE DONBAS." Vitaly knew there was no point denying that he was now part of a full-on information war, but he told himself he was just finding idiots and giving them what they wanted.

And so like most people do in jobs, Vitaly settled into a routine. He would find a photo of Angela Merkel and superimpose a Hitler mustache onto it.[10] He took a photo of Ukrainian prime minister Arseniy Yatsenyuk's head and Photoshopped it onto a traditional Ukrainian woman's dress, arranging the figure so that Yatsenyuk appeared to be clutching a suitcase full of dollars in one hand and a wad of cash in the other while running away from the Verkhovna Rada (Ukraine's parliament), with the caption "Time to get out of here."[11] He turned Ukraine's president, Petro Poroshenko, into a pig.

It was all designed to make the Ukrainian government look ridiculous and the threat of Ukraine's supposed "fascists" look grave. Central to this was Pravy Sektor, the far-right group that played a large part in the Euromaidan protests. It was in reality a fringe group whose leader received barely any support in the first post-Euromaidan Ukrainian presidential elections. Nonetheless, endless photos and memes were created to push the idea that Pravy Sektor was a huge fascistic organization, linking to articles that detailed the group's supposed atrocities. Often Ukrainian army actions in Donbas were blamed on Pravy Sektor. Any photo he could find of far-right Ukrainians he would spread.[12]

As well as attacking Western and Ukrainian leaders, the goal was also to boost the separatists. One memorable meme featured Natalia Poklonskaya, the attractive prosecutor general of Crimea (who joined the separatists when Russia invaded), dressed in a sexy uniform carrying a machine gun. The words "Crimea" and "Russia" topped and tailed the cartoon, linking to an article entitled "Crimea Is Ours—and So Are Visas," which claimed that residents of Crimea would get EU Schengen visas.[13] The goal was to play on the patriotic feelings of Russians who felt Crimea was theirs.

It was awful work. Vitaly spent a lot of time on social media talking to his friends and reading up on the news. More to the point, his job was seriously getting to him. He was now undeniably part of an information war that clashed directly with his liberal principles. He started to rebel in small ways. Sometimes he worked against the operation from the inside by deliberately not spreading "news" that he knew would be popular. Sometimes instead of anti-Ukrainian news he spread anti-Russian news. One fake article he just refused to share. It was about an LGBT activist from Euromaidan who purportedly harassed a straight man who, in turn, killed the "sodomite." The goal here was clear: to delegitimize the Euromaidan protests by associating it with the LGBT movement, which, in Russia's deeply homophobic society, is anathema. He was given the article, told it was top news, and instructed to spread it widely. It was one of the few instances when he openly defied his superiors.

It was now clear to Vitaly that he had to quit. He had originally intended to work at the farm for six months, but now, after around three and a half months, it was all too much. He started having issues with his nerves. He couldn't stop thinking about the type of "shit" he was doing. He felt dirty. Long after he quit, he still couldn't get the experience out of his mind.

By this point there had been a couple of exposés of the troll farm in the Russian media. Everyone in St. Petersburg with the slightest interest in politics knew about it, and it became uncomfortable having to tell his friends what he did for a living. So at the end of 2014 he told Anna he wouldn't be continuing with his contract. She took him to the canteen and immediately began questioning him on the reasons for his decision. He was honest, and told her that he didn't believe in what the farm was doing.

After he left, he felt he had to do something to make amends, so he began contacting St. Petersburg media to see if they'd be interested in having him write a story on his time at the farm. At first nobody responded, but then a news website, www.sobaka.ru, did. He wrote the article anonymously and pretended to be a woman (like the majority of the farm's employees).[14] The article came out three weeks after he left. It caused a stir. Even opposition leader Alexei Navalny tweeted a link to it.

Vitaly had tried to remain anonymous but he was worried that it would be easy to work out who the real author was. He was right. An hour after the article came out Anna sent him a long and abusive message saying that he had behaved like a bastard who couldn't do anything for himself but only go behind people's backs and spoil things for others. "You may think of yourself as a hero," she wrote, "but in reality you're just a little son of a bitch."

Then the phone calls started. "What the fuck do you think you're doing? People can get punched in the face for doing this sort of stuff," a gruff male voice growled down the phone at him a day later. He got several more calls like that over the next week or so; the number was always blocked. For a while he was afraid to walk the streets alone.

When, toward the end of our interview, I asked Vitaly if he considered himself to have been an actor in the Ukraine war, he replied that yes, "unfortunately," he had been—and he was right. When Vitaly joined the troll farm he enlisted in the Russian army. He may not have worn a uniform or carried a gun, but he was a soldier nonetheless. While Anna used Facebook to enable her to become a warrior on the ground, Vitaly was a virtual one, fighting a narrative battle at the discursive level of war. Every meme he created or fake article he wrote was just one more virtual bullet he fired into the social media space. And every person who linked to that article on Facebook or Twitter or shared that meme enlisted, too. With a single press of the Share or Tweet button, they became their own little propaganda machine for the cause. And in this army there are almost no barriers to entry. It's the virtual form of total war, in which anyone with an Internet connection can take part.

This is what makes it so dangerous. "In these times," Vitaly continued, "Russian journalists must take a stand for or against Ukraine. A journalist in Russia can be neutral if he's writing about pop culture, models, or show business, but even if you're writing about culture or sport you often touch upon Ukraine. A film called *The 8 Best Dates* recently came out in the cinema. It had nothing to with politics, but the main actor is a Ukrainian who spoke publicly in favor of the Ukrainian army. At the premiere there were lots of demonstrations against him and the film. Even the critics talked more about the politics than the film. Everything in Russia is politicized now.

"Russian taxpayers pay for the troll farm," Vitaly continued. "It's a kind of legalized corruption. And, worst of all, I think the government believes it's a patriotic duty to set up initiatives like this."

In the end, I asked Vitaly, what was the troll farm's ultimate goal? "The troll farm is a continuation of Russian TV—to teach people fake patriotism, to justify the behavior and the actions of the Russian government, to reaffirm that whatever TV says is the reality," he replied. "They are doing exactly what Russian TV does, except on the Internet. Most people in Russia watch state-controlled TV; for those who prefer to surf the Net, there is the troll farm."

The ability of the troll farm to both shore up the Kremlin's base and confuse the narrative was, in the end, flawed but considerable. And it is important to understand how this one outfit stands as the embodiment of Russia's wider twenty-first-century military doctrine. As Mark Galeotti, a Russia expert and a senior research fellow at the Institute of International Relations in Prague, the Czech Republic, told me, "The Russians are painfully aware that they cannot confront the United States or NATO by conventional military means. Instead they look for ways to weaken the resolve, the unity, the coordination within the Western alliance and within [Western] countries themselves. It's not like they have some complex, carefully thought-through strategy. We are in many ways victims of our own assumptions that Russians are all chess-playing grandmasters thinking seventeen moves ahead."[15]

What Galeotti perceives is something more chaotic: "Instead they're throwing everything but the kitchen sink into this campaign on the principle that you can launch twenty different information operations, ranging from paid intelligence officers trying to blackmail someone to random teenagers in Omsk posting stuff on social media, and if only 20 percent succeed, then it's a success."[16]

But what would success mean? When I asked a US State Department official (who did not wish to be named) if the West was losing the information war against Russia, the response was atypically blunt: "Losing what? Pew [the polling company] did a global poll a while back asking people in various countries what their opinion of Russia was. All the countries had a very low opinion of it. . . . The bottom line is that Russians are spending millions and no one is being convinced."[17]

But it is on this precise point that we come again to the dichotomy upon which Russia's information war is based. The goal, as Vitaly had discovered, is twofold. The first is to convince and reassure those who want to be convinced and reassured. This is simple enough. The second goal is, as Galeotti observes, to sow discord and disharmony within the West, to confuse and to obfuscate—mostly through the spread of disinformation and, critically, through a knowledge of the West's weak points. This is Russian propaganda or disinformation, *dezinformatsiya*, for the twenty-first century. It may even be able to convince a small minority of those beyond its Russian-speaking base.

The West is seeing the rise of populist, antiestablishment parties and politicians, from France's National Front, to which the Kremlin extended an $11.7 million loan to in 2014, to Donald Trump, whom

Putin personally praised on several occasions and whom RT television consistently promoted and supported throughout the 2016 US presidential election campaign.[18] Trump, in return, repeatedly hailed the Russian president as a better leader than Barack Obama, and even, staggeringly, appeared on RT America to criticize US foreign policy. Over the course of the campaign he also repeated, almost verbatim, the Kremlin line on various issues such as Ukraine as well its denial that Russian hackers had infiltrated the Democratic Party.[19] RT also adamantly supported those advocating for Britain's withdrawal from the European Union in the June 2016 referendum campaign in order to weaken European unity—an issue that split the British electorate into two bitterly opposed camps. The divisions are there to exploit. The Kremlin can reach those on both left and right who question liberal democracy in its time of crisis. It can reach those of an anti-EU or anti-Washington bent. It even reached the winning US presidential candidate. Who knows how much Russian propaganda may now start to enter the US political mainstream.

The more doubt you can sow in people's minds about *all* information, the more you will weaken their propensity to recognize the truth when they see or hear it. This is the overarching goal at the heart of Russia's propaganda—and it is one that Vitaly ultimately came to understand. At the end of our interview he looked genuinely depressed. Clearly our conversation had brought back bad memories, but it was when I asked him about the ultimate effects of the operation that he became truly downcast. "Look," he told me, "my parents use the Internet. They used to read these sort of comments and articles, to look at the memes and cartoons, and they used to believe them—like so many other people. Now they know it's probably almost all fake. Now no one believes anything anymore."

7

THE POSTMODERN DICTATOR: ADVENTURES IN UNREALITY

Russian president Vladimir Putin understands the times in which he lives. When he annexed Crimea, Putin invaded and lopped off part of another country. His desire to steal other people's land was atavistic. US secretary of state John Kerry called it a "nineteenth-century" move; it would have been equally at home in the ninth century.[1] But his methods were irretrievably twenty-first-century.

Putin never officially invaded Crimea. No war was declared; no Russian soldiers ever officially crossed the border. Instead, several hundred troops marched into Simferopol and seized its regional parliament and Council of Ministers. They were masked and wore green uniforms without any identifying insignia. Of course everyone knew they were Russian, not least when they hoisted Russian flags over the captured buildings. Then, over the next few weeks, the "little green men" took control of the region, and on March 16, in a controversial, Russian-sponsored referendum, more than 96 percent of Crimeans purportedly voted to join the Russian Federation. Moscow had annexed a chunk of another sovereign state without officially invading it, or even firing a shot. It was, Putin said, democracy in action.

In one sense this is nothing new. The Russians call it *maskirovka*, military deception that "is carried out at national and theater levels to mislead the enemy as to political and military capabilities, intentions and timing of actions. In these spheres, as war is but an extension of politics, it includes political, economic and diplomatic measures as well as military."[2] Russia's revered Marshal Georgy Zhukov developed it as a doctrine in the 1920s, but it is perfect for Putin, who is a new breed of autocrat.

In his book *The Dictator's Learning Curve: Inside the Global Battle for Democracy* William J. Dobson argues that today's successful despots are the ones who have understood the need to evolve. Totalitarianism is a fundamentally twentieth-century phenomenon. Idi Amin, Pol Pot, and Saddam Hussein are passé—they all tried it and they all failed. The yearning for democracy is, as the Arab Spring showed, global. Its promotion, as Dobson points out, is an international industry stuffed with an array of human rights, election monitoring, and development organizations, not to mention the passersby who will broadcast your every sadism to the Internet.[3] Become too overtly homicidal and you are Syria's Bashar al-Assad; wall yourself up from the world and you become North Korea's Kim Jong-un.

Putin has internalized these lessons. You can behave to all intents and purposes like a dictator, but you must look like a democrat. Putin's Russia has replaced Soviet brutality with more understated forms of oppression, scrupulously coated in a veneer of democracy and the language of human rights. He has replaced the gulag with zoning violations to shut down the offices of dissident newspapers, the firing squad with audits to bankrupt recalcitrant businessmen. Elections (though rigged) are observed; the constitution (though liberally interpreted) is sacred; opposition parties are created rather than banned. Democracy is "managed." And you can't go around invading countries or killing people en masse. This is something

Ukraine's former president Viktor Yanukovych never understood, and his brutality during the Euromaidan uprising proved to be his downfall. Yanukovych was a modern dictator; Putin is the first postmodern one. Yanukovych was analog; Putin is digital.

Even Russia's revanchist adventures in Syria—in which tens of thousands have died so that Moscow can both prop up its ally Assad and promote a vision of an imperial Russia designed to placate Putin's decreasingly prosperous population—have been "managed." First, Syria is an outlier, an overt show of Russian force in a region to a large degree vacated by the United States during the Obama administration. Second, the Syria action was cloaked in the guise of one of the twenty-first century's most sacred geopolitical tropes: fighting terrorism.

In eastern Ukraine, despite considerable evidence that Russia has sent both military equipment and its Spetsnaz (special forces) to aid the separatists, the Kremlin still denies overt Russian involvement. Ukraine is fighting the separatists and by proxy Russia, but no war has been declared and its ultimate enemy doesn't officially exist. Soviet strategy with a twenty-first-century twist.

Journeying throughout eastern Ukraine as the cities and towns fell, almost daily, to pro-Russia separatists in early spring 2014 was a gradual immersion into the surreal realities of postmodern warfare. The effects of Russia's information blitzkrieg were ubiquitous: online content had seeped into the offline world and was reinventing reality for those it targeted. Every city I visited was in a state of civil and military chaos, but amid it all, certain key tropes kept reappearing—ideas and motifs, parroted to me by eastern Ukrainians, that could have come directly from Vitaly's virtual pen on Savushkina Street. It was surreal. But behind the chaos was clarity. Putin's Russia understands perfectly the power of narratives in wartime, and employs them more adeptly than any other state in the world. In the Estonian presidential palace, President Toomas Hendrik Ilves, whose country has its own Russian-speaking minority and also fears possible Kremlin actions, summed up the reasoning behind Russia's efforts:

> Occupying Ukraine is beyond the means of Russia; it would not work at this point given the politicization of the Ukrainian people. On the other hand, if you can keep it off balance and unstable, if you can promote the narrative that these guys are a bunch of corrupt Nazi jerks, then you've won anyway because sympathy for Ukraine lessens. This narrative has taken hold in some parts of Europe to the degree that it mobilizes opposition to EU aid packages. I mean, we're not going to abandon Ukraine but it's going to be hard. You see the argument now: Why should we give them money when it all disappears [into the hands of corrupt politicians]? So if you create that narrative you don't necessarily need Russian occupation troops because you help create dire poverty and an inefficient, impotent state. So the narrative is both a military and political tool.[4]

My experiences in Ukraine exposed me to nearly all the practices associated with twenty-first-century warfare, and in particular the increased use of "non-kinetic" (nonmilitary) means to make war, especially those brought about by Web 2.0. To compound the sense of vertiginous unreality, all of these themes played out within the context of a "gray zone" conflict, in which all parties existed in a state of neither war nor peace. What I witnessed was a clear example of Emile Simpson's war as "armed politics." Russia had put troops and separatist proxies on the ground in eastern Ukraine, but it was clear that its primary objective was not to defeat the Ukrainian army, which it easily could have done. In fact, that was so far from being Moscow's primary objective that it never even bothered to declare war, and while it sent troops and machinery across the border to aid the separatists, it never did so to the degree that would have been required to defeat the enemy. Instead, as Ilves notes, its focus went toward weakening the Ukrainian state by getting eastern Ukrainians to subscribe to a particular narrative. Again, the purpose of military operations was to support information operations.

As Mary Kaldor has noted, those most successful at "new wars" are those who are most able "to avoid battle and to control territory through political control of the population."[5] This was exactly what Moscow was doing on the ground. Just as Emile Simpson notes that the goal of British soldiers in Afghanistan became not to defeat the Taliban per se but to convince the local population to support the Afghan government, Russia's actions were designed to get eastern Ukrainians to subscribe to the Kremlin narrative and in so doing attack the Ukrainian state without having to conquer its capital or defeat its army.

In this can be seen Putin's masterstroke. With a combination of carefully orchestrated propagandas backed up by limited military force, he had created the very definition of a gray-zone conflict:

> Gray zone conflict is best understood as activity that is coercive and aggressive in nature, but that is deliberately designed to remain below the threshold of conventional military conflict and open interstate war. Gray zone approaches are mostly the province of revisionist powers—those actors that seek to modify some aspect of the existing international environment—and the goal is to reap gains, whether territorial or otherwise, that are normally associated with victory in war. Yet gray zone approaches are meant to achieve those gains without escalating to overt warfare, without crossing established red-lines, and thus without exposing the practitioner to the penalties and risks that such escalation might bring.[6]

What this meant in practice was that the opportunity for outside powers to intervene on Ukraine's behalf was and is severely restricted. Without a declaration of war, international powers could not openly

accuse Putin of being an outright aggressor. Senior international figures condemned Russian actions (and of course knew the truth of the
situation), but that mattered little. Russia did suffer for its behavior
in the form of sanctions. But it gained Crimea and it continued to
destabilize Ukraine, safe in the knowledge that, short of it commit-
ting massacres or rolling its army into Kyiv, the world will talk but
do almost nothing. The world has not yet caught up with Russia: it
still believes that words, propaganda, and partisan narratives are less
dangerous than tanks. What Russia accomplished was the definition
of twenty-first-century warfare carried out with chilling efficiency
and aplomb.

"Novorossiya! Novorossiya!" the man bellowed as he swigged from
a bottle containing an indeterminate clear liquid that, whatever it
might have been, was clearly getting the job done. It was late 2014,
and I was standing outside a cafe in Donetsk, in eastern Ukraine, trying to make a phone call. He leaned in, his breath reeking of spirits—I
began to fear he was actually drinking straight alcohol—and jabbed
a finger at me. "Kyiv—fascist junta, fascist junta!" he repeated in broken English. "Bandera, ptui!" he added, referring to the Ukrainian
nationalist Stepan Bandera, who collaborated with the Nazis during
World War II, as he spat on the ground. I stepped back a few paces,
but it made no difference; he grabbed my arm. "Putin, he strong! He
strong!" he concluded, bunching his free hand into a fist for further
emphasis. What Vitaly had produced in the troll farm had, it seemed,
made its way directly onto the battlefields of Ukraine.

Meanwhile, Russian TV, mainly the channels Vesti, Russia 24,
NTV, Channel One Russia (ORT), and RTR Planeta, continued to
maintain a stranglehold on the east Ukrainian imagination. The
Donbas region was former Ukrainian president Yanukovych's base,
but after the Euromaidan protests the government made no attempt
to reach out to the east to reassure the people there, many of whom

were sympathetic to the president and had watched the revolution with unease. Russian TV and Internet stepped in to fill the void. Vitaly and his colleagues entered the battlefield.

A special news report on Russia 24 featuring one of Putin's favorite journalists, Dmitry Kiselyov, that ran on April 13 (and again on April 27), at the height of the separatist takeover, encapsulated the Russian strategy. Kiselyov used the broadcast to hammer home two or three simple messages that have formed the basis of Russia's propaganda attacks on Ukraine throughout the crisis. "Kyiv is totally under American control; it has lost its sovereignty," he thundered. Pointing to the presence of (in reality small) far-right elements among the protesters, such as the political party Svoboda and the militia group Pravy Sektor. He claimed that Euromaidan was a "Russophobic and fascist" uprising that had overthrown a democratically elected president. Pravy Sektor, he warned, was sending its violent ultranationalists to terrorize eastern Ukraine.

"All media," said the Canadian philosopher Marshall McLuhan, "are extensions of some human faculty—psychic or physical."[7] In eastern Ukraine it was as if Putin's central nervous system was on display. The people I spoke to did not articulate complaints so much as repeat mantras about fascist juntas and the ubiquity of Pravy Sektor terrorists, mantras that existed only on Russian TV and the Internet—that is to say, in the Kremlin's imagination. The influence of domestic Russian-language channels on elderly eastern Ukrainians and of the articles and memes on VKontakte among the youth I met was almost total. Old men parroted geopolitical concepts that descended straight from Putin's lips, even as they struggled to explain what those concepts meant. Teenagers laughingly showed me racist memes of Obama on their smartphones. Beliefs in fantastical notions, such as Kyiv wanting to "destroy" the speaking of Russian in Ukraine, or that Pravy Sektor was ubiquitous and always about to strike, were sincerely held. The troll farm, with its production of memes, doctored photos, and endless video clips and articles, had played its part in the wider information war. It wasn't the promulgation of a narrative: it was the reinvention of reality.

And it centered on social media's ability to maximize centrifugal impulses. Just as new technology brings people together, it also amplifies their divisions—an ability Moscow used to great effect on swaths of disenfranchised pro-Russia Ukrainians across parts of the country's east. On April 6, 2014, in Kolika Square, a wide, flat concrete expanse in central Odessa, I saw my first pro-Russia demonstration. Several hundred protesters, many carrying Russian flags (though even more waved the hammer and sickle of the USSR), filled the square, where they listened to Soviet marching songs and a succession of speakers extolling the virtues of Russia. At the front of the crowd a man proudly waved a banner depicting Joseph Stalin as Arnold Schwarzenegger, muscle-bound and holding a huge machine gun. "Those of you who want to join Europe, take out your lubricant," yelled the speaker to roars of approval from the crowd. Most were of pensionable age. "America wants to conquer us! It wants to buy our country!" he continued. More cheers.

A heavily made-up lady of around sixty explained the protesters' position to me. "If Russian troops come here I will welcome them with bread and salt," she declared grandly. "They [the Kyiv government] hate us," she continued. "They want to destroy our language. If you go to Lviv [a strongly pro-Ukrainian city in western Ukraine] they won't even sell you milk if you speak Russian."[8]

I heard this complaint in every single occupied city I visited. It was a major problem for the government, as Ukrainian member of parliament Olga Bel'kova later confessed to me as we sat drinking coffee at a table outside a cafe in central Kyiv. "People in the east have this constant flow of information telling them that things are bad because they are Russian speakers and the idiots in Kyiv don't listen to them," she said. "The economy is almost dead . . . but all they can talk about is the language issue."[9]

At the side of the square a group of masked men in uniform, armed with bats and clubs, stood watching the demonstration. "We have intelligence that Pravy Sektor is coming to Odessa to burn down our tents at 4:00 a.m.," said the group's leader, Oleksandr, "and we are ready for them." He did not want to live in a country run by a "fascist junta." It was time, he said, to separate from Ukraine. Feeding them a diet of Russian TV and social media propaganda, the Kremlin had driven citizens of the same country to splinter into utterly opposing camps. The cognitive disconnect between what eastern Ukrainians believed and what was actually taking place in their own capital, just 275 miles away, was almost total.

A few days later I arrived in Donetsk and saw the same process beginning. Several hundred separatists had stormed the city's central administrative building, declared the foundation of an independent People's Republic of Donetsk (DNR), and were now publicly urging Russia to send in a military force to protect them. A large banner hung from the building's balcony: PEOPLE'S REPUBLIC OF DONBAS, it declared.

The protesters who gathered outside the building on Shevchenko Boulevard wanted Donetsk to follow Crimea. Chants of "Re-fer-en-dum! Re-fer-en-dum!" mixed with deep-throated cries of "Ros-si-ya! Ros-si-ya!" Some Russia media arrived, much to the crowd's delight: "Russia Today tells the truth! Russia Today tells the truth!" they bellowed, cheering the RT crew.[10]

East Ukrainians have legitimate grievances with Kyiv, which has neglected their region for twenty years. Unemployment in Donetsk in 2014 was around 2 percent higher than the national average, and its main industry, mining, is dying. There is also bitterness stemming from the widespread belief that the east subsidizes the rest of Ukraine. In 2013, the eastern cities of Donetsk and Luhansk contributed 11.7 percent and around 4 percent, respectively, to Ukrainian GDP.[11] Many of the protesters I spoke to felt they had been shortchanged. But apart from some vague ideas about better pensions, there was noticeably little discussion of what the tangible benefits of joining Russia would be.

Putin's sustained media war on Ukraine had successfully exacerbated long-standing regional grievances to help create the conditions for the east's destabilization. Stage one was complete. *Maskirovka*—the covert military action that followed—would be stage two. Eastern Ukraine broke into outright revolt just days after my visit to Donetsk when, on April 12, armed separatists stormed and occupied the police station in Sloviansk, a hitherto insignificant industrial border town of some 130,000 people. I was one of the first journalists to arrive on the scene, in the late afternoon. Bouts of occasional gunfire burst through the air. An hour earlier I had encountered a separatist checkpoint controlling the approach to the town, where armed men surrounded the car I was traveling in and ordered me and another journalist out at gunpoint, demanding to see my identification and accusing me of being an American spy.

Barricades had been erected around the police station, sealing it off from the street entirely. Access was through a small gap controlled by an armed man using a riot shield as a makeshift door. I tagged on to the end of a group of protesters and made my way inside. Middle-aged couples chanted pro-Russia slogans while excited teenagers took turns taking selfies in front of the neon-blue POLICE sign. Masked men in uniform, impervious to the chaos around them, guarded the area, their fingers resting by the triggers of their machine guns, which they kept pointed downward at all times—the classic pose of the professional soldier. They stood together in groups of two and three and communicated via radio. They refused to speak to me, but their dress and behavior were identical to those of the soldiers who had captured Crimea. The little green men had returned to Ukraine.[12]

This time, though, Russia was more brazen, openly sending in Russian nationals to lead the rebellion, notably Igor "Strelkov" Girkin. Girkin is believed by Ukrainian and Western military officials to be a colonel in the Russian special forces, or Spetsnaz, and he quickly emerged as the "commander" of the Donbas People's Militia, based in Sloviansk. There he headed up a core of Russian officers, many of whom had fought in Chechnya and Afghanistan, who trained local militia before moving on to other occupied cities in the east.[13] By mid-April Kyiv had arrested more than a hundred Russian citizens for separatist activity.

Over the following months convoys of military equipment, including tanks and missiles, flowed steadily across the border from Novoshakhtinsk, a checkpoint fifty miles from a training camp near the Russian town of Rostov, allowing the rebels to fight on in the face of superior numbers and firepower. A lot of military assistance came into Sloviansk disguised as humanitarian aid. Fridon Vekouah worked with the separatists while secretly reporting back to Kyiv. "A call would come in saying, 'You are getting a package: 50 percent is humanitarian aid; 50 percent is something else,'" he recalled.[14]

The Kyiv government and its security officials, still reeling from Crimea's annexation, could only mount a confused political and military response.[15] After Oleksandr Turchynov, then acting president of Ukraine, launched an "anti-terrorist operation" on April 13, a series of offensive and counteroffensives between Ukraine forces and the rebels saw the fighting spread to more towns and cities throughout the southeast. Dozens of Ukrainian army helicopters and planes were shot down using Moscow-supplied weaponry, while the Ukrainian army shelled separatist positions in the occupied cities. Hundreds were killed. On May 11, the DNR held a series of referendums, which Kyiv and international observers deemed illegal, across the Donetsk Oblast, in which 89 percent of the populace "voted" in favor of self-rule.[16] The democratic simulacrum would be maintained at all times.

But Ukraine's crisis was about to go global, for which Putin would need a different set of tools. On July 17, 2014, shortly after heavy losses forced the rebels to abandon Sloviansk, Malaysia Airlines flight MH17 from Amsterdam to Kuala Lumpur was shot down over eastern Ukraine by a surface-to-air missile, killing all 298 people on board. Just after the plane went down, Strelkov posted a message on his VKontakte site claiming responsibility for destroying what he thought was a Ukrainian plane.[17] The post was later deleted, but not before it had been shared hundreds of times.

US and NATO officials believed that the separatists could only have gotten the necessary anti-aircraft missile system from Russia. International leaders lined up to condemn Putin. "This is a defining moment for Russia," tweeted British prime minister David Cameron. "President Putin faces a clear choice in how he decides to respond to this appalling tragedy."[18]

In eastern Ukraine Putin had deployed the medium most effective for his target audience to push his message: TV. But while eastern Ukraine could be confused and subdued through Russian-language TV and social media, the MH17 problem was a global one, requiring an international and—critically—instant response. Social networks would now have to prove their worth to the Kremlin at the global level. As articles on the crash went up around the world, the troll farm kicked into gear.

Thousands of what the *Guardian* newspaper, among other publications, described as paid pro-Kremlin trolls appeared on comment threads to defend Russia, attack Ukraine, and generally confuse the facts.[19] Many of them—and the material they used to advance their cause—came from that bland building on Savushkina Street.

The Kremlin could also take advantage of the tens of thousands of its online fanboys just waiting to tweet or share the official line— critical when you need to react quickly. Hours after MH17 went down, thousands of pro-Russia Facebook pages and Twitter feeds began to parrot Kremlin rhetoric and shift blame onto the Ukrainians: it happened over Ukraine, so it had been Kyiv, or the Americans. Or even, as many pro-Russia memes on VKontakte suggested, collusion between the Americans and the Ukrainians. Conspiracy theory, denial, and blame-shifting: the building blocks of Russian propaganda laid bare, shared and tweeted into infinity.

The majority outside of Russia and eastern Ukraine dismissed these absurd claims, but for Putin that didn't matter—that wasn't his goal. Convincing his supporters—most of whom wanted to be convinced—that Russia had nothing to do with the massacre of innocent civilians was easy. The plan for the real target, the watching world, was equally simple: discombobulate and confuse, for which social media's various platforms, and the ability they have endowed upon users to spread narratives, were the perfect tool.

More problematic was the political fallout. After the crash, enraged diplomats discussed the possibility of a new round of financial sanctions on Russia, which in a globalized world can be devastating. But globalization cuts both ways, which Putin understands, almost instinctively. His entire political philosophy is based on the belief that twentieth-century geopolitical paradigms are obsolete.

And he is right. Russia knows that international corporations have become more powerful than international institutions. Finance itself is multinational. Cameron may have talked tough on sanctions, but Britain is in hock to Russian cash. Britain's public schools and art galleries are reliant on it. London's high-end property market is based on it. In 2014, London's commercial lawyers received 60 percent of their work from Russian clients.[20] The British-based BP has a 20 percent stake in Rosneft, Russia's biggest oil company, and its outgoing chairman, Lord Livingstone, warned that British banks would suffer from further EU sanctions on Moscow. Sanctions duly came on July 29, 2014, but their effect was noticeably limited. Russia's oil industry was targeted, but the EU's addiction to Russian gas (as distinct from oil) left that sector untouched.

Ukrainian MP Anatoliy Hrytsenko, former minister of defense and a former presidential candidate, was gloomy, almost bitter about all this when I met him in his office in Ukraine's parliament in early 2014. Chain-smoking Marlboro Lights, he told me, "People talk about interconnectedness, but don't they realize that Ukraine's problems affect everyone? Putin annexed a part of our country large enough to settle several European countries in. Who will be next? Estonia,

Transnistria? This will have destabilizing consequences in thirty or forty years' time. By then Cameron and Obama will be off fishing somewhere and other people will have to face the consequences of their actions. Globalization," he snorted. "It means that Putin can get away with murder."

Putin, despite the fastidiously calibrated democratic laminate, is a true totalitarian. He doesn't just want control of your business or your politics. He comes for your senses: Russian troops aren't in eastern Ukraine. They never invaded Crimea. What you saw you did not see. New media allows him to push his message in ever more effective and pervasive ways. Locally, it reinvents reality to create the conditions for war; internationally, it harnesses the engine of public opinion to either justify or confuse it. Arrayed against him is a citizen army, empowered and given form by social media. Centralized state power faces off against diffuse civilian power, while the West, caught in a web of globalized finance, looks on, largely powerless to act. This is what twenty-first-century war looks like. And Vladimir Putin is its master practitioner.

8

THE INTERPRETER 1:
FROM THE BEDROOM TO THE BATTLEFIELD

Eliot Higgins was battle-scarred but relentless. He would never stop fighting. The Alliance versus the Horde; humans, Dryads, Dwarves, High Elves, the Keepers of the Grove, the Tushui Pandaren, and the Worgen: he had either fought or allied with them all at various points in wars that had lasted for weeks at a time, often over years of conflict. He was a natural leader. He had both the temperament and the organizational skills needed to keep dozens of people in line under the most strenuous of circumstances. Strategy and tactics had to be perfect if victory was to be ensured. And for Higgins, victory was all: he was fanatical about it, despite the hardships involved in managing his various bands of followers, most of whom were dispersed throughout the world, and most of whom he'd never met.

Higgins was an obsessive player of *World of Warcraft*, the world's most popular massively multiplayer online role-playing game (MMORPG). Almost every day he would get online, rally his troops, and disappear into the Internet. Marathon game-playing sessions were a regular occurrence. Once he was in his alternative reality, nothing else mattered. An entire day might be taken up with

a twelve-hour session, and as the world outside his window continued to turn, Higgins paid it no notice. He didn't know it then, but
each day he spent on the Internet drew him one step closer to what
he would eventually become: an online sleuth able to use the power
of freely available social media tools to debunk the lies of one of the
world's most powerful nations—without ever even having to leave his
room.

"Game-playing taught me most of the skills I need for my current
job," says Higgins with a laugh as he leans back and takes a sip of coffee in a noisy Café Nero on the Strand in central London.[1] The coffee
shop we are sitting in is bustling with lunchtime customers. Forget-
table pop music wafts out of speakers placed at each corner of the
seating area. "I've always used the Internet," Higgins tells me. "From
1996–97 onwards, when it became something a normal person could
access. I quickly became part of different Internet communities.
With gaming, I started with Ultima Online, a MMORPG based on
a popular role-playing game series at the time. It was an intense online community with different guilds and groups. Then I graduated
to *World of Warcraft*. It can get quite intense because you're asking
thirty or forty people to spend hours online at a time. You need to
get people organized, you need to keep tempers down—people get
annoyed, there are cock-ups. And over time you come to understand
the different personalities of people in Internet communities. You see
the same thing with our people on Twitter now, the different kinds
of characters that you must learn to manage: the worrier, the person
that panics about every tiny thing, and gets really stressed, so you
have to keep them balanced and focused—you can never totally calm
them down. Then you need to identify the leaders as well. They are
proactive: they get out there and do stuff, and then everyone kind of
falls into line behind them. Anytime I joined a guild I ended up being
the leader—I can't just sit back and go with the flow. I need to keep
pushing and organizing, getting stuff done."

He continues: "This transferred into my current work well. During my gaming days I would always become focused on one thing. Everything else became less interesting to me. It's the same now: if I'm working on a research project, I'm constantly thinking about it from every angle, thinking about what I can do next. But it's also about being organized. It's great thinking about these things but you need to be organized enough to make stuff happen."

Higgins is in his late thirties, pale with dark hair flecked with gray, tall with the heft to match. With his rectangular glasses and pleasant demeanor, he looks like any one of the millions of Londoners heading to work each day, perhaps a lawyer, computer programmer, or young academic. But he is none of these things. He is something new. So new that describing what he does still defies easy categorization. But the impact of his work is undeniable. From the war in Libya to the Syrian civil war, his presence continues to be felt, perhaps nowhere more so than in the Russia-Ukraine conflict. It began in the months following July 17, 2014, when flight MH17 from Amsterdam to Kuala Lumpur was shot down over eastern Ukraine. Higgins, from the confines of his own house—and occasionally just in his underpants—with only a few fellow unpaid volunteers was able to almost conclusively prove what not even Western intelligence services seemed able to do: that the Russian army had provided pro-Russia separatists in eastern Ukraine with the Buk missile that shot down the aircraft. The importance of this fact—that responsibility for those 298 civilian deaths lay ultimately with Moscow—would prove to be of enormous global significance in the war between Russia and Ukraine.

Higgins has no background in the intelligence services or the military. He does not have access to classified information. He is not a hacker or an IT whiz. Indeed, his most notable previous employment was arguably as a payments officer at a women's lingerie company. But, along with just a few others, through the power of open-source information—that is to say, information anyone can access—available on social media, Higgins was able to prove Russia's culpability. Such was the quality and strength of his output that the Russian

Eliot Higgins,
the Interpreter.
(Courtesy of
SKUP.no)

Foreign Ministry has, on more than one occasion, been forced to
publicly respond to his claims. To restate: a major arm of the state
apparatus of the world's largest country has been forced to publicly
refute his findings. There is no clearer example of the shift in power
from hierarchies to individuals and networks of individuals than the
case of Eliot Higgins. He, from the comfort of his own home, as a
private citizen, has directly affected the narrative war surrounding
the Russia-Ukraine crisis to a degree that would have previously been
unthinkable, let alone possible. All he needed was an Internet connection and an obsessive personality.

The emergence of Web 2.0 transformed Internet users from mere pas-
sive consumers of content to individuals capable of using a variety of
platforms to create their own. At the center of these platforms are the
abilities to create networks and broadcast (hence the terms *social* and
media). People now use LinkedIn to network for business opportunities, Facebook to keep up with friends and show off their glamorous
vacations and children, and Instagram to pose for selfies. Now able
to produce content, people produce endless streams of it—mostly for
social purposes.

But these abilities are also utilized by everyone from Farah, who broadcasts Palestinian suffering, to Anna, who mobilizes volunteers and collects donations. "Produsers" (users who also produce) create content, and all content is data, which social media companies greedily vacuum up to sell to advertisers so they can tailor their products to us. But during times of crisis and war, content becomes data of a different kind. Every YouTube video posted from Ukraine or Syria becomes a possible piece of evidence about a suspected atrocity on the ground, every tweet a possible source of confirmation or refutation of a rumor. Social media is merely the aggregation of nearly endless streams of content and data, the scale of which—especially in wartime—is so vast that it can be overwhelming. Russia takes advantage of this cascade to confuse and distort, to spread falsehoods and disinformation. But if you can learn to interpret that data, if you are *Homo digitalis* of the most advanced kind, you can do truly remarkable things. And you can influence wars in ways that have never been previously possible.

It all started with Libya. In addition to game playing, Higgins was involved in online discussion boards from their beginnings. He then began to contribute to the *Guardian* newspaper's Liveblog site, and come the summer of 2011—by which time he had been involved in online communities for over a decade—the Libyan civil war was raging. He kept seeing dozens of illuminating videos posted from Libya that the media ignored. As he argued online with people over what the government and the rebel forces were doing, he often used YouTube videos being uploaded by those on the ground to back up his argument. Invariably, his opponents would fire back: "Well, how do you know the video is real?"

He decided he would start to try to prove that the videos were indeed real—basically just to win online arguments. His big chance came when government forces and rebels began fighting over the Libyan city of Brega, on the Gulf of Sidra. Both the rebels and the government subsequently claimed they had captured the city, and the dispute was tearing the *Guardian* Liveblog apart. What made things confusing was that both sides were posting videos that appeared to back up their claims. Obviously they couldn't both be right, so Higgins decided to do some detective work. He tried to find out where the videos were filmed by looking at Google Maps—and that was the start of everything.

Google Maps gave Higgins access to something vital: satellite imagery. It enabled him to see the areas in the online videos from space, which proved vital when he stumbled across a seemingly innocuous video that would eventually solve the mystery of who was really in control of the city. The video was as basic as it got: about five minutes long, it consisted of a rebel simply walking through a street with the camera facing himself (essentially an extended selfie shot). The viewer could see the background behind him, which was just the road as he walked through it. Critically, the viewer could see the intersections as he walked past them.

The obsessiveness Higgins had honed over years of online gaming immediately kicked in. He decided to draw out a map by hand: as the rebel in the video walked down the road, Higgins drew out the various twists and turns he took. There were no major landmarks in the video, so the shape of the road was the only thing that would be easily noticeable from space. He duly mapped out the road and was then able to match its layout to a road on the satellite imagery. Once he did that the smaller features became easier to spot. Through matching that single rebel video to the satellite imagery he was able to deduce that though the rebels were in Brega, they were on its farthest outskirts, which he knew was a newly built residential area called New Brega, in the east of the city. He then used similar techniques on government-produced videos. The truth became clear: both sides were lying. Neither had captured Brega outright. Rather, government forces had captured the western half of the city, while the rebels had captured the eastern part. Each was filming from their side and claiming they controlled the whole city. This showed Higgins that he could verify where videos were filmed: a technique that would become a founding principle of his work, sorting truths from lies in wartime.

In March 2012, Higgins—now married with an infant daughter—thought he'd set up a blog, which he decided was far better than immersing himself in online forums. He could just pick it up and put it down whenever he wanted, he thought, leaving him free to be the family man he now was. He could not have been more wrong.

He called the blog *Brown Moses*, after the title of a Frank Zappa song that he liked. He thought it had a good ring to it, and it gave him some anonymity. By this time the civil war in Syria was starting to escalate; once again the information coming out of the region seemed confused and contradictory, and once again he was drawn to try to work it out. People began posting videos of fighters using various types of weapons, so he started looking them up to teach himself about weaponry—all from open sources, even sites like Wikipedia. He became obsessed with posting only content that he was sure was correct. His experiences of online discussions over Libya, where, to his mind, people had posted endless crap without bothering to verify it, had left an ineradicable mark on him. He didn't want to be like every other sucker posting stuff they had no clue about—especially on a subject as serious as war.

And slowly a new career began to emerge. Using open-source materials gleaned from social media combined with his own tireless dedication and willingness to obsessively pursue even the smallest of details, he began to shine a deeper light on the Syria conflict. It was sorely needed. Because of the danger involved, the war suffered from a lack of foreign journalists on the ground. Misinformation and fakery were rampant. Both the government and the rebels made various claims that could not be verified. Or so they thought. In actuality, traditional media simply did not yet know how to use the tools available to them, which Higgins was fast learning to employ.

His work was beginning to capture mainstream attention, and in January 2013 he went international. By now, Higgins was an expert in the various forms of weaponry being used by both sides in the Syrian war, and early in the month, while watching Syrian state TV, he noticed something odd: the presence of M79 Osa rocket launchers, which have a unique and easily identifiable design. As his blog states, the M79 is "originally a Yugoslavian anti-tank weapon, designed in 1979, and still manufactured and used in countries that once made up the former-Yugoslavia."[2] He then saw the same weapons on the YouTube channel of the jihadist organization Ansar al-Islam. No way should jihadists be getting weapons from abroad, he thought.

Higgins was so ahead of the curve with his findings that even the *New York Times* was struggling to catch up.[3] Eventually the paper's veteran war correspondent C. J. Chives teamed up with Higgins, and together they uncovered an illicit trail of weapons originating in Croatia that had ended up in the hands of jihadist rebels.[4] Again, a lone individual was able to move faster and more effectively than a long established institution bulging with bureaucracy. Indeed, even intelligence agencies were reportedly noticing his work. Higgins told me that certain elements within the French intelligence services were overjoyed at his findings because they had long argued against arming the Syrian rebels for the reason that any weapons supplied would end up in the hands of jihadists.

The ramifications of his work were starting to reach the political level as politicians and diplomats began to cite it. There was no doubting it anymore: Higgins had gone from a mere blogger to an actor in conflict, one able to debunk myths and publicly expose lies faster than established institutions stultified by bureaucracy and staffed by people who did not fully understand the new information environment in which the world was now operating. Higgins was slowly showing both the media and government agencies the way forward—and he was about to go global.

July 17, 2014, began as an ordinary day for Eliot Higgins. The British summer was typically absent, and he was indoors on his laptop working on his latest research project. At the end of 2013 he had set up a company, Brown Moses Ltd. After a Kickstarter crowdfunding campaign on July 14 raised £51,000, Higgins had set up a new website called *Bellingcat*. The name came from the classic fable "Belling the Cat," about a group of mice seeking to combat the threat of a dangerous cat. Higgins was now able to devote his time fully to open-source investigation. After an hour or so he thought he'd sit down and have some quiet time—with Twitter, naturally, still open in the background. His "relaxation" was precipitously interrupted when news came in that a plane had been shot down over eastern Ukraine. Higgins, who until then had been focused on Syria and wasn't following the Russia-Ukraine conflict that closely, started to scour social media for details. Within a couple of hours a video appeared online. It showed what appeared to be a military vehicle carrying a missile launcher heading down a two-lane highway with large trees running along the middle. A lot of people were talking about it, trying to work out exactly what it was, whether it was real, and, crucially, where it had been filmed.

Higgins had to run some errands, so he fired off a tweet asking if anyone wanted to have a go at geolocating the video of what appeared to be a missile launcher driving out of a town: "Gold star sticker to the first person who geolocates this video."[5] He returned fifteen minutes later to find around ten replies, nine of which pointed to the same location: an area south of the central part of the Ukrainian town of Snizhne. He assumed the respondents had seen the two-lane road with trees running down the middle and located it fairly easily, given that there is only one road like that in the area, which runs right through the center of Snizhne. The video was quickly deleted from YouTube, but Higgins had learned long ago to immediately download any online video of interest to his own computer.[6]

Higgins then verified for himself, using geolocation techniques, that the video had indeed been filmed in Snizhne, and he wrote an article for *Bellingcat* detailing what those techniques were so that anyone could re-create his findings.[7] The investigation had begun. All sorts of other images and photographs were now appearing online, and the informal community of open-source investigators, many of whom followed him, was having a go at verifying them. One particular image, taken from a garage forecourt, that emerged the following day was of special interest: it showed a truck with the same missile launcher on the back of its loader. Higgins was trying to verify it but kept coming up with nothing—and without verification of its location, the image added nothing to the investigation. It was just a photo of a truck with a missile launcher. It was incredibly frustrating.

Just under twenty-four hours later and four thousand miles away in Charlotte, North Carolina, Aric Toler was relaxing at home at the end of another arduous working week. Toler worked the Sunday-to-Thursday day shift at Bank of America–Merrill Lynch, so the Friday after MH17 was shot down was his day off. Unlike Higgins, he was an intelligence specialist, though in corporate security. Bank of America–Merrill Lynch has offices in fifty countries, with thousands of employees, and Toler was part of a division that monitored open-source data for information on anything that might possibly pose a threat to its employees or facilities, from terrorist attacks to natural disasters. If something happened, he and his colleagues needed to be the first to find out—even before CNN. In fact, if something happened and CNN reported it before he was on the case, it was already too late. CNN won't report anything until all the facts are verified, so he generally had around a fifteen-minute window. It was a 24/7 operation, with teams working both day and night shifts. Toler focused on Europe and had his TweetDeck and other social media platforms open constantly.

He enjoyed his work, but there were a number of serious issues with it that frustrated him. The structure wasn't the best, there wasn't a lot of room for advancement, and there was a lot of bureaucracy—not as much as in government, but frustrating nonetheless. There was some room for creativity, as he had good bosses, but the layers upon layers of bureaucracy were a bind. Once more, the case of Toler would prove how established institutions, stifled by bureaucracy, simply cannot compete with networks of individuals empowered by social media.

Toler got to know Higgins mainly as a Twitter source for breaking news, especially in regard to conflict. Like Higgins, he had an obsessive nature, but he had honed his talents in a different arena. As a graduate of the University of Kansas in Slavic languages and literature, Toler had spent years developing the hermeneutic skills necessary to analyze literary texts and narratives, to discern patterns and influences. He spent hours poring through source materials like personal correspondence and essays to try to dig up biographical data and doing line-by-line close readings of texts. "When you are trying to determine the truth about something, for every 99 bits of information you read only one will be useful—so you are constantly looking for needles in haystacks," he told me.[8] The methods and focus required for his studies and his job were the same, only now his source materials were links, videos, and posts instead of poems and novels.

Toler's studies had given him an added advantage: he spoke fluent Russian, which would prove vital for verifying the photo from the garage forecourt that Higgins was struggling with. Lounging around and enjoying his day off, he was surfing Twitter at home when, in the late morning, he noticed that Higgins had posted a photo of what he had now identified as a Buk missile, asking if anyone could geolocate it.[9] Everyone suspected the photo was from Snizhne, the town from which the first video had emerged, but it still needed verifying. Toler could see that in the background of the photo was a shop, with its name written across the top in Russian. Unfortunately, a tree in front of the shop sign made only part of its name visible. "Too blurry to read the yellow sign on the right. The store on the left is _ _ РОЙ ДОМ or _ _ ТОЙ ДОМ," he tweeted at Higgins.[10]

But, just as he would with a literary text, Toler was determined to puzzle the problem out. He could see the second word of the shop sign, which was the word *dom*, which means "house"; the first word was the problem—due to the tree in front of it he could only see its second half, which was *roi*. Then it clicked: it must be *stroi*, "to build."[11] Once he worked that out, he realized that it was the name of a chain of hardware stores, and he duly alerted Higgins and several others on the Tweet string: "Got it. It's СТРОЙДОМ, (stroy-dom.com). I'll check for addresses for these stores in Snizhne," he tweeted triumphantly.[12]

He Googled the shop name and could find no reference to one in Snizhne, but he did discover one in Torez, its sister city to the west. Now he needed to find the exact address so he could match the photo to satellite maps. He did a search on Torez and Stroi Dom and found a wiki-type site that lists notable features of streets in the town. He discovered that there was a street called 50 Years of the USSR that had a Stroi Dom on it, but, infuriatingly, the site didn't give the exact address. After more Googling he finally turned up a court document with the name of the shop and its address as part of testimony from a witness. Armed with all this information, he was then able to identify the location on Yandex maps (Russia's version of Google Maps).

But Toler wanted to be doubly sure. He needed, if at all possible, to *see* the exact address of the shop to confirm that its location matched up with the photo. He knew that in Russia and Ukraine people love dashcams, which they often use for insurance purposes in case of crashes, but which has led to a strange phenomenon of people (almost always men) filming themselves driving around town, generally set to music. The dashcams always have the date and in effect provide those who watch the videos with their own personal Google Street View of wherever is being filmed. He entered the search terms "Torez" and "50 Years of the USSR" into both Google and YouTube, hoping he would get lucky—and he did. There were two videos from the same guy driving down the street (with, of course, two different songs in the background). They were both from the same year, one on a foggy day and one on a clear day, so he was obviously a local. Toler watched the videos closely and eventually saw the Stroi Dom shop. He was sure it was the right place, as the footage also showed a distinctive black-and-white-striped building to its right.

The location was now established. The next thing to do was to establish the time the photo had been taken. For this task, Higgins once more entered the story. His method was to use a publicly available website called SunCalc.net. The site allows you to post an image to it and then, with a cursor or slider, move the position of the sun by sliding it through various positions. The shadows the sun casts change throughout the day and by matching the shadows in the photo with the shadows the sun casts as you slide the cursor across the image it is possible to determine the rough time of the day in any photo. Higgins and Toler were fortunate because in the case of the Torez photo the sky was clear and they could easily see the direction of the shadows. Half of one of the buildings in the photo was in shadow but the other half was not. They could, accordingly, determine that the photo had been taken somewhere between noon and 1:00 p.m. "Currently using SunCalc to figure out the time of day the Buk photos were taken using shadows http://suncalc.net/#/48.024,38.6146,19/2014.07.19/10:05 . . . ," Higgins tweeted.[13] "Yep, I'm getting somewhere between 8am–10am. The times are in SunCalc are our local times, not Kiev time, right?" Toler tweeted back.[14]

"All these bits come in and you piece them together to end up with something coherent," Higgins told me with a smile as he sipped his coffee. "It's a classic form of people working together online." Once more, the combination of new information technology and networks of people was proving that nothing was impossible.

Now Higgins and his team had the initial Snizhne video and also a photo that had emerged from the town that a blogger named Andrew Haggard (now also a part of Higgins's investigative team) had verified on the website Korean Defense, which normally looks at North Korea.[15] Crucially, it showed the Buk without its trailer truck—moving on its own steam via its caterpillar track—at around 2:00 or 2:30 p.m. Then there was a video, also posted on July 17, from the town of Zuhres, which was easy to verify because it had the coordinates on it. But Higgins and a few others double-checked these just to be sure, and also verified the time of day by the shadows using

SunCalc once more. The informal band of sleuths was beginning to establish the route of the Buk on its journey through Ukraine.

Around a week later, on July 25, the team caught a break. The French tabloid *Paris Match* published a photo of the Buk, which one of its journalists, Alfred de Montesquiou, tweeted was taken in Snizhne. His tweet caused all sorts of confusion among the Twitterati, as the image had a billboard pole in the background, but no billboard pole like that existed in the town.

During our conversations, Higgins repeatedly mentioned the "wow factor" involved in his work—similar to that of a magician. Nothing perhaps better illustrates this than the fact that people were able to geolocate a photo by a single billboard pole—a simple steel pole with a few steel struts jutting horizontally out of it (the billboard itself was not actually visible). There were two stages to the process. The first was that the truck carrying the Buk had a Donetsk phone number written across its side. The phone number was then Google-searched, which gave the address of the company it came from. *Paris Match*—amid all the online questioning over its claim that the photo was taken in Snizhne—phoned the number, which turned out to be a vehicle rental company in separatist-controlled Donetsk whose proprietor told them that pro-Russia separatists had stolen several of his vehicles earlier that month.[16] Now the team knew that truck's exact starting point, the vehicle rental company's address in Donetsk. They then used Google Maps Route Planner between that address and the Zuhres video (which was the next point on the map from Donetsk) to discover what was the fastest route—and therefore the most logical one for the truck to have taken—between the two points. Once that was established, they used Google Street View to "travel" down that route, as if they were in the truck itself, until someone eventually found that billboard pole in exactly the same location. Higgins double-checked it and saw that even the tree branches were in the same position, which is as good as it gets when it comes to verification. It was painstaking work. But they had succeeded, and had done so using tools available to anyone. *Paris Match* had to issue a sheepish correction stating that the image actually came from Do-netsk. Meanwhile, the route of the Buk was becoming even clearer.

Soon Higgins and his team had enough information to establish exactly what had happened in Ukraine. Pro-Russian separatists had stolen a truck from the vehicle-rental company in Donetsk in the morning, and *Paris Match* had photographed the truck around 9:00 a.m. The truck had then proceeded from there to Zuhres, where it was seen in a video at 11:40 a.m.[17] From there it was sighted in Torez (in the photo Toler had verified) before being seen in Snizhne at 1:30 p.m., both in the photo Andrew Haggard had verified on Korean Defense and in the first video Eliot and his followers had verified, which had kicked off the whole process. Finally, the Ukrainian Ministry of the Interior had published a video of it (which was then verified) later on in the day—clearly after shooting down MH17—leaving Luhansk minus one missile. The actual launch site, in a field just east of the village of Chervonyi Zhovten (the name means "Red October"), south of Snizhne, had first appeared in a photo posted on Twitter almost exactly three hours after the downing of MH17 and had been verified almost immediately.[18] All the pieces were now in place.

On July 21, several days after the Ukrainian Ministry of Interior had published the Luhansk video, the Russian Ministry of Defense convened an hour-long press conference in response. During the conference it presented various pieces of "evidence" to refute the accusation that the video was from separatist-controlled Luhansk. Their major claim was that the Ukrainian video from Luhansk was actually filmed in Krasnoarmeysk—in Ukrainian government territory. It took Higgins and his followers little time to debunk this theory using simple geolocation techniques. What so astounded Higgins was that the counternarrative the Russians presented at the press conference had been floating around Russian social media sites for a couple of days—the official Russian spokesman was merely parroting Internet rumors.

Higgins was not yet on Russia's radar, but that would soon change. On July 28 he wrote up the previous weeks' investigations into a single post on his blog.[19] He and a few others had, to his mind, categorically proved that the Russian government had lied shamelessly about where the Buk missile had been fired. As he said to me with a laugh that day: "It's one thing to say the Russian government is lying. It's another to prove it in a PowerPoint presentation." Higgins and his team had, they believed, mapped out the route the Buk had taken once it was in Ukraine. Proving it had come from Russia, which therefore bore ultimate responsibility for the tragedy, would be an entirely different matter altogether.

Higgins was operating under the same principles as Farah: in the world of *Homo digitalis*, anyone with an Internet connection can become an actor in war. Higgins, an obsessive online gamer, spent hours each day trapped in a virtual world he preferred to a fairly basic job that held little interest for someone of his intelligence. And yet it was the very attributes that made him such a successful gamer—the obsessive personality, the familiarity with Web 2.0 technologies (in this case online role-playing games)—that enabled him to go further than even the Arab Spring protesters or Farah. Unlike them, Higgins was not on the ground in the center of a conflict. In fact, he was thousands of miles away behind a computer screen.

Social media broadcasts and amplifies messages—and in so doing it also creates data. Higgins understood early on that social media, if harnessed properly, can interpret that data as well as simply broadcast it. It is a tool that can be used to bring meaning to the often endless streams of information emerging from war zones, which are, because of their sheer volume, chaotic and confusing. Just as social media platforms spread falsehood, they can also be used to debunk it, empirically and forensically. Higgins employed the Web 2.0 technologies spreading disinformation to discredit it. It was inevitable that he would eventually find himself up against the Russian state.

9

THE INTERPRETER 2:
MAN VERSUS SUPERPOWER

The rain outside Café Nero is getting worse. It's pelting the glass window of the store like a ripple of applause as Higgins continues to detail the intricacies of open-source investigation to me. He speaks rapidly. I struggle to keep up, my fingers whizzing across my Apple keyboard. I'm grateful my recorder is running; his churning mind never stops, and he flies off on the occasional tangent. London is overcast and gloomy, but Higgins's cheerful manner is undiminished. I bring him around to MH17 again. He pauses to take a sip of coffee and then resumes his narrative.

After Higgins's July 28 post on *Bellingcat* detailing from start to finish the Buk's route from its starting point in Donetsk to it leaving Luhansk minus a missile after MH17 was shot down, things had gone relatively quiet.[1] He still kept an eye on the story, but with the global emergence of Islamic State, his mind was drawn once again to Syria. His initial work, however, had attracted the attention of the official Joint Investigation Team (JIT) investigating the tragedy.[2] In September, the British police contacted him on behalf of their Dutch counterparts, who wanted to interview him about all the research

Bellingcat had done. Higgins went to his local police station in the city of Leicester to meet officers from the JIT, who had flown over especially to meet with him. They made him go through his findings line by line.

It made Higgins think. If *Bellingcat*'s work was already of interest to the JIT, how much more might be achieved if he threw additional resources and time into the investigation? He decided to put together a team dedicated solely to MH17—most pressingly, to find out where the Buk had originally come from. Who, ultimately, bore responsibility for the tragedy? He knew it would a difficult undertaking, one for which, if it was to be successful, he would need the best people possible.

Iggy Ostanin was getting tired of playing *Championship Manager.* He loved it, but his life was disappearing into a black hole of endless online gaming. It was August 2014, and he was living with his brother in the Netherlands.[3] Ostanin is Russian and spent the first nine years of his life in an obscure city called Izhevsk, known only for being the manufacturing base of the AK-47. He then moved around with his family for a while before eventually settling in the United Kingdom. In late 2013, he had been accepted to study law at the University of York in Northern England, but his course didn't start until October the following year. With a lot of free time on his hands, he had gone out to the Netherlands, ostensibly to spend time with his girlfriend, Julia (who was studying there), and his brother, but, as it turned out, mainly to play *Championship Manager* on his computer. The hours he spent researching the various strengths and weaknesses of respective soccer players exasperated Julia. Frankly, she said, it bordered on the obsessive. "Do something useful with your life," she told him—on more than one occasion.

He knew she was right. And so he began to turn his attentions elsewhere. As a Russian, he had been following the news closely since Moscow's March annexation of Crimea from Ukraine and the subsequent turmoil in the eastern part of the country. He wasn't a big Twitter user, but he had read about Higgins in the *Guardian* and liked the sound of his work, though he hadn't given it much thought afterward.

But when MH17 was shot down, it was a national tragedy in the Netherlands. The plane had taken off from Amsterdam, and of the 283 passengers and 15 crew killed, the majority were Dutch nationals. The country was in mourning. He had nothing else to do, he had an obsessive personality, and he was in Holland, where the MH17 story was ubiquitous. It was a triumvirate of forces he was powerless to resist.

He began to trawl Russian-language social media sites to see what he could find out about the situation in Ukraine and eventually wrote up a couple of stories. He gave one of them to the online magazine *The Interpreter*, which had a daily live blog devoted to covering the war.[4] Remembering Higgins from the *Guardian* article, he sent the other to *Bellingcat*. He wanted to remain anonymous, so he sent it through the email server XMail. Higgins was interested and pressed Ostanin for an author name. Ostanin decided on "Magnitsky," after Sergei Magnitsky, the Russian lawyer and auditor who was killed in 2009 in Russian custody after allegedly getting close to revealing evidence of mass corruption.

By late August Higgins still knew him only as Magnitsky. But as the Dutch press continued to report on the MH17 investigation, Ostanin just couldn't get the July 25 *Paris Match* photo out of his mind—especially the remnants of markings and symbols he could see on the side of the Buk. He decided to try to find any other images of it that were available. For four days he barely slept, hammering his espresso machine as he searched for any videos that might have been uploaded to either YouTube or VKontakte. He used hashtags on Instagram like пво (the Russian abbreviation for *protivovozdushnaya oborona*, "anti-aircraft defense").[5] Eventually he found something: a photo of a Buk in the Russian city of Stary Oskol, in Russia's Belogrod Oblast, 384 miles south of Moscow.[6] The person who uploaded it claimed that the Buk was part of a large column of about eighty to a hundred military vehicles, which had a few Buks among it. Ostanin could see the date the photo had been taken: June 23, 2014. The user also claimed the vehicles in the convoy all had the area code 50 on their license plates—information that would prove vital later on.

At this point Ostanin didn't think it was the Buk that had downed MH17. Stary Oskol wasn't close to the Ukrainian border and the photo had been taken almost a month before the tragedy. But "what the hell," he thought, "let's keep trying." Now he had at least the date and place of a definitive Buk sighting. He assumed that people might have uploaded photos of this Buk without knowing what a Buk was, so he started thinking of any search terms that people might use to describe what was in the photo: "column," "military vehicles," and a common Russian phrase, "*voennaya tekhnika* (military technology)."

He narrowed his searches for videos and images to that time and location and soon found a video of the column on VKontakte in a place called Alexeyevka a day later, on June 24.[7] It was a long video, around eleven minutes, filmed by someone standing outside a supermarket, who captured the entire column as it went past. Then Ostanin saw it: a Buk with markings on its side similar to the ones on the *Paris Match* photo. Specifically, there was a clear "3 x 2" marking on the Buk in the Alexeyevka video, remnants of which could be seen in the *Paris Match* photo (it being standard practice for Russian army units to paint over markings on their vehicles just before they enter Ukraine). He was stunned. He watched the video over and over to be sure. Frustratingly, the resolution wasn't as clear as it could be; he needed to find more videos to be certain.

Using a program called Pixifly, which allowed users to search geotagged Instagram posts by date, time, and location, he decided to work backward, searching through what he thought was the most logical route between Stary Oskol and Alexeyevka on the relevant days.[8] After a day of scrolling through endless videos, he found it: a video of the column on the motorway outside Stary Oskol, filmed on June 23. The resolution in this video was much better, and he was able to screenshot the Buk and look at it closely, which he did repeatedly.[9]

The markings matched. There was now no doubt in his mind: this was the Buk used to down flight MH17.

This was potentially a discovery of international importance, and Ostanin, in a great state of excitement, got to work so that he could send it off to Higgins as soon as possible. Altogether, he had by now found around half a dozen videos of the column, including one of it heading into Alexeyevka on June 24.[10] It was high resolution, and as Ostanin watched it he made a list of the vehicle number plates that he could see—all of which contained the number 50. He remembered the first Instagram post he had found, which mentioned that all the vehicles in the column had license plates with the number 50 in them. Ostanin searched online to find out which Russian army units used that number on their license plates and also had Buks. He discovered on Wikipedia that all brigades in the Moscow Military District used the license plate number 50, and from the website ryadovoy.ru—a military enthusiasts' forum where people talked about military technology—he learned that only two Moscow units had Buks: the 5th Brigade, based in Shuya, and the 53rd Brigade, based in Kursk.[11] He was able to rule out the 5th Brigade because he discovered it had been moved out of the Moscow Military District and into the Western Military District, based in St. Petersburg, which used the license plate code 43. Ostanin had now, to his mind, proved that the Buk that had shot down MH17 had come from the 53rd Brigade of the Russian army, based in Kursk. Helping corroborate this was the fact that the earliest video Ostanin had discovered in terms of the convoy's chronology had been taken just outside Kursk.[12] Put together, the information was explosive. Higgins and the others agreed, and they published their findings on September 8.[13] And that could have been the end of that—but things had been happening at Higgins's end to ensure that it wasn't.

While Ostanin had spent August in the Netherlands embarking on what would become a new career, back in the United Kingdom

Higgins was busy putting a together a team dedicated solely to un-covering as much information about the MH17 tragedy as possible. Toler had already proved his worth, so he was a no-brainer, and Os-tanin had more recently done the same, so he was in, too, as were a couple of others who had demonstrated their investigative skills over time. It was a small group, consisting only of about five or six people, but Higgins thought it would be enough. They were now ready to do a deep dive into MH17.

The first thing he needed to do was to centralize the whole pro-cess. Every single member of the team lived in a different city or country, or even on another continent. He decided to use an app called Slack, which consists of chat rooms (channels) that can be organized by topic and also allows private groups to communicate among themselves. The app can be used to create different "rooms" or feeds where particular topics such as missile launchers or members of a particular brigade (a subject that would become vital to the inves-tigation) could be discussed. Higgins also liked it because it worked well with links: if you posted a tweet, it would show the full tweet; if you posted a YouTube video, it would embed it. All the information would be there at their fingertips.

The MH17 investigation group kicked into gear with the aim of publishing the most comprehensive report on MH17 yet written. Slack was a place where they would bounce ideas off each other late into the night, exchanging tips as well as sharing tasks. Ostanin and Toler, Russian speakers both, were tasked with searching Russian social media sites for any information they could find. Ostanin's re-search had proved that the Buk had come from Kursk with the 53rd Brigade, but at that point they didn't have visual evidence of the col-umn entering Ukraine. Early October arrived, and Ostanin started his law degree at York University. While his fellow students were attending freshman events and getting drunk together, he spent his nights on Russian social media, turning up to seminars short on sleep and feeling he could be doing something far more important.

Ostanin and Toler continued their investigation of the Russian social media space. Ostanin was keen to discover as much as he could about the 53rd Brigade, as he thought it might provide further confirmation that it had been the unit that took the Buk all the way to Ukraine. The first thing he did was to check if the brigade had a VKontakte group. It did. Then it was a question of clicking on any public profiles and scrolling through them to see what information they yielded. In one profile a soldier had posted various images including a vehicle, the license plate of which matched a license plate from the June 24 video.

Meanwhile, Toler was doing exactly the same thing on a similar message board called Mat Soldata (Soldier's Mother). Because of conscription in Russia and a tradition of widespread bullying in the army, Russian parents, girlfriends, and wives are always concerned about which regiment their son or partner is being sent to. What are the conditions like? Is there a lot of hazing? Questions like these were commonly posted on forums dedicated to providing information about the Russian military for anxious relatives. Toler found the forum beneficial for two reasons. First, as eighteen-year-old conscripts, the soldiers generally would much rather have been back home playing video games or chasing girls, so they cared little about security issues. Many of them were also unsophisticated youngsters from remote villages who were keen to show off, and had sent home photos of themselves posing with the convoy as it headed toward Ukraine, photos that their mothers had, in turn, proudly shared. One mother who had been receiving photos from her son in the 53rd Brigade throughout his military service wanted to surprise him with a photo album of his time in the army when he returned home. She included all the photos he had taken of himself with the Buk heading to the Ukrainian border in an album on the forum, showing off to the other mothers, telling them what a great present she had waiting for her son when he came home. He wasn't the only one who got a present. For Toler, it was pure gold.

By late October the team had everything: evidence that the Buk originated in Russia and had been part of the 53rd Brigade convoy that headed toward the Ukrainian border between June 23 and 25, the movements of the Buk in eastern Ukraine on July 17, and finally the vehicles seen in the same convoy leaving Luhansk after the July 17 downing of MH17. On November 8, after months of work, their first major report was published, detailing all their findings.[14] As far as they were concerned, they had Russia dead to rights.

As soon as Higgins and his loose band of followers began their work on MH17, Ukrainians had taken note. Hundreds, if not thousands, of Ukrainian Twitter and Facebook users began sharing and tweeting their posts. Official Ukrainian government Twitter accounts, NATO accounts, and foreign ambassadors to Ukraine also began to retweet and share their findings. Estonia's president, Toomas Ilves, was a big fan. For the Ukrainians, *Bellingcat*'s findings were becoming a potent weapon in their narrative war against Russia. But it was after the deep dive in September and October, when the *Bellingcat* team went beyond merely tracking the Buk in Ukraine to allegedly proving it had come from the 53rd Brigade in Russia, that the Russian authorities began to take notice.

And they began to respond, first slowly and more informally, using their various media arms, before intensifying their attacks and raising them to the official level. Higgins had long been used to amateurish pro-Kremlin trolls attacking him on Twitter every time he wrote a post on MH17. "I've had trolls longer than I've had children!" he told me on that rainy afternoon in London. But a few months after the group's November 8 post, Sputnik, an official Russian media outlet founded by the government-controlled news agency, Rossiya Segodnya, which has been repeatedly accused of being little more than a propaganda mouthpiece for the Kremlin, came out to attack him.[15] Sputnik claimed that the *Guardian* had been forced to correct an article that Higgins, "a self-styled 'citizen journalist,'" had written. This was, it claimed, because "Sputnik news agency learned the newspaper's reporter had himself jointly authored the research on which the story was based."[16] The article then went on to hint at links between Higgins and Western intelligence services—a common line of attack on anyone (most often journalists) deemed to be producing output seen as hostile to the official Kremlin narrative. "Higgins is a research fellow with the UK based security and intelligence organization CENTRIC, based at Sheffield University. CENTRIC's website boasts the organization has 'close collaboration in security research and activity started between Sheffield Hallam University and Law Enforcement Agencies and whose board comprises of individuals from UK policing and the British intelligence community,'" the article read. It then challenged him "directly on whether he and his Bellingcat group had any links to the well-documented CIA-front organization, the National Endowment for Democracy." It finally strayed into outright conspiracy theory, declaring ominously that "records held by Companies House reveal that Higgins' business 'Brown Moses Ltd,' which owns the Bellingcat website, was established in December 2013, just months before the Kiev coup took place in February 2014."

Then, inevitably, RT got involved. In a segment entitled "Clerk Promises 'Truth' About MH17 Ahead of Official Report," which aired on October 8, 2015, an RT reporter named Anastasia Churkina, speaking flawless English with an American accent, posed several question to the viewers: "What does it take to shape public opinion and be a newsmaker over the conflict in Ukraine, finding answers and solutions that have eluded even the brightest political minds? Can a cozy couch and a laptop and Internet access to endless social media posts be enough to paint the full picture?"[17] The report went on to describe how, even before the official investigation into the crash had reported its findings, Higgins, a "36-year-old laid-off office worker" with "no background or training in weapons," had claimed to have solved the puzzle. It then detailed how *Bellingcat*'s findings had been taken at face value by the "mainstream media" but at least one publication, the German newspaper *Der Spiegel*, had subsequently been forced to issue an apology. RT then sent a reporter, Nimrod Kamer, to "doorstep" or ambush Higgins, who in that segment appeared to be evading him. Finally, it quoted experts dismissing his methods and analysis, before pointing to his links to the Atlantic Council, a US think tank, which it correctly stated received some of its funding from US and foreign government agencies.

When I challenged Higgins on these allegations over email, he replied that they "did our analysis and they [*Der Spiegel*] found people who disagreed with it and published that. Later the same images were analyzed using professional imagery analysis software and it turned out we were right all along. But that doesn't stop the likes of RT and Sputnik bringing it up all the time." Then he pointed me to a link on the website Arms Control Wonk to back up his claim.[18]

Regarding what looked like his attempt to avoid talking with Kamer, he responded equally forcefully: "He [Kamer] actually messaged me on Twitter to arrange an interview, I was too busy so I told him I could do it in a few days, so when he turned up in Leicester anyway at my office (which I wasn't at anyway) it was clear he was trying to pull the same bullshit hit piece he did on SOHR [Syrian Observatory for Human Rights] a couple of weeks earlier, and I wasn't going to play that game with them."

Higgins also sent me a spreadsheet with twenty-seven (mostly Russian) articles published attacking both him and his work.[19] It was clear he had annoyed some important people in Moscow. The extent of this became clear when Russia's Foreign Ministry spokeswoman Maria Zakharova gave a public briefing in Moscow on April 6, 2016. During the briefing she directly attacked *Bellingcat* in a press release titled "Bellingcat as an Instrument to Divert Attention from Investigating the Tragedy of the Malaysian Boeing over Ukraine."[20] She made Russia's position unequivocal: "We understand the purpose of this group's activities," she said. "Acting jointly with the current

Ukrainian authorities, they continue to use all possible 'fakes,' to create quasi-evidence to blame Russia [for the downing of MH17]."

In response to accusations of the use of "fakes" in *Bellingcat*'s work, Higgins wrote to the Russian Ministry of Foreign Affairs (MFA), along with the Russian Defense Ministry (which had made similar allegations), asking for evidence of fraud or fakery on *Bellingcat*'s part.[21] After some back-and-forth, the MFA responded with a rather sarcastic letter ("Your persistence would find a better use if you did put some effort to performing your self-proclaimed Internet sleuth role," it began.) It then included the purported examples of fakery that Higgins had requested.[22] The only problem was that Higgins was able to prove that the examples used in the ministry's response had been plagiarized from a LiveJournal blog, *Albert Lex*, one of which had been posted just a month earlier. There were four major claims, which Higgins forensically debunked one by one in a *Bellingcat* post entitled "The Russian Ministry of Foreign Affairs Publishes 'Their' Evidence of MH17 Fakery" on April 22, 2016.[23]

Regarding the plagiarism, its brazenness is plain to see. In its letter, the Ministry of Foreign Affairs had written, "В качестве доказательств—десятки фотографий из социальных сетей, на которых изображены какие-то солдаты с размытыми лицами, боевая техника с плохо читаемыми бортовыми номерами, к тому же непонятно где находящаяся" ("The proof presented is dozens of photos taken from social networks showing some soldiers with blurry faces and military vehicles with poorly visible side numbers in unknown locations.") The blog *Albert Lex*, meanwhile, had written: "В качестве доказательств—десятки фотографий из социальных сетей, на которых изображены какие-то солдаты с размытыми лицами, боевой техники с плохо читаемыми бортовыми номерами, к тому же непонятно где находящейся." Such is the extent of the plagiarism that no English translation is even required: the wording is almost identical. As Higgins pointed out on his blog, the "only difference between the two texts is that the MFA letter used an en dash (double-hyphen turned into a longer dash in MS Word), while the *Albe[r]t-Lex* post only used a single hyphen."[24]

The MFA's sloppy response brought to mind something Aric Toler had said to me: "It just blows my mind how bumbling these people are. I can't imagine the DoD or State Department being one-tenth of this stupid—for all of their many faults."[25]

On July 15, 2016, *Bellingcat* produced its most in-depth report on MH17 to date. Entitled "MH17—The Open Source Investigation, Two Years Later," it was forty-two pages long and outlined, in forensic detail, the investigation team's findings, which had now stretched to two years' worth of work. In response, a group of Russian bloggers with links to the state, calling themselves "anti-*Bellingcat*," produced a report designed to refute *Bellingcat*'s key findings.[26] The authors of the report made their views clear from the beginning, stating that "analysis of Bellingcat journalistic investigation's course shows, that from the very beginning so-called independent experts chose and coherently followed pro-Ukrainian (pro-American?) version of militiamen's guilt for the aircraft's crash."[27] Describing the team as "so-called sofa researchers," the report goes into confusing depth about the variety of different types of Buks and the difficulty of distinguishing one from another. It also claimed that their "opponents" stated that the Buk in the *Paris Match* photo was "covered with a canvas, but air missile launcher 'Buk,' clearly covered by a camouflage net." The report is a classic example of Russian disinformation: written in poor English, almost impossible to follow, and based on spurious evidence or outright fabrications, its goal is clearly to confuse the narrative as well as to cast blame elsewhere, in this case on Ukraine and/or the United States.

The most remarkable thing here is not the plagiarism or the absurd anti-*Bellingcat* report: it's that the Russian government was forced to publicly battle a group of mostly unpaid civilian volunteers (though after receiving funding from Google in December 2015 Higgins had taken on Aric Toler and some others as full-time, paid members of staff)—a battle that would have been both unnecessary and unthinkable just ten years ago. The power of *Homo digitalis* could no longer be ignored, not even by the government of a major power.

For much of the world, the question of who shot down flight MH17 was officially put to rest on September 28, 2016, when the JIT, just over two years after the tragedy, released a report concluding that the Buk missile that had downed flight MH17 had come from Russian territory at the request of Russian-backed separatists and returned to Russia the same night. The report used cell phone recordings, witness statements, and, crucially, social media sources as part of its investigative methods.[28] Higgins's work and the subsequent interviews he gave to the JIT team—a total of ten to twelve hours, in which he took the team through all the group's findings step by step, as well as the sources the group had used—were all present in the report. Open-source investigation had been incorporated into one of the largest and most important international investigations of the twenty-first century. On the day of the report's findings, Higgins posted a comment on Facebook: "Just got mobbed by the media."[29] Beneath it were two photos of him surrounded by a thicket of microphones and video cameras as reporters scrambled to get his thoughts on the report. Just like a young girl in Palestine, the former payments officer for a women's underwear company was now a star.

Perhaps the greatest problem surrounding the case of Eliot Higgins lies in deciding what exactly he is. As he told me: "I am one of the few people that do this. I am like the queen bee of open-source investigation. We are all free agents doing this, just a handful of people: you could probably put us all on a minibus and drive us off a cliff and set the whole process back by twenty-five years! In twenty or thirty years' time I want there to be thousands of people doing this—I am patient zero." When I asked him how he would describe himself, he chose the term "researcher," but that seems inadequate. The element of ratiocination—of detective work—that results in findings that can impact both criminal investigations and the political activities of state organs moves him beyond the realm of mere researcher. At the same time, he cannot accurately be called a detective, at least not an official one. He has no powers to arrest or apprehend; he can merely present his findings and rely on the media and willing politicians to disseminate them to the wider world. His power remains purely at the discursive level of war.

However, there is no denying that what Higgins does is having a profound impact on wartime intelligence gathering. According to Higgins, he has a friend at the US State Department who told him that each morning the entire US intelligence service would check his blog. More than that, Higgins added, he was seen as a model to emulate: "One guy told me that senior intelligence operatives in the US were using my blog to ask their subordinates, 'Why aren't you doing what this guy is doing for free on his blog? We have a huge budget—how can you justify it when you can't even get the stuff he does?'"

This might be somewhat overstated; certainly Higgins is proud of the work he does and unashamed in pointing to his successes. But it does point to a deeper truth, one that everyone from Anna Sandalova to Farah Baker to Eliot Higgins has shown: that freelancing individuals, brought together by social media, are able to form networks that can react faster and more effectively to events in wartime than bloated state bureaucracies with endless chains of command and multiple competing agendas. It was precisely this problem that Aliza Landes had fought against during her time in the IDF Spokesperson's Unit, and it is the lack of this problem that has helped Higgins to stay so far ahead of the curve.

The military historian Lawrence Freedman, emeritus professor of war studies at King's College London (where Higgins also lectures), summed this phenomenon up. "In the end, social media information campaigns have got to work with realities as they appear on the ground," he told me.[30] "The Russian information campaign is, accordingly, a complete failure. The most effective performers on social media are the counterpropagandists, people like Eliot Higgins. There is a command-and-control issue here. People think there is a presiding genius that orchestrates [Russia's information wars]. In fact, different people are responsible for different bits, and it gets messy. . . . It's too complicated to control social media messages. One of the strengths of the West in all this is that there isn't a presiding genius, just a lot of free individuals, and they are actually more effective than the clunky hand of the state."

Describing Russia's information warfare as a complete failure is, once again, to overstate the case. Its primary goal, as has been discussed, is generally not to convince but rather to confuse, and in the case of eastern Ukraine even to reinvent reality. But Freedman's point remains a percipient one. When I asked Higgins why he seemed able to prove facts on the ground in wartime faster and more conclusively than government agencies, he replied without a pause: "The intelligence agencies are still hanging around jihadi forums waiting for someone to announce the next 9/11, while all the jihadis are sharing selfies on Instagram."[31] His response may have been glib, but it encapsulates, once more, the shift in power from established institutions to individuals and networks of individuals that social media has brought to war, and to life in general. Individual people react to change far more easily than institutions, and the reasons are as much cultural as technological. Most of the major government institutions in the West are still predominantly staffed—at the senior level, at least—by middle-aged white men who are out of touch with new media and the degree to which the West has changed, socially and culturally, since the turn of the century. They govern like twentieth-century officials in a twenty-first-century world, and it shows.

Put simply: twentieth-century institutions adapt more slowly than twenty-first-century people. During our interview Higgins recounted an instructive anecdote. On July 20, 2014, just days after MH17 was shot down, US secretary of state John Kerry publicly stated that all the evidence pointed to pro-Russia separatists in eastern Ukraine as being responsible. "We know because we observed it by imagery that at the moment of the shootdown we detected a launch from that area," he said. "Our trajectory shows that it went to the aircraft."[32] Kerry claimed to have seen a photograph of the launch site that would be made available to the public. It was highly anticipated by the press. The imagery was duly produced and released on various US embassy sites, but the result was disappointment all round.[33]

Journalists had been expecting a photograph, but what actually appeared was a low-resolution satellite composite image of what was allegedly the launch site. It was, in Higgins's words, "rubbish." If anything, it confused the situation more than it elucidated it. "The White House put this out and it was just laughable—it was embarrassing," Higgins told me. "The authorities are just not up-to-date with social media. They are getting more interested in it. The CIA has said it is going to use more social media and open-source information and integrate it with other intelligence, which is what they've got to do. But I've been doing that for the last two years, so why are they only thinking of it now? They're behind the curve, because they have a very conservative culture."

Unlike the White House, Higgins had quickly learned another valuable lesson, one that Peter Lerner, Daniel Rubenstein, and Aliza Landes had long understood when it came to getting IDF material across to an audience: war is now a consumer commodity. If you want people to click on your tweets or posts, you have to make them appealing. You have to ensure that your audience, that is to say, your consumers, won't scroll past your link in a twenty-first-century world of shortened attention spans and dopamine hits of likes and retweets. Higgins found it frustrating, but he had no choice. He began to imitate the US website *Buzzfeed*'s style of posting his articles with a question as the main title. It worked—the number of visitors to the *Bellingcat* website doubled. If he used an image as well, it would double the number of visitors again. As Lerner well knew, visuals on social media are the key to everything. Higgins told me, somewhat forlornly: "I have come to accept that no matter how good your research or data is, unless you've got a question in the title and it has a nice image, it won't be looked at. You have to present it in such a way that someone giving it two seconds' consideration will decide to read it. It's why we write reports. If we do a blog post, no one cares, but if we do a report, then it gives the media something substantial to write an article around. If you want to pretend to be a doctor, wear a white coat and everyone will believe you. Put your findings into a PDF and it's a report, so it gives you credibility. Most people don't bother reading it, but they can go to the *Guardian* to get the summary. I doubt that more than 5 percent of the people who read about our report in the press actually read the report itself. But the opinion-formers read it—and they are the ones that matter."

If opinion-formers are reading Higgins's work—and they are—we're left with the question of impartiality. This is a war, and there are sides. Is Higgins as unbiased as he claims, or are his findings skewed toward a specific point of view? "I don't want to be seen as someone taking sides," he told me. "I'm pro–human rights and anti–people being killed. If my research showed that Ukraine had shot MH17 down, I would have published it; it makes no difference to me whatsoever." That Higgins believes himself to be impartial I do not doubt, nor do I doubt his claim that had his research proved the Ukrainians had shot down MH17 he would have published it. Rigorous analysis of his work reveals it to be honest and backed up with plentiful evidence. But whether he accepts it or not, he has chosen a side. His links with the Atlantic Council make clear that he has aligned himself with a particular political outlook. This is not to say it is the wrong one. Higgins finds himself on the wrong side of Russia for the simple reason that the Russians have, in Ukraine, acted reprehensibly, and Higgins—and, indeed, the Atlantic Council—has correctly called them out on it. Higgins is definitely an actor in the war, and he has chosen a side.

Our interview draws to a close. Higgins finishes his second cup of coffee. My tape recorder shows that we have spoken for two hours in our final meeting. The skies outside have darkened, and the rain has slowed to a drizzle. I pay the bill and we leave. Higgins will be leaving to go abroad soon. His work has changed his life. He is now a visiting research associate at King's College London's War Studies Department, a visiting research fellow at UC Berkeley School of Law's Human Rights Center, and a nonresident senior fellow at the Atlantic Council's Digital Forensic Research Lab. He also sits on the Technology Advisory Board of the International Criminal Court.

Out on the street, it's cold; Higgins adjusts his sweater. In the beginning, Higgins says, his family was skeptical about his work. Now they complain that he travels all the time and they never get to see him. "Whenever my wife complains that she wants me home, I tell her: 'You should have just let me continue playing *World of Warcraft*,'" he says. Smiling, he disappears off into the London gloom. I watch him recede into the distance, just another anonymous figure in a city of millions.

Eliot Higgins has become a player in wartime intelligence gathering, able to exercise influence on everyone from the JIT to the Russian MFA and MOD; he also now briefs various elements of the US government, NATO, and the Latvian, Ukrainian, UK, and Dutch governments. His real strength, however, lies less in the role he plays in war—though that is both inescapable and integral to defining him; without war there would be no Eliot Higgins—than in the role he occupies in the emerging media landscape. New information technology has created new ways of disseminating information, which, as we have seen, have ruptured traditional forms of newsgathering. Higgins would not be possible without the information he gleans from social media posts and tweets as well as the videos uploaded by people in war zones. Higgins would not be possible without people like Farah.

From Libya to Syria to Ukraine, Higgins has relied on information provided by those on the ground. What makes him different from traditional journalists or researchers is the way he has used that information. In an article titled "Start Making Sense: A Three Tier Approach to Citizen Journalism," the academic Matt Sienkiewicz discusses the still-traditional structure of news in the digital age, which is two-tiered.[34] The first tier consists of "amateur producers" who "expose new truths via online technologies." The second tier consists of legacy media outlets like the *New York Times* and the *Wall Street Journal*, which now often rely on the work of the first tier for their own reporting. What Sienkiewicz both identifies and calls for in this article is the existence of a third, intermediary tier, not yet fully understood, but emergent and vital to the correct dissemination of news. He calls this tier the "interpreter tier." In his own words: "Not only do the journalists who make up this middle tier interpret and verify potentially important citizen-produced news content, they also follow stories across long periods of time, following new developments even when mainstream outlets are temporarily uninterested in a story."[35]

He continues:

> This interpreter tier, as it is currently situated in the still-emerging field of citizen journalism, can be identified through three defining characteristics: (1) members possess a wealth of contacts both among mainstream journalists as well as individuals involved in the production and uploading of citizen reports, with an emphasis on the latter; (2) members develop long-term commitments to a specific region or story, following it even when mainstream sources have ceased to focus on it; and, (3) members' work is dependent on active collaboration, via user-oriented online tools such as interactive wiki-maps, "open newsroom" forums and popular social media platforms such as Twitter and Facebook.

The above could be an exact description of Eliot Higgins and his MH17 team. Indeed, Sienkiewicz cites Higgins in his article, which challenges what he describes as a "celebratory narrative" that emerged during the 2009 Green Revolution and the 2011 Arab Spring. This narrative holds that citizen journalist user-generated content has now "entered the mainstream," with amateurs on the ground providing the raw data (be it videos or tweets or posts) that professional journalists, with their own set of skills, then turn into accurate reporting.

The truth is, as Higgins shows, vastly different. He has skills and options that traditional journalists lack. And they are sorely needed, not just because fakery is extensive but because the sheer volume of information emerging from conflict zones needs to be verified in new ways—it needs to be "interpreted." What Higgins has done is to take his ability to interpret new media emerging from war zones and use it to prove or disprove what is being produced. Farah produced content that was real, but she was not impartial: she was a Palestinian under attack by Israel and could not accurately say (and most likely did not even know) whether Hamas was using her as a human shield or not. Equally, had IDF soldiers saved a Palestinian child from harm, it is doubtful she would have tweeted it. Throughout his career, Higgins has unquestionably tended to highlight things more unfavorable to one side, but he has reported the truth, backed up by forensic analysis and the public display of his methods. In so doing, he has been able to alter—at the discursive level, at least—the course of conflict in an entirely new way. War will never be the same again.

10

THE RECRUIT:
FRIENDS ARE CLOSE BUT ENEMIES
ARE CLOSER

'm sitting in a bistro in the shadow of the Palace of Versailles, to which in 1682 the Sun King, Louis XIV, moved the royal court from the center of Paris, making this previously insignificant town on the capital's outskirts a defining symbol of French absolutist splendor. The palace looms in the background, managing to be both tasteful yet almost absurdly grand: a building fit for France's most famous, and most ostentatious, king. I am waiting for Sophie Kasiki, a thirty-four-year-old French woman, originally from Senegal, who has come to tell me her story. I sip Sprite and eat *steak frites*. She arrives twenty minutes late, having had to wait for her babysitter to arrive. She is charming and articulate, and speaks softly, gesticulating with delicate hands that feature immaculately polished nails. She is wearing a beige top with a black scarf draped loosely across it. Her dark skin is set off by black hair woven into neat, short braids. A tiny silver stud glints in her nose. She starts to talk.[1]

Any military entity, from a state army to an insurgent group or even a terrorist cell, needs to recruit members. In the absence of conscription, state militaries and non-state actors have to convince recruits to join up. Traditionally, states have drawn upon a few set narratives to do this. In peacetime, recruitment is usually powered by the narrative of enlistment as a career option, stressing the opportunities for education, adventure, and travel. In the aftermath of World War II, with the ending of wartime conscription, 55 percent of all US recruitment posters played upon these themes, attempting to convince Americans that the military was a good career choice.[2] But perhaps the most common narrative, especially during times of conflict, is patriotism: the need to defend one's country. In World War I, for example, 42 percent of all US army recruitment posters used patriotism as their guiding theme.[3]

For non-state actors, narratives are just as important, if not more. Lacking the military means of states, such actors are often forced to fight by nontraditional methods (often against civilian targets) that we classify as "terrorism." The narratives such groups espouse must be especially powerful to justify both such actions and the fact that those recruited will become "terrorists," hunted men and women. Groups like the Irish Republican Army (IRA) and Hamas thus rely on narratives centered on resistance and the need to "liberate" land. Sometimes these narratives are grounded in truth, and non-state actors seek to battle genuine oppression, as the African National Congress (ANC) did with its battle against the apartheid South African state in the latter half of the twentieth century (though its violent arm certainly committed terrorist acts).

Propaganda—defined as "information, especially of a biased or misleading nature, used to promote a political cause or point of view"—is a type of narrative.[4] It has distinctly negative connotations, and what is deemed propaganda is always subjective. All state and non-state actors push narratives that are accused by their enemies of being propaganda. Sometimes the boundaries are blurred. Any coalition soldier who enlisted in the run-up to the 2003 Iraq War to help rid Iraq of weapons of mass destruction (WMDs)—which did not exist—was arguably a victim of propaganda, even if it was propaganda likely based on error rather than design. The critical element of successful propaganda is that it has at least an element of truth, however small. Saddam Hussein may not have had WMDs, but he *was* a barbarous dictator and a threat to regional stability. Hitler was a deranged Nazi, but his arguments that Germany had been ill-treated in the aftermath of World War I *were* valid. There *are* fascists in Ukraine, even if their number is minute.

If not the largest, then certainly the most sophisticated and rapid recruitment drive and propaganda campaign since World War II has occurred with the emergence of Islamic State. At its peak, throughout the latter half of 2014 and 2015 the group gradually occupied an area of land across Iraq and Syria the size of Great Britain. With its goal of reestablishing an Islamic caliphate (an Islamic area governed by strict sharia law and led by a caliph, a religious figure who must be a descendent of the Prophet Muhammad), Islamic State needed to recruit not just soldiers but the civilians required to perform a variety of functions within its "state."

The group's recruitment rests on its use of new media, especially social networks. According to Abdel Bari Atwan, author of *Islamic State: The Digital Caliphate,* "Without digital technology it is highly unlikely that Islamic State would ever have come into existence, let alone been able to survive and expand."[5] Moreover, he continues, "from recruitment and propaganda, to directing simultaneous military actions at great distances apart and consolidating allegiances with like-minded groups, ISIS has used the Internet and digital communications with great skill and inventiveness, competently fending off threats from global intelligence bodies and military opponents."[6]

To understand how Islamic State became so successful so quickly, it is necessary to understand the group's history, and how central the evolution of information technology has been—especially social networks. At the ideological level, the progenitor of Islamic State's unique characteristics was Abu Musab al-Zarqawi, a Jordanian who went to fight in Iraq after the 2003 invasion, eventually pledging allegiance to Osama bin Laden and in 2004 forming the Iraqi branch of the terrorist group al-Qaeda. Zarqawi displayed the traits that would come to define Islamic State. He was a showman, he was interested in eschatological material, and he had a fervent antipathy to the Shia branch of Islam and its adherents. But above all he had an understanding of the need to use propaganda to shape conflict and even the battlefield itself.

Al-Qaeda had always been technologically savvy, and under Zarqawi it would become more so. According to Bari Atwan, the group was the first major jihadist network to understand the potential of the Internet, initially using it to covertly share plans and disseminate ideological tracts. While the Taliban were smashing TV sets in the 1990s, al-Qaeda was using email lists to disseminate information and encrypted communications to orchestrate major attacks, notably the 1998 embassy bombings in Nairobi and Dar es Salaam. By 2000 the group had set up its first website.[7]

Then came the realization that the Internet was of far greater use for overt means. Now al-Qaeda could switch from having to rely on legacy media to broadcast grainy videotapes of its leader Osama bin Laden's speeches to setting up its own online news service, the Voice of the Caliphate, which it did in 2005.[8] But it was Zarqawi who truly took jihadist propaganda to the next level. On July 9, 2005, Ayman al-Zawahiri, then a senior figure in al-Qaeda (and now its leader), sent Zarqawi a letter warning him against being too brutal in his attacks. "I say to you," Zawahiri wrote him, "that we are in a battle, and that more than half of this battle is taking place in the battlefield of the media."[9] Zarqawi took this advice to heart, though not in the way his jihadist counterpart had intended. As he continued to fight against both coalition forces and Iraq's Shia population he understood the need to broadcast ISIS's every success—and in this he was enabled, in no small degree, by the emergence of what would become one of the most popular social media platforms, YouTube, the very same year. As Bari Atwan observes:

> [He] pioneered the tactic of recording every successful attack on Coalition targets in Iraq on digital video, complete with cries of "Allahu Akbar" ("God is Great") and a soundtrack of the rather beautiful, stirring *nasheeds*. (These Islamic hymns are specifically written for the purpose of praise, adoration or prayer, and are typically addressed to a deity or to a prominent figure.) YouTube . . . provided the perfect forum for these videos, as well as for the filmed posthumous "wills and testaments" of suicide bombers, which could be uploaded anonymously.[10]

The chaos of postwar Iraq allowed jihadism to flourish; jihadists' increasing understanding of new media allowed them to compound their successes. Bari Atwan points to the example of Anwar al-Awlaki, a US-born youthful cleric prominent in al-Qaeda in the Arabian Peninsula (AQAP). Al-Awlaki pioneered the use of social networking platforms, creating his own blog, Facebook page, and YouTube channel to spread jihadist material for publicity and recruitment purposes, earning himself the nickname the "Bin Laden of the Internet."[11]

Islamic State's social media efficacy is built on the efforts of older jihadist groups, but it honed and perfected their techniques to a degree of success unparalleled in the history of modern terror groups. Critical to this achievement was the war in Syria, which Alberto Fernandez, the former coordinator of the Center for Strategic Counterterrorism Communications (CSCC) at the US State Department—the body charged with countering Islamic State propaganda—described to me as the "first social media war."[12] Islamic State became what it is today in 2013, when Islamic State of Iraq (ISI), which had been established in 2006, became transnational through contact with the war in Syria and fully embraced the use of social media, especially Twitter. Terror groups like Hamas and al-Shabab (a Somali jihadist group allied to al-Qaeda) had previously used the platform, but not in any meaningful way. With legacy media barely able to cover the Syrian war on the ground because of the extreme danger involved, social media became the primary way for actors to get their message out to a wide audience and in a variety of languages.

The unholiest of trinities created Islamic State as we know it today: the experiences of Iraq, which generated ISI; the group's contact with Syria and subsequent embrace of Twitter; and its use of foreign languages made the group into a global terror organization the likes of which the modern world had never seen.

On April 8, 2013, the leader of Islamic State of Iraq, Abu Bakr al-Baghdadi, announced in an audio statement that he was merging the group with Jabhat al-Nusra (a Syrian offshoot of al-Qaeda) to create Islamic State in Iraq and Syria (ISIS, or what is here referred to as Islamic State). Just over a year later, Islamic State emerged as a fully grown entity with its capture of Mosul, Iraq's second-largest city. With Mosul under the group's control, on June 30, 2014, Baghdadi proclaimed the official establishment of the caliphate.[13] From that point Islamic State's propaganda went into overdrive. Social media was the platform of choice, and the group began to produce material aimed at drawing people from across the world to its newly established statelet. Tweets, memes, videos, and texts in languages ranging from English, French, and German to Azeri, Kurdish, and Russian began to appear.[14]

They had an almost immediate impact. As Bari Atwan told me, "Islamic State is only two years old. Many people all over the world know about it because of the Internet. If they had emerged thirty years ago it would have taken them twenty years to reach a quarter of the audience they have. They are making use of the latest Western invention—the Internet—and managing to recruit everyone from experts in IT to fighters from the West and Muslim worlds to graduates from highly reputed Western universities to put themselves on the media, political, and military map."[15] Islamic State's social-media-empowered ability to recruit is staggering. It is estimated that by late 2016 the group had managed to persuade at least thirty thousand foreign fighters from around a hundred countries to make the journey to Syria and Iraq.[16] Incredibly, more foreign fighters have gone to Syria, most of them to join Islamic State, than went to fight in Iraq when American troops invaded or in Afghanistan during the decade-long Soviet-Afghan war. This simply cannot be explained without the recruiting power of social media.[17] In the past jihadist groups like al-Qaeda would use the technology to disseminate official information. But Islamic State had an army of networked individuals under its command, all with their own Twitter, Facebook, WhatsApp, and Skype accounts, who could act as individual broadcasters and recruiters. Instead of just one central organization producing propaganda, Islamic State became a hydra, with innumerable heads spouting their poison across the Internet and throughout many countries. And, just like the Hydra of Greek myth, for every head that was cut off (or shut down), two would regrow in its place. The decentralization of its broadcasting ability would allow the group to reach across the world, even to people not naturally attracted to its message. This would prove tremendously effective, not least in the case of Sophie Kasiki.

When Sophie Kasiki was nine years old, her world fell apart. Up until then she had enjoyed a nearly idyllic childhood in Senegal with her mother, whom she adored. Her life was secure and rested on the bedrock of that relationship. Her mother was a nurse, a born nurturer. Sophie was, she told me, living in what she later realized was a cocoon. Her father had died when she was a toddler, but her mother's love was enough. Then, after a long illness, her mother died as well. Her remaining family decided that Sophie—the youngest of five now orphan children—would join her sister in France. The move took place almost immediately, and while she didn't mind the move to another country so much, what really pained her was the absence of her mother.

But Sophie was forced to adapt, and she did. She completed school and went on to qualify as a social worker—just like her mother, Sophie wanted a job where she could help people. She also got married, at twenty-eight, to someone who had first been a friend. The relationship was a happy one, and they had a child, Hugo.[18] But still she felt a void in her life, an emptiness that lingered from her mother's death—something that neither her job, which she enjoyed, nor her son, whom she adored, could fill. She came from a Catholic family and as a child back in Senegal had been religious; each week she had looked forward to church on Sunday, where she could put on her best dress and go with her mother to listen to the priest's sermon. But as she grew up in Paris she began to question her faith. If God exists, why had he taken her mother from her? she repeatedly asked herself. She also came to question whether Catholicism was the right religion for her or merely something she had been born into. She started to read about other religions. First she studied Buddhism with some friends, but she didn't agree with all of its precepts. As a social worker, Sophie worked mainly in the run-down *banlieues* (suburbs) of Paris, which contained large Muslim communities, so she began to study Islam. From the beginning it just felt right, and she began to find answers to the questions that had plagued her for years.

She went online and began to read surahs (verses) from the Quran. She found YouTube especially valuable, because it enabled her to listen to Islamic prayers and beautiful *nasheeds* (Islamic songs). She also bought children's books on Islam designed to explain the faith to beginners. When she had begun to question her faith her sister had told her to go speak to the priest or go to confession. In Islam, however, there was no intermediary: it was just Sophie and God. In July 2013 she finally made the decision to convert. As a Catholic, she had assumed conversion would be a long process, but to her surprise the local mosque gave her an appointment within a week of her first phone call. When she showed up, with the requisite two witnesses, she was informed that she would merely have to recite a single sentence, the "Testimony of Faith" (known as the *shahada*). And so, with excitement and trepidation, she pronounced the required Arabic words: "La ilaha illa Allah, Muhammad rasoolu Allah" (There is no true god but God [Allah], and Muhammad is the messenger of God).

Only two people were aware of her conversion: the witnesses she had taken along with her. None of her friends or family or even her husband, a fervent atheist, knew. It was a personal decision, and Sophie knew they would not have agreed with it. She would, she told herself, tell them later on, when they could see how much the conversion had improved her life. Though she had no idea then, she had just taken the first step in a journey that would eventually lead her and her son to Syria—and into the arms of Islamic State.

It's March 21, 2016, almost nine months before my meeting with Sophie at Versailles. I make my way through the throngs smothering central London's Oxford Street and turn into a side road just by a Dr. Martens shoe store to arrive at a nondescript building near the corner. The glass doorway reveals little about the various offices within. Pressing the buzzer, I enter. I then take the elevator up to the fourth floor, where I come into a large open-plan office with rows of desks, five or six across. One side of the wall is covered with windows, but the blinds are pulled down; a kitchen area with a kettle and packets of opened chocolates and cookies stands at the far end. It looks like any other central London office. But the people here engage in an activity quite different from those in the surrounding retail outlets and restaurants.

I am at the Institute of Strategic Dialogue, a key center of the United Kingdom's counterextremism efforts, to meet with Melanie Smith, a researcher and project coordinator for the center's Women and Extremism program. Part of Smith's work involves running a database that uses social media platforms to monitor women who have left their country of origin—mostly Canada, the United States, Australia, or Western European countries—to join Islamic State in Syria or Iraq. She is polite and intelligent, answering my questions methodically as we retire to a meeting room with black faux leather chairs surrounding a long rectangular table. "The push factors for radicalization of women," Smith tells me, "revolve primarily around a social identity crisis, young women who don't know where they fit in society. In France, 60 percent of them are converts and generally have only a nascent knowledge of Islam.[19]

"It's rare for women to be radicalized or recruited offline," she continues. "Men are radicalized more in social settings than women. Men can form groups and share ideas. For women, the idea is more shameful, and they are more likely to do it in isolation online. As such, you mostly see them leave to join Islamic State alone or in isolated groups, often from the most surprising of circumstances. Social media has been a game changer in terms of people being radicalized; it's also a game changer in the way they are radicalized. The manner in which they are drawn in is very different to what we have seen previously, due to the way in which groups like Islamic State have been able to radicalize people through harnessing the immediacy of social media."

This is vital, she continues, because there is almost invariably a personal element to radicalization and recruitment. "Social media sits at the center of the process, but it alone is generally not enough." It is unlikely that someone will make the long journey from Paris or London to Syria merely because of watching Islamic State propaganda. A woman will almost certainly come into contact with someone else who draws her in and helps to recruit her, whether someone within her community or, more often, someone who has already joined Islamic State and is now in Syria or Iraq, from which they communicate online, she tells me. "Social media," she concludes, "allows them to engage: it's a bi-way process." Though neither she nor I knew it then, Smith had just described—almost exactly—the journey that would take Sophie from Paris to Syria.

Most of Sophie's job revolved around a community center in an impoverished Paris *banlieue*, where she had started working in 2012.[20]

The idea was to give people a place to go and keep those most at risk, usually young males, off the streets. Sophie's job was to monitor certain families to make sure that everything was going all right and to flag any problems that arose, as well as helping children with their homework and organizing trips to places of cultural interest in Paris, to show them something beyond the *banlieue*. Idris, Suleiman, and Mohammed were three regulars at the center. They were young guys, all between the ages of twenty and twenty-four; all were practicing Muslims, but they were not extreme and they didn't proselytize. They ate halal food, but they also wore trendy clothing and spoke freely with women. One worked for a major French company, while the other two were in school. Sometimes they talked about the situation in Palestine or the history of colonialism, but these were normal discussions—intellectual inquiry was encouraged. They were ordinary young Muslim men from the *banlieues*.

Then one day they disappeared. It was October 2014, just a few months after Islamic State took Mosul and the group began to dominate global headlines, when one of Idris's sisters called Sophie, crying. Her brother, she explained, along with Suleiman and Mohammed, had all told their respective parents that the three of them were in Syria. He didn't say what they were doing there, only that they were safe and happy. She told Sophie her mother was sick with worry, and Sophie went to their house to offer support. While she was there, Idris called, with the others in the background; the connection on the phone was bad, but they reiterated that they were in Syria and that they were okay, and apologized for leaving so abruptly. Idris's mother was hysterical and screamed into the phone, "Come back, come back, it's not too late. It's just a small mistake, nobody will know."

Sophie heard little more about it until a couple of weeks later, on December 9, 2014. The date is forever fixed in her memory. She had just come out of the hospital after a throat operation and hadn't eaten properly for days; she was tired and unwell and getting ready for bed when she got a Skype call. It was from an unknown ID, but she answered anyway. "Guess who it is?" said a lighthearted male voice at the other end. Sophie was in no mood for games. "Tell me who it is or I'll hang up," she snapped. "It's Idris," came the reply. Sophie immediately switched on. She knew how worried Idris's family was about him, and everyone at the center was also worried about the three of them, so she thought she'd try to get as much information from him as possible, and perhaps even convince him to come home.

She was speaking to Idris, but she could hear the other two in the background—it sounded like he was on speaker. Idris told her they were in the Syrian city of Raqqa (the capital of Islamic State's "caliphate") and he wanted news about his family. They asked after people in the social center and how things were in the neighborhood—everyday questions. But Sophie wanted to make them aware of the pain they were causing. She told Idris that his mother was in a terrible state and his seven-year-old sister was always asking after him, that the younger brothers of the other two were no longer going to school, and that everyone was upset. The conversation lasted less than five minutes. At the end they said they would call back. "Yes," she replied, "call back—and come back."

The next call came about two weeks later, and a regular correspondence began from there. Sophie was still feeling ill after her operation; she was also depressed, and work wasn't going well. She had become a social worker to help improve lives, but instead she was tasked merely with monitoring people. It was intensely frustrating, and in a way the calls became a relief. She started to think of herself as a conduit between three lost young men—still boys, really—and their families. She thought if they simply understood how much pain they were causing their loved ones, they would catch the next plane home. Each time she spoke to them she made sure to update their worried parents. She even felt special—they had chosen her as their messenger. But slowly things began to change. They began to ask about her, and because she was feeling vulnerable, she opened up. The fact they were on a different continent also meant she felt able to speak to them more freely than she could to people around her. She liked their childish, cheeky *banlieue* humor—they cheered her up. Often they would quote a surah from the Quran that opened up a new perspective on life for her. At all times she thought she was in control, but sitting across the table from me at the bistro near Versailles palace, she tells me that she now realizes they were slowly, as she put it, "brainwashing" her. They knew she was an orphan, that she was an Islamic convert, and that she was depressed—and they played it.

Although Sophie was unaware of it, she was being subjected, via new information technologies like Skype and WhatsApp, to an emerging recruitment campaign straight out of Islamic State's playbook. In its report "Why ISIS Flourishes in Its Media Domain," the American Foreign Policy Council notes, "It is surely a mistake to think that individuals are radicalized by themselves or solely by the consumption of radicalizing social media. There is usually a personal dimension—a friend or relative or neighbor—or a virtual individual dimension providing remote intimacy through Skype or Twitter or instant messaging."[21] The three men had first provided Sophie with something she craved, intimacy, but the vital element was that the intimacy was remote; the fact that they were far away enabled her to open up to them.

Then there was their message. Since Islamic State first emerged, the global media consistently focused on the brutality of its propaganda, broadcasting its every atrocity, from the beheading of the American journalist James Foley to the immolation of the Jordanian pilot Muath al-Kasasbeh, to millions around the world.[22] In the public consciousness Islamic State propaganda is associated with extreme violence packaged in slick videos with dramatic music and high production values. But its real strength in recruitment lies in something far different. Charlie Winter, senior research fellow at the International Centre for the Study of Radicalization at King's College London, identifies a positive vision at the heart of the group's propaganda. Their recruitment narrative is built around an alternative way to live that is based on piety and religiosity but also on a defiance of the status quo.[23] Alberto Fernandez expands on this, identifying three elements that together make up Islamic State's propagandist appeal.[24] The first is a Salafi jihadist worldview. Salafism is the belief that Islam must return to its "pristine" form as practiced by its first three generations, collectively known as *al-salaf al-salihin* (pious predecessors), who are "held to constitute a golden age of authenticated and orthodox Islam."[25] Salafi jihadism is the worldview that violence must be used to achieve this end. Most Salafists are nonviolent, are often apolitical, and reject the idea of a pan-national caliphate, whereas for jihadist Salafists, its establishment is a strategic goal. Salafi jihadism and the establishment of a caliphate stand at the center of Islamic State's ideology, and the group has produced reams of material highlighting its achievement of these goals, material that proved a powerful way of drawing Muslims from around the world to the black flag.

This was not of interest to Sophie, who was no Salafist and certainly not a jihadist. When it came to religion, she was more spiritual than doctrinaire. Indeed, her husband still had no idea that she had even converted. Instead, as Winter and Fernandez identify, the men pushed the second and third parts of Islamic State's message, namely, the positive vision of life in the caliphate. This is the limb of Islamic State propaganda that speaks to potential recruits on an individual level, appealing to their desire to be part of something greater than themselves—a state-building project.[26] In an article for the BBC, Winter examined Islamic State's online output, broadcast across a variety of social media platforms, over the thirty days of the month of Shawwal, which, according to the group's own calendar, began on July 17 and finished on August 15. Over that time, he states, the group's official propagandists created and disseminated 1,146 separate units of propaganda from thirty-five different media outlets.[27] Much of it was predictable in highlighting the group's abhorrent violence, but what struck him was how much of the message was far more concerned with promoting a positive image of the caliphate:

> Coming immediately after the holy month of Ramadan, Shawwal
> begins with a day of celebration, Eid al-Fitr. Predictably, IS wanted

to show this off. Its media team needed to demonstrate to their audiences, both within and without the so-called caliphate, that Eid "IS-style" was unmatched. As such, the initial focus was fixed upon two central aspects of the IS utopia—the religion and social life of its "citizens." The propagandists made great play of the alms-distribution among the needy in Syria and Libya, and spent a huge amount of time documenting celebratory prayers and the general "ambiences" of the festivities. Kids played on fairground rides, toys and sweets were handed out among orphans, fighters at the front lines sang, drank tea and laughed together.

The final appeal is to youth and rebellion—elements that almost certainly factored into the radicalization of Sophie's young male recruiters—and to action and agency. This type of narrative is summed up by Junaid Hussain, a British Muslim who went to Syria and became one of Islamic State's most effective propagandists (changing his name to Abu Hussain al-Britani in the process). "You can sit at home and play *Call of Duty* or you can come here and respond to the real call of duty," he tweeted. "The choice is yours."[28] It was this type of call to action (albeit not of the violent jihadist kind) that the three men played upon, and which would prove the deciding factor in Sophie's eventual decision to make the trip to Syria. The message they gradually sold her presented her with the opportunity to go from, as she put it, being a spectator in her own life to being an actor in her own life.

As the three men slowly turned the tables on Sophie they stopped asking questions about their life back home and began to tell her about life in Raqqa. "Sophie, you must see the beauty of this city, it is magical," they told her. They were, they continued, serving a "great cause"—though what that cause was, they never explicitly mentioned. They began to send her photos via WhatsApp and Viber of themselves in a bakery stocked full of goods, laughing in a restaurant, and sailing in boats on the Euphrates River. They were, they told her, being truly useful for the first time in their lives. They had never felt integrated into French society: they talked resentfully about how they had witnessed their parents breaking their backs for nothing. They talked about the racism they had experienced, the fact that despite being born in France (unlike Sophie) they had never felt French, how their neighborhood was lacking in opportunities. But in Raqqa, they told her, it was different. They belonged; they were doing good. Listening to them on the phone, Sophie thought they sounded euphoric, as though they had finally found a purpose in life.

The men were providing her with exactly the same direct, personal message that Winter identified, backed up with plenty of images—photos from thousands of miles away in Raqqa that, because of apps like WhatsApp and Viber, she was able to receive instantly and frequently. The power of social media allowed them to provide her with a complete narrative—critically, both verbal and visual—of an almost utopian life under Islamic State.

Central to this narrative was something they knew would appeal to Sophie in particular: the women's hospital in Raqqa. This treated large numbers of female refugees who had fled all parts of Syria to escape the tyranny of its president Bashar al-Assad. The hospital, they told her, had a large maternity ward. Many foreigners had come to help the beleaguered Syrians, but there still weren't enough women working there. Syrian children were being born by the dozen and the place needed her help. "I'm not a doctor," she told them. "It doesn't matter," they replied; "you're trained to care for people." They knew she loved children and that she could bring her skills as a social worker to help those in genuine need, as opposed to performing her perfunctory monitoring duties at her current job, which she had told them on more than one occasion she wanted to quit. In Raqqa, they told her, she would find everything that was missing in her work and personal life.

Sophie felt useless, and here was a positive state-building project that needed her help. It was the perfect match. France and modern life, they told her, made everyone a slave. The line struck a chord.

Sophie had recently been to Gorée Island in Senegal, the so-called slave island, where she had visited the "Door of No Return" monument, commemorating the final exit point of slaves from Africa. She found herself telling them that the only thing that made her get up in the morning was being a mother. Sophie had also watched the news of the Syrian humanitarian crisis—she, like millions of others around the world, had seen the images of people suffering at the hands of Assad—and now she was being offered the chance to help.

But still she had doubts. Raqqa was in a state of war. Surely it was dangerous there. "That's bullshit, Sophie," they replied. "The roads are full of trees and flowers. The war is far away—we've never even heard a rifle shot. Don't believe the newspapers—here all Muslims live in peace, here we truly serve something." For every question she asked, whether it was about security, comfort, hygiene, or health care, they had an answer—in fact, they had multiple answers. They were, they told her, living in *dar al-Islam* (the house of Islam). Yes, they conceded, there was suffering there, but life went on, and it meant that people like her were needed even more urgently.

"They were trying to feed me with a disgust for Western life compared to the life they were living," she tells me in the bistro. "They fed me repeatedly with the idea that in France I was a spectator in my life, in Syria I could be an actor in it." In short, they promised her agency—the chance to take back control. It was everything she wanted. They had played it beautifully.

During our interview I ask Sophie how she was able to reconcile her burgeoning online relationship with these men when she must have known what a brutal terror group Islamic State was. When the Paris office of the weekly satirical newspaper *Charlie Hebdo* was attacked by two gunmen on January 7, 2015, killing twelve people, she tells me, she was appalled. Almost simultaneously at a Parisian kosher supermarket four people were killed by a lone gunman, Amedy Coulibaly, who pledged allegiance to Islamic State. But she simply couldn't make the association in her mind between Idris, Suleiman, and Mohammed and those kinds of people.

"I thought I was in control of things, but I realize now that they almost certainly set out to recruit me from the beginning," she tells me. It was only with time that she came to understand what had happened. She believes the recruiting process started with the first call. She wasn't the only person they called, she realizes in hindsight. "Every question they asked me was designed to further the process of recruiting me." She thinks they were probably paid for every person they could get to go to Syria, especially women, who could come and make babies—to be, in effect, wombs for the caliphate. "None of these calls were innocent," she concludes. "They knew I had a desire to help people—they used the fact that I was complaining about my daily life here to go somewhere where I could be useful."

Social media is many things, but above all—as we have seen with Farah Baker, Anna Sandalova, and Eliot Higgins—it empowers the individual. Specifically, at its most powerful, it is a tool of the powerless, the voiceless, the marginalized. The French scholar Olivier Roy discusses whether much of the jihadist violence we see involves the radicalization of Islam or the Islamization of radicalism. By Roy's reading, joining Islamic State becomes a way of rejecting bourgeois, Western norms in a vein similar to those who in the past became Communists, anarchists, or even hippies. Today these kinds of people go online and watch videos the group produces, which often employ video-game-like imagery and show fighters driving stylish BMW cars to promote the idea of "jihadi cool," an alternative lifestyle that flies in the face of everything the bourgeois West stands for. As Yaroslav Trofimov wrote in the *Wall Street Journal*: "What if the real issue is that nihilistic misfits and violent malcontents in the West turn to Islamic State simply because it is the most obvious foe of the system? What if Islamic State, with its *'Call of Duty'* style propaganda, merely harnesses the fury that it didn't create?"[29] And there is nothing, of course, better suited to harnessing, giving voice to, and ultimately mobilizing the fury of the marginalized and malcontented than social media.

The appeal of Islamic State is in fact a question of both the radicalization of Islam *and* the Islamization of radicalism. The overwhelming majority of its recruits hold a Salafi jihadist worldview and understand full well what they are signing up for. But Sophie was looking for answers to fill a void she had felt since the death of her mother; it is instructive that she looked at other religions before finally settling on Islam. Had she been born forty years earlier, her substitute might well have been Communism or even existentialism. The one thing that is clear above all else throughout her narrative is that she was looking for an alternative to a life in which she felt useless and powerless.

Sophie never referred to herself as being "radicalized"; rather, she preferred the term "brainwashed." In the sense that she was never radicalized into a Salafi jihadist worldview and was never convinced of the righteousness of Islamic State's cause, she is probably correct. But whether or not she can admit it, the three men succeeded in radicalizing her by getting her to agree to travel to the heart of the caliphate. After more than two months of dialogue with her recruiters, Sophie had faith in the narrative they sold her—and, perhaps most important of all, she had faith in them.

It was at this point that Idris first began to talk to Sophie about the system of "invitations" to Raqqa. He wanted, he said, to invite his dad over to show him the city and the luxury in which they all lived. As it was supposed to, it put the idea of going to Raqqa into Sophie's head, especially since she would also finally be able to see the hospital she had heard so much about. Her relationship with her husband had worsened over time, and she needed a change of surroundings. Idris was enthusiastic about the prospect of her coming, but she still had questions, and kept asking him to confirm that she would be able to return. He assured her leaving would not be a problem. He also brushed aside her concerns over the treatment of women, claiming that they were treated with the utmost respect in *dar al-Islam*. They wanted her to bring her son with her, and they told her that the two of them would live in a good apartment and that Hugo would have other children to play with. When she was online with them, it was all so convincing, but when she closed her laptop the doubts returned. She understood that Syria was at war, and that even if what they said about Raqqa was true right now, it would not be safe forever. Nonetheless, the time had come to make her decision, and so she did. She would go.

She agreed with Idris that she would go for a month to see what it was like, and at that point she would make a decision about whether to stay long-term. Then it was a question of the logistics. She didn't want to tell her husband where she was going, so instead she told him she was going to Istanbul with their son, Hugo, to work in an orphanage for a month. Her husband had looked after Hugo while she traveled to Senegal to visit Gorée Island, so he was glad for the break.

She booked a one-way ticket to Istanbul for February 20, 2015, with the intention of coming back on March 10. Idris told her she would be reimbursed for the flight later on. Still, Sophie wavered. She bought her ticket only two days before she was scheduled to leave; she was still of two minds about the whole thing. But once she was on the plane, she was in their hands—reliant on them as they laid out to her, via WhatsApp, every step of her journey to the caliphate. They told her that once she got to Istanbul she would be met by someone, but they couldn't say who, and told her not to ask any questions. She duly landed at Istanbul's Atatürk airport, where she was met by a tall, thin North African man who spoke a bit of French and maintained constant contact with Idris. They then took a taxi to the center of Istanbul, where they stayed with a French-speaking family for a night and left the following day at around noon. Everything was a blur. From Istanbul they took a bus to the town of Gaziantep, on the Turkish-Syrian border, from where they crossed into Syria together on foot, avoiding the checkpoints. Once safely across, they walked for about five minutes until Sophie saw a car waiting to take her to Raqqa.

The men in the car wore long robes and carried weapons; they looked like typical jihadists. It was unnerving. As they drove she saw a destroyed plane on the road, and the car passed through several checkpoints before they arrived in the city. Her first impressions of Raqqa were ambivalent. As Idris and the others had promised, it was a functioning city. It was indeed quiet and there were no sounds of war. But what struck her the most was the sight of people going about their daily lives in the street, all seemingly normal except for one small detail: nearly all the men were armed. Her spirits lifted when she saw Idris, Suleiman, and Mohammed. But at the same time she saw that they too were armed. Why, she asked, did they need to carry weapons when they were doing humanitarian work and the city was not in danger? They brushed her questions aside politely and said that the first thing they had to do was take a taxi to buy Sophie a *niqab* (a type of veil worn by Muslim women when outside the home that covers the entire face) because she was only wearing a headscarf. It was a surprise to her, but if that was what she had to do to live there, she thought, she would abide by the rules.

The *niqab* would turn out to be a portent. Wearing it was difficult; Sophie could barely breathe or see. She was installed in an apartment that, she found out, had been seized from its original Syrian owners, who had managed to take some of their possessions but had left most behind. After she had spent a few days settling in, she was taken to Islamic State's women's hospital.

Sophie was horrified by what she saw there. The hospital was overwhelmed, with rows of women giving birth without the proper medical care. The foreign women who had supposedly come to help the Syrian women persecuted by Assad treated the patients like dirt. A clear hierarchy existed, with the foreign fighters and civilians at the top and the Syrians squarely at the bottom. The care was so bad that it often amounted to maltreatment. Doctors seemed to perform

Caesarean sections on almost everyone, often with no anesthetic; in far too many cases the mothers died. Women and babies screamed constantly. The whole enterprise was like a factory line designed to populate the caliphate. She even began to suspect that medical services were offered almost free of charge as a way to make the local population beholden to Islamic State. When she complained, she was told that she was thinking like an "arrogant French woman"; at the same time, she was also told that, as an African, she should be used to these conditions. "You've never set foot in Africa," she replied indignantly. "My mother was a nurse there, and she never would have stood for conditions like these."

Outside the hospital, things were no better. Idris and the other two guys would talk about the Syrians like they were animals. It seemed to Sophie that Islamic State, far from being a benefactor, was in fact an occupying army. After about seven days in Raqqa she contacted her husband and told him everything: where she was, how she didn't want to go to the hospital anymore, how she didn't want to be like the other Western women there. They began speaking as often as possible. He got in contact with a deradicalization team in France, which impressed on him the need to avoid making Sophie feel guilty. Rather, they advised him to remind her of all the positive aspects of her old life. He sent Sophie an old photo of her smiling with their newborn son; she looked so happy. She was astonished to realize that she didn't even recognize the photo; it was as if she had been under anesthetic for months. But now, finally, she had woken up.

She began harassing Idris and the other two almost daily, constantly telling them that she wanted to leave. They got angry, took her apartment key away from her, and barred her from leaving the building without permission—they even brought food to the apartment so she didn't have to go out for it. They told her she was a coward; couldn't she see the project they were building here? One day they came to her apartment to take Hugo to the local mosque; she roared at them to leave him alone, and got a punch in the face for her pains. "You disgust me!" she screamed at them. "You make me not want to practice this religion, and I hope you never get to paradise!" They beat and insulted her, and then she finally understood: the cheeky *banlieue* boys were gone; the men in front of her were fanatics, a danger to her and her son. She had to get out.

That would prove more difficult than she ever could have imagined. After her constant complaints had crescendoed into confrontation and physical violence, she was sent with Hugo to a *madaffa* (guest house). It was home to dozens of foreign women whose goal was to marry Islamic State fighters, whom they revered; it was also, in essence, a prison. Worst of all was the TV room, in which videos of Islamic State's endless atrocities were broadcast to the appreciative women, whom Sophie remembers clapping and cheering as they watched the video of the Jordanian pilot being burned alive.[30] Critically, the *madaffa* played not just videos of the enemy being slaughtered but also of the hideous fate meted out to those perceived to be traitors to Islamic State. It was clear that this type of propaganda was considered vital to keeping the city's population under control.

Sophie was trapped and desperate. The woman who oversaw the *madaffa* was in effect the house jailer and made sure to keep the doors locked at all times. But Sophie was about to experience her first stroke of luck in a long time. On her second day in the house, a jihadi fighter came to propose to one of the women there. As the *madaffa* matriarch sat in with the soon-to-be betrothed, Sophie saw that she had shut the front door but not locked it after his arrival. She seized the opportunity to flee. Leaving all her luggage behind, she put just a few layers of clothing on Hugo and left.

She walked for a few streets to check that no one was following them. She had decided to go to a private hospital in the city to see if someone, anyone—even someone from Assad's side—could help her and her son. But when she arrived the doctor wasn't there and the secretaries didn't speak French. They couldn't give her a room to stay in, so—utterly desperate—she took a taxi back to her old apartment and hid in the garbage area until it was prayer time and she could be sure Idris and the others would be at the mosque. Her only remaining option was to contact a neighboring family in the apartment block who had cooed over Hugo a few weeks earlier, in the hope that they would help. It was a desperate gamble, but it was all she had.

It worked. At great risk to their own safety, the family took Sophie and Hugo in and hid them for the night. It was all she needed. During the previous weeks, Sophie's husband had put together a plan. The woman in charge of the deradicalization program in France was in touch with a Syrian activist on the ground, who put them in contact with the Free Syrian Army (FSA), an anti-Assad militant group originally consisting of officers from the Syrian army. For a fee of 30,000 euros, which Sophie's husband raised from relatives, the FSA agreed to exfiltrate Sophie from Raqqa. But Sophie had to be careful; because she wore a *niqab*, she could not be recognized, but Hugo is light-skinned and would attract attention. Sophie carried him in the folds of her long dress to hide his skin as much as possible.

After nearly missing their connection, Sophie's FSA contact took her to a safe house in the city, where they spent the night. The following morning, on April 24, they took a motorbike, with Sophie hiding Hugo under her robes, and drove toward the border. They drove at high speed, and at one point Sophie fell off the bike—she was lucky to avoid a broken back. Hugo was screaming the whole time; it was a nightmare. They eventually arrived at the Turkish border. As they were scrambling through a fence, Sophie's *niqab* caught on the wire. She tore it off in disgust.

After just over a month, she had escaped Islamic State. Had they been caught at any time they would have been killed, most likely in an extremely brutal fashion to serve as an example to anyone with similar thoughts of escape.

Once in Turkey she took a taxi to a designated shelter, where she met with people from the French consulate and the Turkish authorities, whom she debriefed about her experiences. Back in Paris, she was reunited with her relieved husband, debriefed by the French intelligence services, and then swiftly put in jail. She was sentenced to four months for child kidnapping, but served only two at a prison in

Versailles. Before she went to jail her husband showed her a photo that Idris had sent him via WhatsApp while Sophie was in Raqqa. It was a picture of Hugo, barely four years old, holding an automatic rifle.

Sophie was at a vulnerable period in her life when her recruitment occurred, but she is educated and intelligent; moreover, she is not a jihadist or even a Salafist. What emerges above all from her story is the professionalism of Islamic State's recruitment strategies and its reliance on certain specific elements that are almost unique to social media. Sophie's recruitment (or "brainwashing," as she described it) is not in itself new. But one thing that is new is the fact that social media has enabled groups like Islamic State to recruit remotely and, therefore, internationally. Through social networking platforms like Skype and Viber (as opposed to broadcasting platforms like Facebook and Twitter), Sophie was recruited by people thousands of miles away, whom she never met face-to-face even once throughout the entire process.[31] Another new element is the speed at which social networking platforms enable groups like Islamic State to recruit. A propaganda tweet or post can go viral and reach an audience of millions in just minutes. At its peak, Islamic State was recruiting the extraordinary figure of two thousand foreign fighters per month.[32] Sophie's recruitment moved at a slower pace than normal, but, as Melanie Smith explained, because she was a woman, her radicalization was more likely to take place in isolation (which it did) and hence be a far more gradual process than was typical of men. According to a report by the Soufan Group, a strategic security intelligence service, at the end of 2015 the number of foreign fighters who traveled to join jihadist groups in Iraq and Syria (overwhelmingly Islamic State) more than doubled in the course of just eighteen months.[33] In September 2014 alone, six thousand new recruits had signed up in just two weeks, thirteen hundred of them foreign fighters: these numbers testify to a reach and speed in terrorist recruitment that are utterly unprecedented.[34]

Despite all this, it is important to bear in mind that there are roughly 1.6 billion Muslims across the world. Islamic State has been able to radicalize, at most, several hundred thousand. The group's recruitment drive is thus paradoxically both highly successful and proportionally tiny. Yet any counterargument that Islamic State propaganda is not extraordinarily successful because it has radicalized only a minute part of the whole fails to understand how revolutionary movements work. The number of people radicalized to leave the comfort of the West to travel to a war zone is unprecedented in the history of jihad.[35] And this is all that is needed. History shows that groups with extreme ideologies, from the Bolsheviks to the Nazis, are never mass movements, but rather are relatively small groups of true believers who take power and then impose their worldview on the masses.

As I have said, social media is both centripetal and centrifugal. It brings people together and splits them apart. Islamic State has used social media's centripetal abilities to unite Muslims across the world, just as Sophie's recruiters did, by painting a virtual vision of a utopian caliphate. The irony is that jihadists' use of social media was, in large part, enforced. As Bari Atwan told me: "When we talk about Islamic State in the world we are living in, it faces a singular problem: How can you reach people when all the Sunni states are fighting you? How can you recruit, spread your ideology, and convince people to join your ranks across the Muslim world and rest of the world? How can you reach people when you are not allowed to have a TV station or newspapers or embassies? Because they are an underground organization they use social media to reach people. They have no other options."[36]

This has proven to be the greatest boon to the group. Social media's role in Islamic State's ability to recruit goes beyond mere propaganda, as the case of Sophie shows. Every detail of the recruitment process is managed via social media, including the logistics of getting a recruit to Syria once that person has decided to make the journey. "Once convinced," Bari Atwan said, "there is a logistics department that looks at 'invites' to get them to Turkey or Iraq. They have their own routes mapped out; once someone arrives in Turkey they have people waiting at the airports, who then get them across the border."[37] Once again, this was exactly what happened to Sophie, who kept in contact with Idris in Turkey via WhatsApp as he directed her, step by step, to Syria.

Now back in France and reunited with her husband, Sophie feels that her life is back on track. Hugo is doing well, and she is slowly emerging from the trauma of her time with Islamic State. She is determined that her case stand as a warning to others thinking about making the journey to Syria, especially for the vulnerable and disenfranchised specifically targeted by Islamic State. When, toward the end of our interview, I ask Sophie what she thought made her recruitment so effective, her answer is instant. "They were just so good at communication," she tells me. "It was like a form of psychological warfare. It was almost scientific—way more clever than I ever thought those uneducated kids could be. I never thought they were capable of using such effective propaganda on me. It was hugely professional—they preyed on all my weak points." She pauses and looks at me. "In the end," she says, "they simply took control of my brain."

Connecting with people on a personal level is the aim of classic recruitment. Islamic State's aims and methods are nothing novel; what is new is the technology, which has allowed it to draw people to its cause more effectively than any equivalent group in the past. Social networking tools enabled Idris, Suleiman, and Mohammed to overcome a vast distance between them and Sophie and, crucially, to personalize the traditional process to such a degree that she never even viewed them as recruiters—only ever as her friends. New media technology has changed recruitment in wartime forever.

11

THE COUNTERTERRORIST: GOLIATH VERSUS A THOUSAND SLINGSHOTS

I t was early 2012 and Alberto Fernandez had achieved the goal of every Foreign Service officer: to be an ambassador. In July 2009, fresh from a posting in Sudan, Fernandez, a career diplomat with almost thirty years' service, had been appointed US ambassador to Equatorial Guinea, a tiny country in Central Africa, measuring just 11,000 square miles with a population of around 1.2 million. Now his time there was coming to an end. Retirement was an option, but he decided to return to Washington for one final posting. In the ramshackle villa that served as the US embassy in Malabo, he looked through the online listing of vacancies until one caught his eye. It was for the post of coordinator of the Center for Strategic Counterterrorism Communications (CSCC) at the US Department of State—the body charged with countering jihadist propaganda. The impetus to set up CSCC had come in 2010 from Secretary of State Hillary Clinton, who, as Alec Ross described to me, was keen from the outset of her tenure to come to grips with power of the Internet.[1] She was especially determined to do something to counter the growing online

Alberto Fernandez, head of CSCC, in a State Department meeting chaired by Clinton; Fernandez is to her right sitting against the wall with a mustache and glassses. (Courtesy of the State Department)

presence of al-Qaeda and other jihadist groups. And Fernandez agreed with her vision.

Islamic State exists on two planes. One is its physical manifestation: an (ever-diminishing) statelet that straddles Syria and Iraq, what might usefully be called the physical caliphate. The other is its online manifestation: encompassing the major social media platforms of our time, notably Twitter and YouTube, something that might usefully be called the virtual caliphate. Indeed, so strongly is the latter idea embedded in the group's thinking that its many fans often refer to the online realm as *wilayat Twitter* (the state of Twitter).[2]

Abdel Bari Atwan christened Islamic State the "digital caliphate" with good reason. For him, it is almost impossible to distinguish between the group's efforts on the ground and those online, as the two are symbiotic:

> Success on the ground means nothing if there is no publicity [to go with it]. If you don't reach the people how can you terrorize them? Islamic State captured Mosul easily because their reputation for brutality—spread throughout social media for all to see—preceded them and the Iraqi army ran away. Media success enables military success: it prepares the ground for it. When you want to conquer a city you need an element of psychological warfare and social media helps them to achieve this. Equally, their online propaganda is not possible without their victories on the ground, which feed their media success. They are two sides of the same coin.[3]

Hamas may have benefited from its citizens tweeting their suffering, but its own online propagandist presence—consisting of belligerent tweets in poor English from one or two official accounts—was feeble. Hamas was and remains a twentieth-century terror group. Islamic State is indubitably a twenty-first-century one. Western governments only belatedly acknowledged the role of Islamic State's (overwhelmingly online) propaganda in its astonishing ability to morph so quickly from a local Iraqi insurgent group to the most successful terrorist brand in modern history. The desire to proactively combat it is now entrenched within their state apparatuses. The major European powers, notably France and Great Britain, together with the United States, now lead the way in the fight against jihadist propaganda. In terms of sheer volume this propaganda has reached levels previously unseen with the emergence of Islamic State.

Several trends that now dominate twenty-first-century warfare are present in the battle fought by nation-states against Islamic State and its propaganda. These center on the inability of sclerotic state institutions to match the effectiveness of *Homo digitalis* and the pervasive lack of faith in these institutions across the West, which prevents them from promulgating effective narratives to adequately compete in the information sphere. This battle is both the culmination of twenty-first-century conflict and the repository of its most distinct practices.

Clinton had seen the need for a department like CSCC as far back as 2010. But, as Aliza Landes had experienced in her struggles with the IDF, the wheels of bureaucracy grind painfully slowly. The State Department initially threw together a mishmash of people headed up by Richard LeBaron, a career diplomat, who worked on an ad hoc basis without an overarching strategy. The Digital Outreach Team (DOT) was taken from another part of the State Department, where it produced online video clips of government officials telling viewers how well the United States treated its Muslim citizens, and assigned to LeBaron. He was not convinced of its efficacy. Finally, in September 2011 President Barack Obama signed White House Executive Order 13584, and CSCC was officially established.

By then, however, LeBaron was coming to the end of his career, and State needed a replacement with a unique set of skills, ranging from public diplomacy experience to fluency in Arabic, all of which Fernandez possessed. Being ambassador to Equatorial Guinea was less important than heading up CSCC, so he left his post in Malabo early and returned to Washington in March 2012. As far as Fernandez was concerned, LeBaron had been an excellent head of CSCC, but Fernandez felt that the department was not producing enough material to directly contest the extremists in the digital space. He was interested in going on the offensive, and for this, he believed, the DOT would be vital.

His staff consisted of around forty people (it would eventually rise to forty-eight) with a wide array of skill sets. The department's budget was a mere $5 million per year, far less than what was needed to mount an effective campaign to push back against jihadist propaganda. What was worse, two-thirds of the budget went on salaries and "keeping the lights on"—essentially it was spent on maintaining the existence of the bureaucracy. The discretionary funds Fernandez had in any given year for anti-jihadist projects was a mere $600,000–800,000.

Fernandez was familiar with the "sausage-making" duties of government. He knew he needed to "feed" the bureaucracy, and so he did, duly attending meetings while his staff wrote analytical pieces and memos. Sometimes their suggestions were taken up; more often they were ignored. As he saw it, he had two challenges. The first was to bypass the bureaucracy and become active in the digital field. "If you're there to counter terrorist propaganda, you have to counter it, not write memos about it," he told me over Skype. "There's nothing wrong with the advisory role, but you have to affect the space, not just write something and send it to the White House, which they'll look at and then do nothing with. A waste of everyone's time."[4]

The second was to use the tiny pot of discretionary money he had available to him to focus on specific projects. Vital for that was the DOT, with its team of operators (tweeting and posting content), editors, and graphics and video experts proficient in Arabic, Somali, and Urdu. It was early 2012, and Islamic State had not yet emerged; much of the jihadist propaganda wasn't even all that slick. There was just so much of it, and so little counternarrative. The problem was not that the United States was challenging the jihadists but losing; it was that they weren't being challenged at all. One of the founding ideas of CSCC was to contest that virtual space. Indeed, its motto, "The media is half the battle," was a subversive take on Ayman al-Zawahiri's letter to Abu Musab al-Zarqawi.[5] Will McCants and Daniel Kimmage of the DOT were, Fernandez told me, the intellectual authors of the idea that CSCC should directly challenge jihadist propaganda online. It was an idea Fernandez embraced wholeheartedly—and one that would cause him significant trouble in the times to come.

The year 2012 was an inauspicious time to start his mission. An Arabic speaker, Fernandez consumed large amounts of Arab media, both legacy and social, and he found that the number one public diplomacy issue in the Arab world was the civil war intensifying in Syria. CSCC had so far stayed away from the Syrian conflict because it was a civil war and Syria was not (yet) a hotbed of terrorism. But the DOT was watching the Arab digital space and noticing how each day the carnage created a more conducive environment for the nascent jihadists on the ground, especially al-Qaeda's Syrian franchise, the al-Nusra Front, which had been formed at the beginning of the year to fight Assad's forces. The West was accused of ignoring the slaughter, and the atmosphere on social media was becoming more sectarian, more toxic, and more extreme. Al-Nusra, meanwhile, was proving itself to be the most effective rebel force fighting Assad and was gaining local support as a result. Fernandez knew that as Syria grew bloodier, jihadist forces like al-Nusra and Islamic State in Iraq (ISI) would increasingly dominate the Arab social media space.

He sought a meeting with Robert Ford, the US ambassador to Syria, and told him that CSCC wanted to start messaging against al-Nusra. Ford agreed, and during 2012–2013 CSCC began to aggressively contest them online. In contrast to previous attempts at countermessaging, Fernandez was not interested in trying to project a positive image of the United States or produce content saying how wicked al-Nusra was. That, he knew, would not work. Instead he ordered CSCC to focus on trying to draw an equivalence between Syria's barbarous president, Bashar al-Assad, and the jihadists. "Don't replace one tyrant with another" was a prominent message. With its minuscule budget, the DOT took to social media with graphics and videos: low-quality, cheap mash-ups. Central to discrediting al-Nusra was the idea that it consisted of foreigners who didn't have the Syrian people's best interests at heart. One video the CSCC produced particularly enraged the terror group. "Annoying/embarrassing questions for Jebhat al Nusra," the title ran. "Syrians know very well who it is who supports them, their revolution, and their national coalition. [It's] the Syrian coalition, which contains the national opposition's forces—people from Hama, Aleppo, Daraa, Idlib, Damascus, and its outskirts. And not the al-Qaeda mercenaries, made up of Tunisians, Libyans, Saudis, Jordanians, Iraqis, and others who want to turn Syria into a base for their reckless adventures, which they previously tried to do in Iraq, Yemen, and Somalia."[6]

But Fernandez could not escape the fact that he worked for the US government. Official policy was not to intervene in Syria, and there was a national debate raging over whether Washington should act to stop Assad's butchery. "Throughout my time we faced a legacy of political decisions that would constrain us," he told me. "Syria was one problem. Another was the fact that we couldn't criticize [then–Iraqi president Nouri] al-Maliki [whose vicious sectarianism alienated large swaths of Sunni opinion]. These types of things made it difficult." During his time as a spokesman for the Bush administration, Fernandez would go on Arab media, where he was always met with questions about the detention of prisoners at Guantanamo Bay and the infamous mistreatment of Iraqi prisoners at Abu Ghraib prison near Baghdad. "When you work for a government you're always chained to its policy," he told me, "for good or for ill."

CSCC had enjoyed limited success against al-Nusra; it was unable to match the volume of content the group created, but it had attracted its attention. That was something, at least. The DOT was, as Fernandez wanted, getting in their faces. But his job was about to become harder than he could ever have imagined. On April 8, 2013, ISI's leader, Abu Bakr al-Baghdadi, announced he was merging ISI with al-Nusra to create Islamic State. Few people in government took the threat seriously at that point. Soon after the group had captured the Iraqi city of Fallujah in early 2014, Obama famously described the group as nothing more than a "JV [junior varsity] team."[7]

Fernandez's team was battling Islamic State online before almost anyone else. As the Iraqi and Syrian jihadist groups merged together, jihadist propaganda went stratospheric. Social media, especially Twitter, was the platform of choice. Tweets, videos, and texts in a variety of languages aimed at a global audience began to flood social media. It was time to take what Fernandez described as "the war of narratives" to the next level.

CSCC went on the offensive against Islamic State, throwing large amounts of time and resources into contesting the group everywhere possible in the virtual space. Once again the department caught the attention of a jihadist group, and Islamic State urged its Twitter fanboys, the so-called Knights of the Uploading, to do anything to get the DOT offline. For Fernandez, it was another small victory. His outfit was tiny in comparison to Islamic State's setup and fan base, but clearly large enough to bother it.

At all times Fernandez had to walk a line. Working in a government bureaucracy was constraining. Too much oversight, endless chains of command, and the scarcity of resources common to almost all government departments meant that CSCC didn't have a lot of arrows in its quiver. But because of the job it was doing, it had a certain amount of freedom. It messaged primarily in Arabic, which meant that for the time being other branches of government couldn't understand what it was doing. The DOT could be as confrontational and subversive as they liked, engaging in ways that senior officials, had they been able to understand them, might feel did not befit the State Department. For the moment CSCC could fly under the radar.

Then on June 10, 2014, came the fall of Mosul, and with it Islamic State's metamorphosis from the "JV team" of Obama's imagination to the most potent terror threat in the world. It was not a surprise to Fernandez, who had been following the group's progress for over a year. CSCC held an emergency internal meeting in which the team decided to drop almost all other projects and focus exclusively on Islamic State. And now he had the full backing of his superiors. When he first took the job, Fernandez had noticed a certain complacency in government after the death of Osama bin Laden; the prevailing mind-set was that the jihadist problem was declining. In April 2012, just one month into his tenure, he attended an academic conference in Washington, DC, in which a high-profile journalist had confidently said that people working on groups like al-Qaeda would become redundant—like the Cold War Kremlinologists of the past.

Now, however, the department was under tremendous pressure from above. The powers that be urged CSCC to take the battle to Islamic State, but the State Department would allocate no additional funds or manpower. Fernandez needed to get creative. In early July, fresh from Islamic State's triumph in Mosul, its supporters created the hashtag #CalamityWillBefallUS, and a deluge of anti-American, pro–Islamic State tweets followed. "#CalamityWillBefallUS Do you want more @BarackObama" tweeted the account @abo3merr, along with photos of coffins draped in the American flag and lines of injured US soldiers, as well as several photos of Islamic State fighters.[8] It was typical of the content being produced, and it needed a response. "Work as hard as you can," Fernandez told the DOT. He had just a dozen Arabic speakers, but they dutifully jumped on the hashtag to try to hijack it, tweeting feverishly, posting videos and photos they had produced. At the end of the campaign they assessed that the hashtag had garnered around 100,000 tweets and that their output was around 1 percent of the total. The score was 99 to 1.

The early weeks after the fall of Mosul saw the zenith of pro–Islamic State propaganda, with supportive hashtags regularly garnering more than 100,000 tweets. That later dropped to an average of around 40,000, but the scale of the problem CSCC faced was clear. Fernandez persisted and maintained a focus on Arabic-language messaging (followed by Urdu, Somali, and then English). The overwhelming majority of what Islamic State produced was in Arabic, and he was determined to meet them on their own terms. But as Fernandez explained to me, on social media you need volume in terms of amplifiers and messengers, and CSCC just did not have that.

Again, the power of *Homo digitalis* is clear: a major arm of the government of the world's most powerful nation simply could not compete with networked individuals operating out of dilapidated buildings in war-ridden Syria or teenagers sitting in their bedrooms creating and sharing content. This state of affairs would have been unthinkable just ten years earlier. From 2014 to late 2015, Fernandez estimates, Islamic State produced eighteen hundred videos. They weren't all hits, but the sheer volume of material it put out and the amount of people sharing it made the group seem ubiquitous. "It's not like we produced eighteen hundred videos to match theirs and theirs were better than ours," he told me. "We were just outgunned. From February 2011 to February 2015, when I left, CSCC produced a total of around just three hundred videos." When ISI moved into Syria and become Islamic State, it gained access to a vast online community, ranging from Islamists to Salafists to Salafi jihadists, able to amplify its message.[9] And then there was Islamic State's own operation. CSCC was battling a group that reportedly then had forty-eight official media offices—one for each self-declared "province" (nineteen in Syria and Iraq, seven in Yemen, and three in Libya, as well as several others in neighboring countries), plus a further nine centrally administered outlets.[10] Fernandez's staff of fewer than fifty people were up against what he calculated to be around ninety thousand pro–Islamic State Twitter accounts across the world. The mismatch was startling.

The department couldn't match Islamic State for volume, so Fernandez believed he had to make the content it produced as striking as possible. And that meant being aggressive. As far as he was concerned, CSCC was in the "attack ad" business. Unlike before and after his tenure, CSCC's output featured no Americans, no videos of Obama or Clinton condemning Islamic State. Instead, the goal was to use Islamic State's language against it—to use its own images and language to try to subvert it. The jihadist space was a countercultural, antiestablishment arena where reasonable voices like government talking heads simply wouldn't fly. The only chance CSCC had, he believed, was to be "edgy."

The CSCC team knew that the Middle East was splintering along sectarian Sunni-Shia lines and that a big part of the Sunni Islamic State's appeal was who they were fighting: Assad (an Alawite and therefore a follower of a strand of Shia Islam) and the Iranian-backed

Shia militias. Central to the team's message was to show that Islamic State also targeted Sunni Muslims. One video produced just two weeks after the fall of Mosul focused on Islamic State's bombing of the Sunni Umm al-Qura mosque in 2011 in Baghdad. The video even featured the voice of the group's spokesman, Abu Muhammad al-Adnani, threatening Sunni Muslims at the end. In its several versions it was viewed about 250,000 times.[11]

Another video compared Islamic State to Assad because both were killing Free Syrian Army fighters and Syrian civilians.[12] Again, the idea was to show that Islamic State, far from being "liberators" of the Syrian people, were just as bad as the tyrant butchering them. Fernandez understood early on that the least believable material was what he described as "soft" propaganda, which promoted the idea that the United States welcomed Muslims, who lived happily in the country. It was output that the White House loved, but according to focus groups, it was the least credible. Fernandez agreed—he was more concerned with getting into his adversaries' heads. "We tried to give the appearance that we were all over the place and challenging them everywhere. It's one definition of trolling, looking bigger and more ubiquitous online than you really are, like some punk kid trolling and tweeting. I read a lot of books on counterinsurgency, which taught me to study the adversary and learn from them: Why are they using these images, these words, and how can we use these against them?" It worked. Islamic State fanboy accounts began to accuse each other of working for the DOT.[13]

It was classic negative programming and advertising. The most successful video the group produced was one entitled "Welcome to ISIS Land" (which Fernandez composed himself).[14] The video was powerful and, as Fernandez intended, aggressive. "Run, do not walk, to ISIS Land" ran the opening line, along with footage of Islamic State fighters throwing the bodies of dead Muslims into a ditch. "Where you can learn useful things for the *ummah* [global Muslim community]. Blowing up mosques! Crucifying and executing Muslims!" This was followed by close-up shots of blindfolded Muslims crucified to wooden stakes and being shot in the back of the head. A decapitated body was shown. "Travel is inexpensive because you won't need a return ticket!" the video continued, showing images of the bloodied bodies of dead fighters. It was all there: visceral imagery and a powerful message dripping with sarcasm.[15] It was edgy and in-your-face, everything Fernandez wanted. It was viewed around a million times.

In our interviews Fernandez was repeatedly clear on the greatest problem he faced in countering Islamic State propaganda: the fact that CSCC was a US government organization. This created two problems. The first was the bureaucracy, which by its nature is slow and overly centralized. Moreover, it is inherently reactive and perennially, infuriatingly cautious. It can never compete with the freewheeling, networked nature of *Homo digitalis*. "Part of the problem was that my vision was too edgy for government and not edgy enough for the space that we were in," he told me. He could use sarcasm and graphic images of Islamic State atrocities, but he could never compete with the group's beheading videos, which were repugnant but also shocking enough to go viral in ways CSCC's videos could not. "We fell between two stools," he continued. "We were too fast for the bureaucratic, risk-averse, clearance-minded State Department, but too slow for the space. Government policy dictated that we could criticize Assad but we couldn't criticize al-Maliki, for example, because we were a government media outlet and had to toe the government line. It's not like Russian disinformation—we could not pretend to be something we were not." In this sense, CSCC's case also highlights the disadvantage democratic states have compared to authoritarian ones when fighting wars at the narrative level. Simply put, they have to abide by a set of democratic norms their Chinese or Russian counterparts do not.

The second problem, which Fernandez discovered from his focus groups, was one of credibility, and it stands at the center of the battle between institutions and *Homo digitalis*. When I made my journey to central London to visit the Institute for Strategic Dialogue, Melanie

Smith had been adamant on this point. "I believe that this type of countermessaging cannot come from government," she told me. "It just undermines the message, which is often bad anyway, but even with a good message or video you shoot down the content with a government logo attached to it."[16] Here the CSCC faced exactly the same problem as the IDF, but even more acutely. As Fernandez knew, of all the voices a disaffected young Muslim would listen to, the last would be the US government, with its perceived litany of crimes in the Islamic Middle East, ranging from the 2003 invasion of Iraq to its torture of prisoners at Abu Ghraib, detention without trial of those held in Guantanamo Bay, and apparent indifference to the slaughter in Syria. As he told me resignedly, "Everything we did had the State Department label on it, and that was a liability."

In December 2013, CSCC had begun a modest project named Think Again, Turn Away, with which it planned to move into the English-language jihadist space. It had already seen, with output like AQAP's *Inspire Magazine*, the rise of jihadist propaganda in English, and believed it was a trend that would expand. Videos like "Welcome to ISIS Land" were part of the Think Again, Turn Away campaign and did succeed. But CSCC faced two major problems. The first was that while the Arabic space was large, the DOT could drill down in it. Knowing the language, it could reach into the nooks and crannies of jihadist sites and platforms. But the English-language jihadist space was so vast and amorphous that it simply could not be targeted with the same accuracy. More than this, however, a new problem arose: now everyone, from the White House to CNN, could understand what the DOT was doing.

"We saw ISIS and their supporters moving into the English language in 2013," Fernandez explained. "And we were prescient in seeing that. But once you start working in English, everyone's a critic. Then it becomes about whether it passes the *Washington Post* test: Is it acceptable to polite society in Georgetown? It becomes a problem of propriety, good taste, and people don't want the State Department logo on this. It brought greater scrutiny into what we were doing, and once Mosul fell, we got 'Why are people still pro-ISIS?' So not only are you doing your own thing and being edgy and aggressive—a big no-no for government—but you're also blamed because it's not working."

And then there was the media. Everyone from the *Atlantic* to TV shows like *Last Week Tonight with John Oliver* began to enter the conversation, commenting on (and often ridiculing) the DOT's work. The DOT was trying to target young Islamic State fanboys in London and Paris, but suddenly everyone from the White House to the *New York Times* was interrupting the conversation. The issue then became about the White House and media consensus, not what an alienated eighteen-year-old Muslim cared about. It was a new obstacle that Fernandez had to contend with, together with the fact that in the mind of the (now watching) world, the DOT, which still worked primarily in Arabic, was now synonymous with its Think Again, Turn Away campaign.

CSCC was battling international headlines externally, but internally they were struggling with the problem at the heart of twenty-first-century warfare: who wins the battle of narratives. The team was countermessaging, trying to subvert Islamic State's propagandist narrative by punching holes in it and by pointing to its hypocrisy and inconsistencies. But what it was failing to do was offer an equally powerful counternarrative in response. This problem existed for two reasons: one more immediate and, while initially overwhelming, theoretically manageable, the other far broader and almost impossible to counter.

The first problem was that Islamic State gained global infamy on the back of a series of startling military successes on the ground. Propaganda does not exist as a Platonic essence. It must have some basis in reality. Sometimes the relation is so tenuous as to be absurd, as with Moscow's labeling of Ukraine's government as a "fascist junta."

But sometimes it is strong. And the fact was that in 2013 Islamic State had conquered the Syrian city of Raqqa, which had a population of a million people—the first time in modern history an al-Qaeda-like group had gained unfettered control of an urban area. Just over a year later, it took Mosul, the second-largest city in Iraq. These successes allowed the group to push a triumphalist narrative online, with plenty of videos and images to back it up, giving it an almost unstoppable momentum. The DOT, conversely, could say little by way of response. Unlike Russia, it couldn't deny or reinvent reality. It could continue to highlight the group's atrocities against fellow Muslims, but it could not rebut the online gloating of Islamic State fanboys. As Fernandez recounted to me: "ISIS propaganda was always sophisticated and highly polished, but the reason we saw it take off in June 2014 was because it was tethered to extraordinary events on the ground. ISIS takes a third of Iraq and takes Mosul and seems to be unstoppable wherever it goes—and we were supposed to counter that with words and videos? We were essentially called upon to make bricks with straw. It was ridiculous."

What Mosul also showed was that the amplification and global dissemination of Islamic State's victories were just as important as the victories themselves. In the months following Mosul's fall, recruitment soared. But because this problem is tethered to events on the ground, it is ultimately manageable. What exists on the ground can be defeated on the ground. And so it proved. Since the heady days of mid-2014, Islamic State has suffered a series of defeats that have seen it lose the vast majority of the territory it once occupied. In spring and summer 2017, the Iraqi security forces backed by US air strikes and Kurdish forces advanced on Mosul, eventually retaking the city. As a result, Islamic State's "victory narrative" has long since receded.

But the group's propaganda remains (albeit not at 2014 levels). This fact points to a recurrent theme also at the heart of twenty-first-century war: that the military dimension, events on the physical battlefield, no longer stands *alone* as the most important arena of conflict. From Ukraine to Gaza to Iraq and Syria, it is clear that the physical and virtual battlefields directly impact each other to such a degree that they now blur together. And this is how Islamic State understands war. As Bari Atwan points out, in its heyday the group used its online propaganda to terrorize the enemy and to coerce acquiescence within local populations. Its ability to produce large amounts of military propaganda from the field as it once did has receded. But rather than see its online presence wither and die, the group has merely shifted its focus.

Islamic State expert Charlie Winter notes that the group's recent propaganda has had a distinctly nostalgic tone. "The caliphate will continue to exist no matter what happens on the ground," he told me. "But it will live on more as a virtual myth than anything else. They have huge archives of video material, which now focuses on the way bureaucracy works and the civilian side of life in the caliphate, so they can say in a few years' time, 'This is what it was like.' If and when they lose more territory, they can point their supporters to this virtual living archive of their past exploits."[17] Islamic State will continue to lose militarily, but the physical battlefield is no longer the single most important arena of warfare. The group and its virtual caliphate will live on.

The second problem CSCC faced in countering Islamic State's narrative was less about being able to refute the group's narrative of success than about not being able to offer an equally powerful counternarrative in response. Think Again, Turn Away, as the name implies, was a negative narrative, calling on people—especially the young and disenfranchised yearning for meaning in their lives—*not* to do something. Set against that was the multifaceted nature of Islamic State's propaganda, which pushed highly stylized ultraviolence designed to appeal to the young and frustrated, offering them a chance to take part in that most dramatic of pursuits: war. And they did so in the most professional of ways, mimicking the cultural tropes and styles of Western culture. Emerson T. Brooking and P. W. Singer cite the work of Javier Lesaca, a visiting scholar at George

Washington University's School of Media and Public Affairs, who studied thirteen hundred Islamic State propaganda videos. He discovered that 20 percent were directly inspired by Western entertainment, including popular video games like *Call of Duty* and *Grand Theft Auto* as well as Hollywood movies like *American Sniper*.[18]

Alongside this was the positive vision of the caliphate that had inspired Sophie to make the journey from Paris to Raqqa. Just as the group pushed Hollywood-style ultraviolence, it also pushed its state-building narrative. Videos like "Eid Greetings from the Land of the Khalifah," which showed children handing out sweets in a mosque, displayed the "softer" side of the caliphate. Prominent in pushing this narrative are videos from the "Mujatweets from the Islamic State" series, which feature scenes ranging from an armed fighter visiting the sick in an Islamic State hospital to a tour around the Raqqa market that highlights the produce on display, up close and in vibrant colors. All of it is designed to appeal to the positive emotions in people, the yearning to be a part of something greater than themselves, and the desire to help their fellow Muslims. Come to Syria and be a hero, or stay in Paris and drive a cab. As Fernandez told me bluntly: "We spent our time telling people not to do things. ISIS, meanwhile, told them to take control of their lives, to join them and take action. There was only ever going to be one winner."

Moreover, Islamic State's narrative dovetails perfectly with the twenty-first-century millennial zeitgeist. Today's twentysomethings have come of age in the aftermath of the 2008 Great Recession: job prospects are bleak, and the future is uncertain. The turn of the century has also seen a loss of faith in the great institutions of the West, from politicians to the financial sector to the press. As Smith, herself in her twenties, told me: "There is a loss of trust in authority in my generation and widespread hysteria around being a millennial. You're constantly told you won't be able to do what you want or find suitable work. If I look at my friends, some [with no prospect of finding decent work] have gone off traveling for three years, while others are working in orphanages and things like that."[19]

Within this general miasma, demagogues and countercultural movements of all stripes now flourish. Both Islamic State and Russian propaganda, as well as the alt-left and the alt-right, with their elements of anti-Semitism and Islamophobia, take advantage of this climate. America's new president, Donald Trump, is the figure around which the alt-right has gathered. He has helped to mainstream their extremist ideology. Jeremy Corbyn, a figure from the hard left, leads Britain's main opposition party. Rebellion against the establishment "elites" that have led the West for centuries is strafing Europe and North America. This has coincided perfectly with the emergence of social media, which has flattened the media space and given these various extremist actors greater ability to project power and to subvert Western institutions than ever before. *Homo digitalis*, like social media, is a force for both good and ill, a revolutionary force that can challenge government narratives and political figures from Washington to London. In this sense, Islamic State is only one part of a larger reality.

And it is a reality the group has seized with cunning and alacrity. As Fernandez said: "People want to identify with something, and it is hard to identify with discredited institutions. And then along comes a 'pristine' organization that is seen as sincere and authentic. The ISIS narrative provides certain cultural, emotional satisfactions; it releases endorphins, inspires in a certain way. If everything around you has been discredited, you will have problems counteracting that. The lack of faith in Western culture prevents us from offering a positive alternative narrative. What moves us is evidently nothing—and you can't counteract them with nothing."

Islamic State also raised an important question of responsibility. When Fernandez looked at the social media space, he saw its platforms, Twitter mostly, being used to disseminate terrorist propaganda. Those spaces had, in effect, been weaponized by the group. Every pro–Islamic State tweet, every video uploaded to YouTube or shared on Facebook had the potential to set a vulnerable young

man or woman on the path to radicalization. If that individual subsequently made the journey to Syria and participated in the group's
atrocities, from the sexual enslavement of Yazidi women to the beheading of Shia Muslims or Sunni dissenters, then the question naturally arose: How culpable were these platforms? Without social
media, Islamic State is just another ragtag bunch of homicidal jihadists (albeit highly successful ones). But empowered by social media,
the group was now a worldwide brand. The US government was losing the narrative war for a variety of reasons, but without social media there would have been no narrative war to fight in the first place,
or at least not one with such potency.

Islamic State was able to take advantage of four things. The first is
the default libertarian worldview embedded into the founding principles of social media companies. The advent of Web 2.0 carries within
it the idea that social media spaces must be arenas where users can
produce whatever they wish (within legal bounds) and free speech
is sacrosanct. As Tarleton Gillespie, a principal researcher at Micro-
soft Research New England, notes, the word "platform" has several
definitions in English, and taken together they suggest "a progressive
and egalitarian arrangement, lifting up those who stand upon it." As
Sam Hinton and Larissa Hjorth comment, "When applied to Web 2.0
applications such as YouTube, Facebook or Twitter, the term suggests
that the role of the company is impartial—they are just there to provide a platform that users can stand on and be treated as equals."[20]

That is the premise upon which people sign up for platforms like
Facebook and Twitter, and it is therefore in the companies' interests
to abide by it. Start censoring too much and they might start to lose
users—something social media companies cannot do for the simple
reason that they are not impartial. They are capitalist enterprises,
businesses that need to make money. That is the second advantage
Islamic State has. Facebook and Twitter, like any other business,
have a "product" to sell, and that product is their users, who generate advertising revenue and whose online habits can be tracked and
monetized. They may have a default libertarian worldview, but more

pressing is their commercial imperative, which is ill-served by kicking people off their platforms, even those pushing jihadist content. And the lobbying power that Google and Facebook (companies that wield more power than many countries) possess at the heart of government makes opposing them a difficult task.

The third advantage that Islamic State had is that the US government shares this default libertarian worldview. It, too, believes social media should be relatively uncontrolled—especially since censorship of the Internet is associated with autocratic states like China and Iran. The United States, conversely, has the First Amendment at the heart of its Constitution. Fernandez found that the prevailing government attitude could be summed up in the (entirely reasonable) cliché that the answer to bad speech was good speech. This view was also embedded within US law enforcement and intelligence, which took the position that it was better to leave the material up so it could be observed—the ability to see who retweeted and shared jihadist propaganda, it was argued, could help these agencies find potential or future jihadists. Focus efforts on foiling actual terror plots rather than worrying about tweets, went the argument. The narrative war simply wasn't privileged to the degree that Fernandez desired.

The final advantage it had was legacy media—another source of great frustration for CSCC. As social media platforms have risen to steal advertising revenues from traditional press and TV, so those institutions have grown ever more desperate in their search for clicks and shares. And for them, Islamic State—a Technicolor terror group—was and is a source of stories that inevitably draw large audiences. Just as Islamic State uses Western cultural hegemony against the West, it also uses the mainstream media news cycle against itself. Like Donald Trump or Kim Kardashian, ISIS is in the news-making business; it does things merely for the purpose of being in the news. Stories it publicizes about establishing its own currency, the Islamic State dinar, or introducing an Islamic State passport—initiatives that never came to pass and almost certainly were never intended to— keep traditional media busy producing an array of output to engage their audiences, as do the increasingly exotic ways of killing people, from beheadings to immolation. But even in these, their strategy is clear to see. The video showing the beheading of the American journalist Steven Sotloff cut away just before the act itself. The group almost certainly knew that no media outlet would broadcast the video had it been included. Islamic State understands the Western media and has weaponized it, too.

As the group has lost ground in the Middle East it has increasingly focused on attacks abroad, especially in the West. On March 22, 2016, Islamic State carried out a coordinated triple bombing in Belgium's capital city, Brussels, which killed thirty-two civilians and injured more than three hundred. Shortly after the attack, they claimed responsibility for the act on the encrypted messaging app Telegram. Islamic State's text was then picked up and published by media outlets across the world hungry to capitalize on a global event (it had deliberately released the statement in English for this purpose). In so doing, those media outlets became broadcasters for the group's propaganda, repeating its line almost verbatim. Fear of the group grew, and with it its perceived potency. It had used the Western media against the West itself.[21] To Fernandez, this is sadly inevitable. As he said to me, "As I know from my time as a press officer at the State Department, in this age of a twenty-four-hour news cycle you just have to feed the beast."

The fact that Islamic State and its fans had, by the time of the Brussels attacks, been largely forced off Twitter and into the world of secure messaging apps like Telegram was largely a result of pressure that even the social media giants could not withstand. A key element in the development of this pressure was the beheading of the American journalist James Foley on August 19, 2014. Here was an American publicly murdered in a dramatic video with high production values. No terrorist murder of a single individual had ever caused such global outrage. Everyone from world leaders to Twitter users was in an uproar, with many refusing to tweet or share the video. The pressure proved too much, and the major social media companies began to suspend accounts and take material down. The State Department's intelligence unit alone oversaw the removal of forty-five thousand items in 2014.[22]

In the meantime, Fernandez had decided that enough was enough. The White House had spent a year drifting and confused, instead of implementing Fernandez's proposed strategy to make CSCC a larger, more permanent, and 24/7 operation. He was disgusted by the vibe of the people he was working with. People like Ben Rhodes, deputy national security advisor for strategic communications, had gone, Fernandez believed, from being supporters to denigrating the hard work CSCC was doing. There was too much drama and back-stabbing. Fernandez was offered a chance to stay on with a position in South America, but in the fall of 2014 he decided to retire after thirty-two years of service, which he did on May 2, 2015. It was a relief.

Fernandez always believed (and still does) in challenging the adversary directly in the social media space. He believed that the US government had to be on it 24/7, put out more material, and work with proxies. But eventually the powers that be decided to get out of the direct messaging business altogether. Fernandez's CSCC had tried its best and scored some successes, but in the end it was not enough.

In late 2015, months after Fernandez had left his post, an independent panel consisting of Silicon Valley experts was tasked with reviewing the work of CSCC.[23] Fernandez's successor had lasted only a few months, and the department was in turmoil. The panel applauded the State Department's efforts to enlist Middle East allies in the propaganda campaign against Islamic State, especially efforts to disseminate material from the group's defectors, who nearly always had horrific experiences to recount. But it questioned whether "the U.S. government should be involved in overt messaging at all." Behind this was the logic that Washington had little credibility with international Muslim audiences, and that direct messaging had done little to stop recruits from joining Islamic State.[24] The White House agreed that the government had zero credibility and that directly engaging the terrorists and their fanboys endowed them with recognition and thus a form of legitimacy. Plus the English-language messaging project had embarrassed them. The decision was made to work entirely through proxies.

Zahed Amanullah, from the Institute of Strategic Dialogue, was unequivocal on this point when I met him in London. "Most governments now realize they cannot be the messenger—and understand the difference between counter- and alternative narratives, and how the latter is far more effective," he said. "Governments need to push alternative—different—visions to pull people back from radicalization. Young people are generally alienated, Muslims especially so. Therefore an alternative vision has to resonate, and for this you need credible messengers: people from the Muslim community to channel this alienation to a political direction, as long as it's not violent. Only people from the communities affected can do this, and they need guidance and training—and they must not be tainted by government."[25]

As Alec Ross observed to me, the US government could come out and say, "'The sun rose in the east and set in the west,' and some percentage of the world would not believe it," on principle.[26] This concept was never lost on Fernandez. He understood that the United States had credibility issues; as he observed, "The most plausible content that would have the highest probability to resonate would be the testimony and stories of those who know the Islamic State best: defectors, returnees, and Sunni Muslim victims and their family members."[27] He also understood better than anyone else the problems inherent in working within a government structure. "A government is always much more bureaucratic, slower, and more risk averse than a terrorist group," he told me. "The insurrectional nature of terrorism makes you faster and less risk averse—that's why you're a terrorist."

But equally he believed there was no one magic bullet to fight Islamic State, and that a successful strategy would require more of everything, including testimonies from proxies and, vitally, being in the space. Just as Peter Lerner recognized that if the IDF was absent on social media it would cede that space to the enemy, so Fernandez believes the same. "Someone needs to be in that space," he told me. "You can't abandon it because you don't want to get your hands dirty."

CONCLUSION

This book was formed in the crucible of twenty-first-century war. My experiences of it, proximate and visceral, in the snows and frost of eastern Ukraine instilled in me a desire to understand the nature of modern conflict. How had it changed and why? And what did this mean for an increasingly unstable world in the years to come? In Ukraine, I grew to understand that new information technology was reshaping almost all the practices of war I saw around me, from the battlefield to cyberspace. That understanding, in turn, began a journey that has taken me across several continents to tell the stories of people at the center of three conflicts who, each in their own way, embody the way social media is reshaping war.

What I discovered is that as well as offering great opportunities, these technologies pose great risks. From all my experiences in Ukraine, and from my study of the rhetoric spewed forth on social media surrounding the 2014 Israel-Hamas war and Islamic State, what ultimately stood out most was the feeling that in each case actors on both sides were unleashing forces they might one day struggle to control. The more Moscow pushed the narrative of a "fascist junta" persecuting Russian speakers, the more its online supporters urged the Kremlin to crush the Ukrainian enemy. The more bloody images that emerged from Gaza, the more people called on Hamas to "exterminate" Israelis. And the cheerleading that accompanied Islamic State's initial rampage across Iraq forced the group to produce ever more extreme content, culminating in increasingly sadistic public killings to both sate its own supporters and keep itself in the news.

In the run-up to World War I, few statesmen had any idea of the destructive powers their actions would unleash, but the pressure for war from their respective populations following the assassination of Archduke Franz Ferdinand became almost impossible to resist. The climate many rulers helped foster made pulling back from the brink a grievous threat to their thrones or administrations. The possibility that one day a state like Russia or Iran, or a terror group like Hamas or Islamic State, may become boxed in by its own aggressive rhetoric is alarmingly close. Empowered by social media, the voices of their own people may be impossible to contain. If that happens, the requisite conditions for a catastrophic global war, which coincided to such disastrous effect in 1914, may well reappear.[1]

The last decade has seen the evolution of social media platforms from niche enterprises—Facebook was originally a small networking site set up for a single university—to global information platforms used by the masses. This transformation has empowered people to a degree previously unthinkable: a simple smartphone now opens up a world of information. The potential for education and for the voiceless to gain a voice—especially in times of war—has never been greater. Equally, governments can now increasingly use those same technologies to police and manipulate their own populations. States track antigovernment movements, as the Iranian regime did during the country's 2009 Green Revolution, while Russia uses social media as a tool to spread disinformation as an integral part of its twenty-first-century military doctrine.

Web 2.0 enabled people to produce content and form transnational networks: it created *Homo digitalis*. And it contains an inherent conflict that Sam Hinton and Larissa Hjorth outline in their book *Understanding Social Media*. On the one hand, they argue, it "promises users empowerment by supporting a new model of media production (and consumption) that does away with the domination of production by a few. On the other hand, it threatens control and colonisation of users' social lives. In this way, Web 2.0 is a contradiction: it is simultaneously empowering and exploitative, a platform for both control and freedom. This paradox and contestation is at the heart of social media."[2] It is tempting to look at social media, and the Internet in general, as an "inherently democratising or emancipatory medium because of the way it seems to empower individuals and undermine old monopolies and systems of power."[3] But it is vital to remember the paradox.

This empowerment of the individual—the creation of *Homo digitalis*—is at the heart of twenty-first-century conflict. Its influence, from Gaza to Ukraine to Syria, has, I hope, been made clear to see. Moreover, it has emerged as a paradoxical force that echoes the constitutional tension of Web 2.0. As a child carries the DNA of its parent, *Homo digitalis* carries within it the DNA of its creator. The hypernetworked individual is above all Manichean, responsible for both good and ill; moreover, the processes that allow for this are merely two sides of the same coin. The networks that stand at social media's heart are inescapably both centripetal and centrifugal, bringing people together and breaking them apart with speeds and scopes previously impossible. Homophily degrades our information ecosystem, and it turbocharges war. Both Islamic State and the Kremlin want their supporters to be cocooned in information bubbles. Drip-fed information by the profit-seeking algorithms of capitalist social media companies, their Twitter and Facebook accounts become mere arenas of ideological reinforcement: Pro-Russia separatists never shot down MH17; Islamic State's caliphate is a joyous thing. Like-minded followers and "friends" combine with information injected into their home feeds to screen out dissenting voices. Thus are they brought together while simultaneously separated from opposing views. Thus do mutual incomprehension and hatred flourish.

Social media not only contains an inherent duality but is also inherently destabilizing, for both good as well as ill. The diffusion of power from hierarchies to individuals and networks of individuals has empowered the powerless, often at the expense of those with too much power. Governments are held more to account; the conduct of soldiers on the field of battle is more scrutinized than ever before. But it also has a negative side that is now understood at the highest levels. When Alec Ross recounted his time as Secretary of State Hillary Clinton's senior advisor for innovation, he outlined to me her growing understanding of the dark side of new information technologies:

> Her response to WikiLeaks [was instructive]. She was really angry, deeply disgusted by the theft of 253,000 cables. . . . WikiLeaks showed how that stuff can be used against you. . . . I remember explaining to her that even with our spectacular capabilities across departments and governments that we were absolutely powerless. I think she was a little disgusted that a bunch of second-tier hackers from Scandinavia or where[ever] the hell else could act against the interests of the world's most powerful country.

Clinton's reaction points to the extent to which social media threatens the state and is indeed inherently anti-state. This works on two levels. The first is the direct threat that the networks it creates pose to hierarchies. The emergence of *Homo digitalis* means that the IDF cannot stop Farah, the NSA cannot stop WikiLeaks, and CSCC cannot stop Islamic State. Moreover, the decentralization of information flows that were once controlled almost exclusively by states and their permitted media outlets, especially in times of war, means that governments are less able to impose state-sanctioned narratives on events. Militaries can no longer as easily cover up atrocities, tyrants are less able to murder their own people with impunity. And the *New York Times* could not now deny the existence of a great atrocity as it did with Stalin's 1932–1933 man-made famine in Ukraine that killed millions.

Also of crucial importance is the threat social media poses to the *idea* of the nation-state, an idea that, perhaps anachronistically, we still adhere to. In this sense it is not merely destabilizing but a force for chaos. Social media creates networks that, by their nature, are not built around the architecture of a single state. They are transnational and care little for borders or nationalism. In this sense, they have both fed into and enhanced a growing global trend that is, in certain parts of the world, tearing the international order apart. Mary Kaldor associates "new wars" with "state weakness" and "extremist identity politics."[4] I observed this firsthand in Ukraine, where after state weakness allowed Russia to annex Crimea without a single shot being fired, large swaths of Russian speakers rejected the Ukrainian state in favor of self-identification along lines of language and ethnicity. Islamic State, meanwhile, took advantage of the fractured post-2003 Iraqi state and a Syria strafed by civil war to emerge and consolidate its power. The destruction of the idea of the nation-state in favor of a transnational caliphate is Islamic State's raison d'être. Indeed, in 2014 the group made a great show of physically demolishing structures marking the border between Iraq and Syria. It doesn't matter whether the foreign fighters it recruits come from France, the United Kingdom, or the United States; once they join Islamic State, they are Sunni Muslims: all other identity is transcended.

As Emile Simpson notes, at the center of the broader change in contemporary conflict is the blurring boundary between war and peace. Social media disrupts the old order in three ways: time, space, and method. It blurs the beginning and end of a war because the informational dimension can start long before active combat and continue long after battlefield operations have finished. In Ukraine and Israel/Palestine, where staccato bouts of fighting burst through the pervading stand-off, the result is near perpetual conflict that lies somewhere between war and peace. In terms of space, social media reaches people beyond the battlefield, speaking to a broader international audience than previously possible.

Central to the change in method is the idea that military operations can become a form of informational operation and seek political rather than specifically military outcomes. In war as traditionally understood, information operations support military action on the battlefield, but today, military operations are increasingly understood to support information operations. War is still fought through military means, but the emphasis placed on these practices alone has receded, as has their efficacy. Israel bombed and invaded Gaza with deadly success, but it still "lost" the 2014 war. Operation Protective Edge had clear military objectives: to deal with the tunnel threat emanating from Gaza and to stop the rocket fire. But in reality, the war was about far more than these goals.

In Gaza, the violence, while horrific, had an almost perfunctory quality to it. Hamas endlessly fired rockets at Israel knowing the majority would be shot down by IDF's Iron Dome missile defense system. Meanwhile, Israel attacked Gaza without the slightest intention of destroying Hamas (which it could easily have done) and imposing a political settlement on it that would finally end the conflict between the two sides. The Clausewitzian paradigm of war was almost entirely absent. The social media arm of the IDF's Spokesperson's Unit flooded Twitter with information about Hamas's use of human shields, while Hamas officials and ordinary Palestinians like Farah tweeted and posted photos of dead children killed in Israeli air strikes. On this level, the war became the physical manifestation of a clash of narratives.

All wars are, to a degree, a clash of narratives, but this strand was so prominent in the Gaza war that it became almost a spectacle played out for an audience. And that audience was not, as in traditional warfare, an "enemy population" that needed coercive "convincing." Both sides, after more than fifty years of fighting, entirely understand the other's position. The audience was the watching world, which, thanks to social media, could follow the action in real time and in greater detail than ever before. In a major way, Operation Protective Edge inverted war's traditional paradigm: it was an information war played out on the battlefield, in which the former was, at times, more important than the latter. It was gladiatorial combat, war as political theater: a truly postmodern conflict.

In this sense, once the tunnel threat was reduced (though not wiped out) and the rockets halted (though not completely), the definition of victory in the Gaza conflict resided in the perception of audiences well beyond Israel and Palestine. The global audience, especially in Europe and the United States, was the key constituency for both sides, which is why many believe that Israel lost the war despite the IDF's unequivocal military victory on the ground. The British journalist Jon Snow, who covered the war from inside Gaza, was blunt: "The Israelis lost the war, unquestionably," he told me. "I genuinely don't believe they can do anything like this ever again because of the global response to what they did, which I think was very much informed by the use of social media."[5] Snow felt able to say this because Protective Edge was not a war fought to achieve a political end but war as politics itself—for which victory in the narrative sphere was the vital component. Stories were more important than tanks.

As Kaldor points out, those most successful in new warfare are those most able "to avoid battle and to control territory through political control of the population."[6] Israel was singularly unable to achieve either of those objectives. It was forced onto the battlefield and demonized in the world's eyes as a result. The case of Operation Protective Edge stands as an example of how in twenty-first-century conflict you can conclusively win on the battlefield but lose the wider war. Conversely, since 2014, Russia has annexed Crimea and destabilized eastern Ukraine. But it has not declared war and admits no official troop presence in the country. What it is deliberately practicing in Ukraine is gray-zone conflict: more than peace but less than war. It has succeeded because it understands the new reality of warfare. Just as the goal for British soldiers in Afghanistan became not to defeat the Taliban but to convince the local population not to join them, Russia's goal in Ukraine was not to defeat the Ukrainian army but to convince east Ukrainians that Kyiv was persecuting them and that their only hope of salvation lay with Moscow and its proxies.[7]

Clausewitzian war is becoming displaced by what Simpson calls "coercive communication," ranging from the use of financial

sanctions to the political encouragement of extremist identity politics.[8] This is both regressive and dangerous. The decentralization of
the western ideal of conflict away from organized, national armies
fighting for the nation-state harks back to earlier, more chaotic forms
of war. Here, multiple actors, often dispersed, fighting either for
"tribal" identity concerns or for financial gain (a large part of Islamic
State's revenue is derived from the sale of looted antiquities and stolen
oil) was the norm. This is the irony of twenty-first-century war: the
latest information technology has created a reversal into the future.

Gray-zone conflicts and armed politics have blurred the distinction between war and peace, which is a dangerous thing. When you
don't desire to defeat your enemy and force him to the negotiating table, then when does war end and peace start? Today the Taliban still
exists and the battle to stop Afghans from joining them still remains.
Does this mean the 2001 Afghan War, called Operation Enduring
Freedom in the United States, is still ongoing? The answer is unclear,
and that's the point. The axiom "You don't make peace with your enemies, you make peace with your defeated enemies" is repeated so
often as to be trite. But how can you make peace when your goal is
not to militarily defeat them? Alternatively, how can you make peace
when your enemy has no interest in making peace? How do you defeat Islamic State when its demands are such that they can never be
met? And how can you defeat it when no matter how many military
losses it suffers, its caliphate will live on virtually?

Western states and their institutions are now behind the curve
in twenty-first-century conflict. CSCC tried its best to battle Islamic
State's narrative, but its fundamental problem was never a lack of resources or numbers (as important as they were) but the very nature
of what it was. As Charlie Winter and Jordan Bach-Lombardo observe: "Governments still have an integral role to play in the communications battle with Islamic State. But they must shift their primary
information activities away from direct communications, to flexibly
supporting and trusting local actors to deliver messages on their

behalf—a model reminiscent of that employed by the Islamic State."[9] In essence, you need *Homo digitalis* to fight *Homo digitalis*. Even the birth of *Militia digitalis*, the first army to fully embrace social media, was insufficient for the IDF to win Protective Edge. This is because it was tainted in the narrative sphere by the nature of what it was: a government institution.

Once more, the shift from hierarchies to individuals and networks of individuals is clear. Networked freelancers, independent of government, can take to social media to battle their equally networked enemies. Here the case of Eliot Higgins is instructive. A networked and social-media-adept individual, he proved far more effective at debunking Russian propaganda, and could do so more publicly and more rapidly, than intelligence services across the world. Higgins's approach is niche, still only practiced by a few people. But using a diffuse, properly funded network of a hundred or five hundred Higginses to amplify anti–Islamic State messaging or to counter Russian disinformation is far more likely to succeed than a centralized bureaucracy. As Alec Ross so aptly put it: "Good ideas die in hierarchies. Social media does not lend itself to a clearance process. It fundamentally degrades the effectiveness of diplomatic institutions."

Until that happens, states will continue to lose the narrative war against citizen journalists like Farah, trolls like Vitaly, and Islamic State. Bloated bureaucracies, risk averse and lacking in credibility, will never defeat the most networked terror group in history. Malicious actors understand that, in the social media age, everyone is now a broadcaster or a fund-raiser or a propagandist. We live in an age of virtual mass enlistment, as can be seen in the numbers of women now playing a role in war. *Homo digitalis* has been weaponized for the worst of purposes. Governments have still not caught up—and unless they change, they never will.

In the meantime, the world continues to grow more unstable— and to look ever more like the years leading up to 1914.

I return again to the words of General James "Mad Dog" Mattis, who dismissed "intellectuals running around today saying that the nature of war has fundamentally changed," and declared that "Alex [sic] the Great would not be in the least bit perplexed by the enemy that we face right now in Iraq."[10] He was right, but only to a degree. Allowing for improvements in weaponry, the physical battlefield may remain largely the same: soldiers still shoot at soldiers, artillery fires from the ground, and planes bomb from the air. But the context within which wars are fought has changed forever. And the blurring between war and politics has come at a time when politics is more unstable than at any other point in living memory—in large part due to social media. The election to the US presidency of Donald Trump, whose tweets had the ability to dominate a news cycle, could not have happened in a pre-social-media age. Complicated, nuanced thoughts that require context don't play well on most social media platforms.[11] These platforms also reward repetition, redundancy, and, given their face-to-face nature, verbal conflict. All these themes were central to Donald Trump's ultimately successful campaign. Never was the media theorist Marshall McLuhan's dictum "the medium is the message" more apt.

Our information environment is sick. We live in a world where facts are less important than narratives, where people emote rather than debate, and where algorithms shape our view of the world. I return again to Oxford Dictionaries' decision to name "post-truth" word of the year in 2016, marking our era as one in which "objective facts are less influential in shaping public opinion than appeals to emotion and personal belief." Social media is now the number one news source for young people in the United States—more significant than TV and newspapers put together.[12] In both the United Kingdom and the United States, public broadcasters have to adhere to guidelines regarding balance and impartiality. No such regulation of social media exists, and the costs are plain to see. Fake news now besets us from all sides, and no institution, no matter how large, is immune to its curse. At the beginning of 2017, the BBC, the world's largest state broadcaster, announced that it was setting up a permanent Reality Check team to "fact check and debunk deliberately misleading and false stories masquerading as real news."[13] Reality Check would also be backed by a team dedicated to exposing false stories being shared on social media.[14]

Facebook, which has been named as the platform most conducive to the spread of false stories (often designed to generate advertising revenue from clicks), also unveiled plans for users to flag false stories that would then be evaluated by third-party fact-checking organizations such as FullFact or Snopes.[15] The need for this is urgent. On December 23, 2016, Pakistan's defense minister, Khawaja Muhammad Asif, publicly threatened Israel with nuclear force on Twitter in response to a false article published on awdnews.com.[16]

The post-truth world has created the post-truth leader, from Vladimir Putin, who can reinvent reality on the ground in eastern Ukraine, to Donald Trump who can lie about the size of the crowds at his inauguration when the evidence that contradicts his claims is on film for everyone to see. The two men remain vastly different—one is a dictator in all but name, the other leads the world's most powerful democracy—but in each case the goal is the same: not to twist the truth like the politicians of old but to subvert the very notion that an objective truth exists at all.

In this sense, this book contains a final character: myself, and the many others like me—the journalists. Everyone can now be a broadcaster, but not everyone can now be a journalist. Most lack the tools, which range from investigative skills to knowledge of how to verify information to even the necessary writing ability. More than this, most aren't interested in being journalists; they merely want to broadcast their version of events. In this sense, everyone from Farah Baker and Peter Lerner to Vladimir Putin and Donald Trump is yet another potential threat to our information environment, a threat that professional journalists are needed to guard against more than ever.

And nowhere is this need greater than in wartime. Like Eliot Higgins, journalists must now be able to interpret the vast amounts of data emerging from war zones—and unlike him, they have to do so not from the comfort of their homes but on the ground amid the confusion. Social media created *Homo digitalis*; it created Eliot Higgins. But because the empowerment of individuals is at its heart, it was inescapable that it would create something else, too: *Homo digitalis* as journalist, the twenty-first-century war correspondent. This phenomenon is now emerging on the battlefields, where journalists harness the same tools that contribute to falsehoods in wartime in order to debunk them. What is crucial here is *how* these tools are employed. For journalists, social media becomes a form of journalistic life support on the ground. It works as a map and as a radio; it enables reporters to "see" other parts of the conflict zone and "hear" what is being said there. It enables them to produce reliable data from inside the war zone, data that someone like Higgins can then use to deduce the wider picture. Twenty-first-century journalists are needed to cover twenty-first-century wars.

In more ways than one, the world of 2017 looks eerily similar to the pre-1914 world. Mass migration flows and their resulting backlash are constantly in the news. We think of globalization as a new phenomenon, but from the mid-nineteenth century to 1914 around sixty million people left Europe in search of better economic prospects in countries like the United States, Canada, and Australia.[17] Then, just as now, new information technologies (like the telegraph and the telephone) increased global interconnectivity.[18] In a report cited in the *Washington Post*, Josh Feinman, chief global economist for Deutsche Asset Management, declared that "the first great globalization wave, in the half-century or so before WWI, sparked a populist backlash too, and ultimately came crashing down in the cataclysms of 1914 to 1945."[19]

From Trump in the United States to the populist Brexit campaign that saw the United Kingdom leave the European Union, from the populist left-wing Syriza party that governs Greece to the rise of the far-right French politician Marine Le Pen and the brutal (and almost certainly insane) president of the Philippines, Rodrigo Duterte, populists are once more dominating international politics. As Feinman points out, politicians back in the pre-1914 age imposed quotas on immigration and implemented trade tariffs—exactly what Donald Trump is doing today. The parallels are not exact, but as Feinman concludes: "Modern globalization has been spurred by some of the same forces that powered the pre-WWI epoch: new technologies, an open, free-trade, rules-based world economic system underpinned by the leading power of the day, and a period of general peace among major countries."[20]

None of this is to say that the world is on the brink of World War III. But several emergent trends, powered by social media, in both the practices of war and its attendant politics have created a global environment more conducive to wide-scale conflict than at any time since 1945. When the new US president refers to NATO, a military alliance that has helped keep the world largely peaceful, as "obsolete"; when the Russian president has already defied a sacrosanct law of the postwar order and stolen part of a neighboring country; when the Middle East is strafed by war and unrest of a degree not seen in almost a century; and when frustrated populations and opportunistic demagogues have discredited almost all of the West's major institutions vital to safeguarding the postwar liberal world—well, the dangers are unambiguous. They must be heeded. Any mass interstate war in a nuclear age would bring devastation the likes of which the world has never seen. And history will have repeated itself, only this time not as farce but as even greater tragedy.

NOTES

Introduction

1. Parts of my opening account originally appeared in this article. See David Patrikarakos, "Ukraine's Pro-Putin Rebels Prepare for a Last Stand," *Daily Beast,* July 10, 2014.

2. See, for example, Anna Nemtsova, "There's No Evidence the Ukrainian Army Crucified a Child in Slovyansk," *Daily Beast,* July 17, 2014.

3. See, for example, Sam Sokol, "Reports of Anti-Semitism in Odessa Highlights [*sic*] Use of Jews in Wartime Propaganda," *Jerusalem Post,* October 12, 2014.

4. Brian P. Fleming, "Hybrid Threat Concept: Contemporary War, Military Planning and the Advent of Unrestricted Operational Art," United States Army Command and General Staff College, May 19, 2011.

5. See, for example, Juliet Samuel, "Searching for the Truth in the Rubble of 'Fake News' from Aleppo," *Telegraph,* December 18, 2016.

6. Emile Simpson, "War and Peace in the Age of the Smartphone," *Newsweek,* July 13, 2014.

7. Author interview with David Betz, London, March 23, 2016.

8. Simpson, "War and Peace in the Age of the Smartphone."

9. Author Skype interview with Emile Simpson, November 19, 2014.

10. Geoffrey Ingersoll, "General James 'Mad Dog' Mattis Email About Being 'Too Busy to Read' Is a Must-Read," *Business Insider,* May 9, 2013.

11. Author Skype interview with Emile Simpson, November 19, 2014.

12. International Institute for Strategic Studies, "Neither War nor Peace: Why the Information Revolution Makes 'Forever Wars' a New Normal," YouTube, November 26, 2014, https://youtu.be/OAR34uz3plE.

13. Emerson T. Brooking and P. W. Singer, "War Goes Viral: How Social Media Is Being Weaponized Across the World," *Atlantic,* November 2016.

14. This term has already been coined, and some literature within technology circles exists on it. Indeed, a book even carries its name; see Natasha Saxberg, *Homo Digitalis: How Human Needs Support Digital Behaviour for People, Organizations and Society* (Amazon Digital Services LLC, July 22, 2015). However, from what I can tell, the term is not in widespread use; my definition of

it was arrived at independently; and my settling upon it was not derived from any previous literature. To the best of my knowledge, I am the first to apply the concept to the field of war.

15. Quoted in Jose Van Dijck, *The Culture of Connectivity: A Critical History of Social Media* (New York: Oxford University Press, 2013), 4.

16. See, for example, Parag Khanna, "Dismantling Empires Through Evolution," *Atlantic*, September 24, 2014.

17. Author interview with Alec Ross, Baltimore, June 26, 2015. The connection element is key to the heart of new social media, which is why I also class network technologies such as Skype and WhatsApp as social media, as they allow for transnational and instant connection, both verbal and visual, without necessarily having an amplification or broadcasting use.

18. Evgeny Morozov, *The Net Delusion: How Not to Liberate the World* (London: Allen Lane, 2011), xiv.

19. On France in 1860: author Skype interview with Nicholas Wright, July 1, 2016.

20. For a fuller discussion, see Mary Kaldor, *New and Old Wars: Organised Violence in a Global Era*, 3rd ed. (London: Polity, 2013).

21. Author Skype interview with Nicholas Wright, July 1, 2016.

22. Alison Flood, "'Post-Truth' Named Word of the Year by Oxford Dictionaries," *Guardian*, November 15, 2016.

23. Ibid.

24. A Palestinian protester films with his mobile phone during clashes with Israeli soldiers on the Israeli border in eastern Gaza City, Friday, October 9, 2015.

Chapter 1: The Citizen Journalist

1. The opening paragraphs of this chapter come, in part, from an article I wrote for *Foreign Policy*: "Hamas Is Ready for War with Israel," June 7, 2016.

2. Peter Beaumont and Harriet Sherwood, "Jerusalem Rocked by Bomb Explosion on Bus," *Guardian*, April 18, 2016.

3. "Israel Says Jerusalem Bus Bombing Was Hamas Suicide Attack," BBC News, April 21, 2016.

4. Sam Hinton and Larissa Hjorth, *Understanding Social Media* (London: Sagel, 2013), 5.

5. Ibid., 2.

6. Mary Kaldor, *New and Old Wars: Organised Violence in a Global Era*, 3rd ed. (London: Polity, 2013), preface.

7. "Information at War: From China's Three Warfares to NATO's Narratives," Beyond Propaganda series, Legatum Institute, September 2015.

8. Mazal Mualem, "Netanyahu Silent on Right-Wing Calls to Avenge Youths," trans. Danny Wool, *Al-Monitor*, July 2, 2014.

9. The entire narrative of Farah Baker's story of the war comes from an interview with the author at her home in Gaza City on April 21, 2016.

10. Fatma Naib, "Growing Up Gazan: Tales of a Palestinian Teen," Al Jazeera America, July 7, 2015.

11. https://twitter.com/Farah_Gazan.

12. Craig Smith, "388 Amazing Twitter Statistics and Facts (February 2017)," *DMR*, February 25, 2016.

13. See for example, this World War II poster, https://gr.pinterest.com /pin/276478864593836146.

14. Naib, "Growing Up Gazan."

15. Francine Prose, "Writing from a War Zone Doesn't Make You Anne Frank," *Foreign Policy*, May 15, 2015.

16. https://twitter.com/Farah_Gazan/status/492779292104081409, July 25, 2014.

17. https://twitter.com/Farah_Gazan/status/491781466666598400, July 22, 2014.

18. Brandon Bolin, "One Brave Girl Tells Her Story from Gaza," Storify. com, https://storify.com/BBOLIN5510/one-brave-girl-tells-her-story-from -gaza.

19. https://twitter.com/drzendn/status/494076920028352512, July 29, 2014.

20. https://twitter.com/Farah_Gazan/status/493878015882182656, July 28, 2014.

21. https://twitter.com/Farah_Gazan/status/493885011557629954, July 28, 2014.

22. https://twitter.com/Farah_Gazan/status/493882107450888192, July 28, 2014.

23. https://twitter.com/Farah_Gazan/status/493878477968642048 /photo/1, July 28, 2014.

24. https://twitter.com/IRELANDreporter/status/493888526652809216, July 28, 2014.

25. https://twitter.com/Renai51ance/status/493913467599224832, July 28, 2014. On Anonymous, see, for example, Alexander J. Apfel/TPS, "'Anonymous' Hackers Attacks on Israel More Hype than Harm," YNetNews, April 7, 2016.

26. https://twitter.com/WillBlackWriter/status/493903312971132928, July 28, 2014.

27. Sam Rkaina, "Sixteen-Year-Old Palestinian Girl Live Tweets Gaza Missile Attacks from Her House," *Daily Mirror*, July 29, 2014.

28. Alexander Smith, "Palestinian Teen Farah Baker Live Tweets Nighttime Bombardment in Gaza," NBC News, July 29, 2014.

29. Azmat Khan, "Sudden Gaza Spokesgirl: 'This Is My Third War . . . but This Is the Worst One," Al Jazeera America, August 1, 2014.

30. See, for example, Radhika Sanghani, "Teen Girl 'Live Tweets Gaza Bomb Attack,'" *Daily Telegraph*, July 29, 2014.

31. Yousef al-Helou, "Social Media: The Weapon of Choice in the Gaza-Israel Conflict," *Middle East Eye*, August 21, 2014.

32. See Chapters 2 and 3.

33. "A World Disrupted: The Leading Global Thinkers of 2014," *Foreign Policy*, n.d. (2014).

34. Prose, "Writing from a War Zone."

35. Author Skype interview with Jon Snow, January 15, 2015.

36. Sadaf R. Ali and Shahira Fahmy, "Gatekeeping and Citizen Journalism: The Use of Social Media During the Recent Uprisings in Iran, Egypt, and Libya," *Media, War and Conflict* 6, no. 1 (2013): 51–56.

37. Ibid., 56.

38. Author Skype interview with Matt Sienkiewicz, July 28, 2014.

39. Ibid.

40. See for example, https://twitter.com/Farah_Gazan/status/493463000 310108161, July 27, 2014.

41. The narrative nature of this part of the chapter means that, where information cannot be independently verified, I am obviously reliant on Farah's version of events. Of particular issue is the matter of what she did and did not believe, which only she can know. But I believe that while she may on occasion have been mistaken, she was truthful when she spoke about what she believed to be true.

42. Moshe Phillips and Benyamin Korn, "Conclusive Proof That Hamas Uses Palestinians as Human Shields," *Algemeiner*, August 7, 2014.

43. Harriet Sherwood, "In Gaza, Hamas Fighters Are Among Civilians. There Is Nowhere Else for Them to Go," *Guardian*, July 24, 2014.

44. "Israel Extends Unilateral Cease-Fire as Gaza Death Toll Tops 1,000," Al Jazeera America, July 26, 2014.

45. Kukil Bora, "Farah Baker, a Gaza Teenager, Becomes Social Media Phenomenon by Tweeting About War," *International Business Times*, August 8, 2014.

46. Khan, "Sudden Gaza Spokesgirl."

47. https://twitter.com/Farah_Gazan/status/490891081840869376, July 20, 2014.

Chapter 2: The Soldier

1. See, for example, Team TOI, "Children of War: Heartbreaking Photographs from Gaza," *Times of India*, August 4, 2014.

2. The entire narrative of Peter Lerner's story is taken from two interviews the author conducted with him at his office in Tel Aviv on April 19 and 20, 2016.

3. Michael Howard, *War in European History* (New York: Oxford University Press, 2009), 49 (emphasis added).

4. Ibid., 54.

5. Parag Khanna, "Dismantling Empires Through Evolution," *Atlantic*, September 24, 2014.

6. It should also be noted that a higher proportion of men are drafted into combat units. Author interview with Aliza Landes, Tel Aviv, March 10, 2017.

7. For the reader's convenience in this and the following chapter, the foreign press branch with the social media department under it will simply be referred to as "the unit."

8. Author Skype interview with Tomer Simon, August 1, 2016.

9. Landes's narrative from this section comes from author Skype interview with Aliza Landes, August 2, 2016, and interview with her in Tel Aviv on March 10, 2017.

10. Author interview with Aviv Sharon, Tel Aviv, February 19, 2017.

11. The name has been deliberately expunged from the email by the author at the interviewee's request.

12. It carries that Web address to this day.

13. Author interview with Avital Leibovich, Tel Aviv, February 20, 2017.

14. Landes's role as the founder of the IDF's social media presence has been well documented. See, for example, Allison Hoffman, "The 'Kids' Behind IDF's Media," *Tablet*, November 20, 2012: "The IDF's new media presence was originally the brainchild of Aliza Landes . . . when, as an officer on the IDF's North American press desk, she piloted the IDF's first forays into virtual warfare during Operation Cast Lead." Also, Brian Fung, "Inside Israel's Social-Media Command Center," *Atlantic*, November 20, 2012: "The IDF's experiment with social media began in 2008 during Operation Cast Lead with 25-year-old Aliza Landes, a member of the IDF's PR team for North American reporters. As with many successes, the IDF's experiment with social media began as a 'pet project' that took on a life of its own."

15. Fung, "Inside Israel's Social-Media Command Center."

16. Noah Pollak, "What YouTube Doesn't Want You to See," *Commentary*, December 30, 2008.

17. Jodi Rudoren, "In Gaza, Epithets Are Fired and Euphemisms Give Shelter," *New York Times*, July 20, 2014.

18. Author Skype interview with Tomer Simon, August 1, 2016.

Chapter 3: The Officer

1. "The IDF's 10 Most Memorable Tweets Ever," IDF Blog, March 21, 2016, https://www.idfblog.com/blog/2016/03/21/idfs-10-memorable-tweets-ever.

2. Sharona Schwartz, "Israel Publishes Video Showing Just How Little Time Some of Its Citizens Have to Seek Shelter from Bomb Attacks—Can You Guess How Long?," *Blaze*, July 8, 2014.

3. "The Gaza Underground," IDF Blog, https://www.idfblog.com/operation gaza2014/#Tunnels.

4. Ibid.

5. See, for example, France 24 video of rockets in front of apartments next to UN building, "Exclusive: Hamas Rocket Launch Pad Lies Near Gaza Home," France 24, July 8, 2014, and then https://twitter.com/IDFSpokesperson /status/496729412046315521, August 5, 2014. Also, "NDTV Exclusive: How Hamas Assembles and Fires Rockets," YouTube video showing Hamas setting up and firing rockets from under canopy next to hotel, August 5, 2014, https: //youtu.be/A_fP6mlNSK8, and then https://twitter.com/IDFSpokesperson /status/496660792993800192?lang=en, August 5, 2014.

6. "Operation Protective Edge," IDF Blog, https://www.idfblog.com /operationgaza2014/#Humanshields.

7. Ibid.

8. https://twitter.com/idfspokesperson/status/489047478998540288, July 15, 2014.

9. See IDF Facebook page, July 11, 2014, https://www.facebook.com/idfonline/photos/pb.125249070831305.-2207520000.1410427987./804544759568396.

10. It must also be noted that the Hague Conventions of 1907, reinforced in subsequent international law, mean that a state has a duty to inform civilians in hostilities when they will be bombing them.

11. See, for example, "The IDF's Efforts to Minimize Civilian Casualties in Gaza," IDF Blog, https://www.idfblog.com/operationgaza2014/#Casualties, and https://twitter.com/IDFSpokesperson/status/503177166117298177, August 23, 2014.

12. IDF, "IDF Avoids Civilians [*sic*] Casualties in Gaza, Hamas Increases Them," YouTube, July 9, 2014, https://youtu.be/VTArVIHDelg.

13. IDF, "IDF Aircraft Calls Off Strikes to Protect Gazan Civilians," YouTube, July 14, 2014, https://youtu.be/PuL-OA84p54.

14. https://twitter.com/IDFSpokesperson/status/268722403989925888?ref_src=twsrc%5Etfw, November 14, 2012.

15. https://twitter.com/AymanM/statuses/493764019237302273, July 28, 2014.

16. https://twitter.com/AymanM/status/493766225516691456, July 28, 2014.

17. https://twitter.com/AymanM/status/493769720760262658, July 28, 2014.

18. https://twitter.com/AymanM/status/493784685684596737, July 28, 2014.

19. https://twitter.com/IDFSpokesperson/status/493787191621849088, July 28, 2014.

20. Ayman Mohyeldin, "Strikes Near Gaza's Shifa Hospital, Refugee Camp Kill at Least 10," NBC News, July 28, 2014.

21. Dell Cameron, "NBC News Deletes Journalist's Claim of an Israeli Airstrike on Gaza," *Daily Dot*, July 28, 2014.

22. https://twitter.com/IDFSpokesperson/status/493900772988682241, July 28, 2014. The "today" in the tweet is a minor mistake since it was posted after midnight, but it was still "today" in the United States.

23. https://twitter.com/gabrielebarbati/statuses/494131918732926976, July 29, 2014.

24. Andrea Mitchell, "Where Does Israel, US Relationship Stand?," MSNBC, July 29, 2014.

25. "Gaza Crisis: Toll of Operations in Gaza," BBC News, September 1, 2014.

26. "Operation Protective Edge in Numbers," YNetNews, August 28, 2014.

27. Adam Horowitz, Lizzy Ratner, and Philip Weiss, eds., *The Goldstone Report: The Legacy of the Landmark Investigation of the Gaza Conflict* (New York: Nation Books, 2011).

28. Author Skype interview with Matt Sienkiewicz, July 28, 2014.

29. There are of course some exceptions, such as when then Secretary of State Henry Kissinger threatened to cut all further aid to Israel if Israeli forces advanced farther into Egypt during the 1973 Yom Kippur War.

30. Yair Lapid, "The Imperative of Integrated Israeli Power," *War on the Rocks*, March 10, 2017.

31. Petros Iosifidis and Mark Wheeler, *Public Spheres and Mediated Social Networks in the Western Context and Beyond* (London: Palgrave Macmillan, 2016), 270.

32. See, for example, its 1981 strike of Iraq's nuclear reactor at Osirak.

33. Gaye Tuchman, "The News Net," *Social Research* 45, no. 2 (1978): 253–276.

34. Ibid., 254.

35. Ibid., 255–56.

36. Ibid., 276.

37. Author Skype interview with Matt Sienkiewicz, July 28, 2014.

38. Ibid.

39. Andrew Tobin, "IDF Was in Own 'Twitterverse' During War, Computer Analysis Finds," *Times of Israel*, September 13, 2014.

Chapter 4: The Facebook Warrior 1

1. Alberto Dainotti et al., "Analysis of Country-wide Internet Outages Caused by Censorship," Center for Applied Internet Data Analysis, 2011.

2. Fred Dews, "NATO Secretary-General: Russia's Annexation of Crimea Is Illegal and Illegitimate," *Brookings Now* (blog), Brookings Institution, March 19, 2014.

3. I cover this ground in my article "In Eastern Ukraine, the Protestors Wait for Russia to Take Charge," *New Statesman*, April 17, 2014.

4. The link for the relevant *Foreign Policy* article had disappeared from the site.

5. Author interview with Anna Sandalova, Kyiv, May 14, 2014.

6. Parts of this paragraph can be found in my article "Ukraine's Facebook Warriors," *New York Times*, December 29, 2014.

7. "Ukraine: Military Budget," GlobalSecurity.org, September 1, 2015, www.globalsecurity.org/military/world/ukraine/budget.htm.

8. Author interview with National Security and Defense Council of Ukraine advisor, Kyiv, April 3, 2014.

9. Author interview with Mustafa Nayyem, Kyiv, April 1, 2014.

10. This quote appeared in truncated form in my article "Ukraine's Underground Army of Civilians," *Mashable*, June 5, 2014.

11. David Patrikarakos, "Ukraine's Underground Army of Civilians," *Mashable*, June 5, 2014, http://mashable.com/2014/06/05/ukraine-euromaydanarmy /#UmOJI9LyjPqh.

12. "Corruption Perceptions Index 2015," Transparency International, www.transparency.org/cpi2015.

13. These quotes are taken from a larger interview I did with Vitali Klitschko for *Foreign Policy*, "'What is Happening in Ukraine Is Dangerous For Russia,'" April 27, 2014. http://foreignpolicy.com/2014/04/27/what -is-happening-in-ukraine-is-dangerous-for-russia/.

14. The final few sentences of this paragraph come from my article "Meet the Ordinary Ukrainians Arming the Country Against Russian Separatists," *New Statesman*, January 8, 2015.

15. The narrative of this section and the next chapter, of Anna's preparation and journey to the East, comes from December 1–3, 2014, when I was involved in a short film for Al Jazeera America, directed by Andrew Smith.

16. Oliver Bullough, "Looting Ukraine: How East and West Teamed up to Steal a Country," Legatum Institute, July 17, 2014.

17. The previous two paragraphs come from my article "Ukraine's Facebook Warriors."

Chapter 5: The Facebook Warrior 2

1. A GRAD is a truck-mounted multiple rocket launcher. *Grad* is a nickname that means "hail" in Russian.

2. Sadaf R. Ali and Shahira Fahmy, "Gatekeeping and Citizen Journalism: The Use of Social Media During the Recent Uprisings in Iran, Egypt, and Libya," *Media, War, and Conflict* 6, no. 1 (2013): 55–69. It is also perhaps worth noting that the first iPhone came out just two years earlier, in 2007.

3. Jennifer Preston, "Movement Began with Outrage and a Facebook Page That Gave It an Outlet," *New York Times*, February 5, 2011.

4. Author Skype interview with Navid Hassanpour, November 17, 2014.

Chapter 6: The Troll

1. Vitaly Vespalov's narrative comes from two Skype interviews with the author on April 4, and April 9, 2016, and an interview in Tymen, Siberia, on April 16, 2016.

2. Emerson T. Brooking and P. W. Singer, "War Goes Viral: How Social Media Is Being Weaponized Across the World," *Atlantic*, November 2016.

3. For a fuller discussion, see Evgeny Morozov, *The Net Delusion: How Not to Liberate the World* (London: Allen Lane, 2011).

4. Prigozhin is also a close ally of Putin, known as his "personal chef"—his Concord catering company not only runs many restaurants in St. Petersburg and Moscow but also is the largest supplier of catering to Moscow's schools and set up the only private restaurant in Russia's Parliament building. He is now a major contractor for the Ministry of Defense. For a fuller discussion, see Alexandra Garmazhapova, "Yevgeny Prigozhin: Caterer to the Kremlin," *Open Democracy Russia*, July 31, 2014.

5. All the websites he had knowledge of from that period have been taken offline except nahnews.org, which continues to this day.

6. See https://vk.com/wall-65275820?offset=17080&own=1&w=wall -65275820_3437.

7. See https://vk.com/wall-65275820?offset=15340&own=1&w=wall -65275820_5712.

8. See https://vk.com/wall-65275820?offset=16020&own=1&w=wall -65275820_5399.

9. See https://vk.com/wall-65275820?offset=16300&own=1&w=wall-65275820_4978.

10. See https://vk.com/wall-65275820?offset=15340&own=1&w=wall-65275820_6327.

11. See https://vk.com/wall-65275820?offset=15340&own=1&w=wall-65275820_6299.

12. See, for example, https://vk.com/wall-65275820?offset=16400&own=1&w=wall-65275820_4863.

13. See https://vk.com/wall-65275820?offset=17000&own=1&w=wall-65275820_3558.

14. www.sobaka.ru/city/city/32942.

15. Author Skype interview with Mark Galeotti, April 11, 2017.

16. Ibid.

17. Author phone interview with State Department official, March 7, 2016.

18. Neil MacFarquhar, "A Powerful Russian Weapon: The Spread of False Stories," *New York Times,* August 28, 2016.

19. Kristen East, "Trump in Hot Water over Putin Embrace," *Politico,* September 9, 2016.

Chapter 7: The Postmodern Dictator

1. Will Dunham, "Kerry Condemns Russia's 'Incredible Act of Aggression' in Ukraine," Reuters, March 2, 2014.

2. N. Iancu, A. Fortuna, and C. Barna, eds., *Countering Hybrid Threats: Lessons Learned from Ukraine* (Amsterdam: IOS Press, 2016), 45.

3. See William J. Dobson, *The Dictator's Learning Curve: Inside the Global Battle for Democracy* (London: Vintage Books, 2013), Kindle ed., location 72.

4. Author interview with Toomas Hendrik Ilves, Tallinn, December 8, 2014.

5. See Mary Kaldor, *New and Old Wars: Organised Violence in a Global Era,* 3rd ed. (London: Polity, 2013), Kindle ed., location 358.

6. Hal Brands, "Paradoxes of the Gray Zone," Foreign Policy Research Institute, February 5, 2016.

7. Marshall McLuhan and Quentin Fiore, *The Medium Is the Massage: An Inventory of Effects* (New York: Bantam, 1967), 18.

8. This paragraph and parts of the previous one come from my article "Meet the Ordinary Ukrainians Arming the Country Against Russian Separatists," *New Statesman,* January 8, 2015.

9. Author interview with Ukrainian MP Olga Bel'kova, Kyiv, April 17, 2014.

10. Descriptions of my trip here can be found in my articles "They Wanna Be Back in the U.S.S.R.," *Daily Beast,* April 8, 2014, and "In Eastern Ukraine the Protestors Wait for Russia to Take Charge," *New Statesman,* April 17, 2014.

11. "Requisitioning of Explosives by Rebels Stops Work in East Ukraine," *Moscow Times,* July 28, 2014.

12. Some of the descriptions of my time in Sloviansk can be found in my article "Inside Occupied East Ukraine," *Daily Beast,* April 14, 2014.

13. "Ukraine: Running Out of Time," Crisis Group Report no. 231, May 14, 2014, 3.

14. Author telephone interview with Fridon Vekouah, Kyiv, September 16, 2014.

15. Author interview, Ukrainian security official, July 4, 2014.

16. "Ukraine's Lugansk Declares Itself Sovereign State," *Sputnik News*, May 12, 2014.

17. https://web.archive.org/web/20140717155720/https://vk.com/wall -57424472_7256, July 17, 2014.

18. "Prime Minister's Statement on Ukraine and Gaza," July 21, 2014, www.gov.uk/government/speeches/prime-ministers-statement-on-ukraine -and-gaza.

19. Chris Elliott, "The Readers' Editor on . . . Pro-Russia Trolling Below the Line on Ukraine Stories," *Guardian*, May 4, 2014.

20. Ben Judah, "London's Laundry Business," *New York Times*, March 7, 2014.

Chapter 8: The Interpreter 1

1. Eliot Higgins's narrative from this section comes from a meeting with the author in London on March 23, 2016, as well as a previous meeting in London on February 27, 2015, and an initial Skype interview on November 13, 2014.

2. "Evidence of Multiple Foreign Weapon Systems Smuggled to the Syrian Opposition in Daraa," *Brown Moses* (blog), January 25, 2013.

3. It should be noted that both Michael Weiss, senior editor at the *Daily Beast*, and James Miller, managing editor of *The Interpreter*, played a significant role in this story.

4. See "How Brown Moses Exposed Syrian Arms Trafficking from His Front Room," *Guardian*, March 21, 2013.

5. https://twitter.com/EliotHiggins/status/489838127591469056, July 17, 2014.

6. "Geolocating the Missile Launcher Linked to the Downing of MH17," *Bellingcat*, July 17, 2014.

7. Ibid.

8. Aric Toler's narrative comes from a Skype interview with the author on September 13, 2016.

9. "Buk Missile System," *Wikipedia*, https://en.wikipedia.org/wiki/Buk _missile_system.

10. https://twitter.com/AricToler/status/490168392918130689, July 18, 2014.

11. See also "Identifying the Location of the MH17 Linked Missile Launcher from One Photograph," *Bellingcat*, July 18, 2014, for Higgins's write-up of Toler's work.

12. https://twitter.com/AricToler/status/490171165244002304, July 18, 2014.

13. https://twitter.com/EliotHiggins/status/490506143132033024, July 19, 2014.

14. https://twitter.com/AricToler/status/490504150191329281, July 19, 2014.

15. "How to Find the Missing Buk System," KoreanDefense.com, July 19, 2014.

16. For a fuller discussion, see "*Paris Match* on the Location of a Buk," *Human Rights Investigations* (blog), July 28, 2014.

17. Between Donetsk and Zuhres it made a slight detour to south Makiivka because there was an overhead bridge that was too low to pass, but that was not known until 2016.

18. For a fuller discussion of this, see "MH17: The Open Source Investigation Two Years Later," *Bellingcat*, July 17, 2016.

19. "The Buk That Could: An Open Source Odyssey," *Bellingcat*, July 28, 2014.

Chapter 9: The Interpreter 2

1. "The Buk That Could: An Open Source Odyssey," *Bellingcat*, July 28, 2014.

2. A JIT is "an investigation team set up for a fixed period, based on an agreement between two or more EU Member States and/or competent authorities, for a specific purpose. Non EU Member States may participate in a JIT with the agreement of all other parties." "Joint Investigation Teams—JITs," Europol, https://www.europol.europa.eu/content/page/joint-investigation-teams-989.

3. Ostanin's narrative comes from a Skype interview with the author on September 21, 2016.

4. See *The Interpreter*, www.interpretermag.com.

5. VK has since made this impossible.

6. See "Images Show the Buk That Downed Flight MH17, Inside Russia, Controlled by Russian Troops," *Bellingcat*, September 8, 2014.

7. See https://vk.com/video135321380_169811617?list=03e8088fdba76 5b187.

8. A photo is geotagged when the addition of specific location information has been allowed. So if your phone has the right settings, it will embed the coordinates on Instagram, which will thus give an approximate location of where and when a photo was taken.

9. See https://drive.google.com/file/d/0B2QMAJOI8GameDB2X2R5dE FJaFE/view.

10. See https://www.youtube.com/watch?v=aLtzYEHolmg&feature =youtu.be&t=1m37s.

11. See https://web.archive.org/web/20140913210044/http:/ryadovoy.ru /forum/index.php?topic=423.0;wap2.

12. See www.youtube.com/watch?v=5TIVzgj7884.

13. "Images Show the Buk That Downed Flight MH17, Inside Russia, Controlled by Russian Troops," *Bellingcat*, September 8, 2014.

14. "Origins of the Separatists' Buk: A Bellingcat Investigation," *Bellingcat*, November 8, 2014.

15. See, for example, Elias Groll, "Kremlin's 'Sputnik' Newswire Is the BuzzFeed of Propaganda," *Foreign Policy*, November 10, 2014.

16. "Guardian Corrects Anti-Russian Story Based on 'Research' of Own Reporter," *Sputnik News*, February 19, 2015.

17. "Clerk Promises 'Truth' About MH17 Ahead of Official Report," *Russia Today*, October 8, 2015, https://youtu.be/PR_bO48IBgs?list=PLPC0U deof3T48YMaClFdtWl6l_D6WDwRW.

18. Jeffrey Lewis, "MH17 Anniversary," Arms Control Wonk, July 15, 2016, www.armscontrolwonk.com/archive/1201635/mh17-anniversary.

19. https://docs.google.com/spreadsheets/d/1hp9QS1HA1cv9JeU-3Wn ZMctTsUZNBBwWdZattWLK9pg/edit#gid=0.

20. "*Bellingcat* as an Instrument to Divert Attention from Investigating the Tragedy of the Malaysian Boeing over Ukraine," Ministry of Foreign Affairs of the Russian Federation, April 6, 2016.

21. "Response from the Russian Ministry of Foreign Affairs to *Bellingcat* Regarding Fakery Allegations," *Bellingcat*, April 14, 2016.

22. Information and Press Department, Ministry of Foreign Affairs of the Russian Federation, letter to Eliot Higgins, n.d., www.Bellingcat.com/wp -content/uploads/2016/04/MFA_response_1_en.pdf.

23. "The Russian Ministry of Foreign Affairs Publishes 'Their' Evidence of MH17 Fakery," *Bellingcat*, April 22, 2016.

24. "Russian Ministry of Foreign Affairs Plagiarizes LiveJournal Posts in MH17 Response," *Bellingcat*, April 22, 2016.

25. Author Skype interview with Aric Toler, September 13, 2016.

26. "The Falsification of Open Sources About MH17: Two Years Later," *Segodnia*, www.segodnia.ru/sites/default/files/pdf/The%20Falsification%20 of%20Open%20Sources%20About%20MH17.pdf.

27. Ibid., 1.

28. Somini Sengupta and Andrew E. Kramer, "Dutch Inquiry Links Russia to 298 Deaths in Explosion of Jetliner over Ukraine," *New York Times*, September 28, 2016.

29. https://www.facebook.com/photo.php?fbid=10154441448564627 &set=pcb.10154441448604627&type=3&theater.

30. Author Skype interview with Sir Lawrence Freedman, November 17, 2014.

31. It was a quote he would subsequently use in newspaper interviews.

32. Dominic Rushe and Shaun Walker, "MH17 Crash: Kerry Lays Out Evidence of Pro-Russia Separatists' Responsibility," *Guardian*, July 20, 2014.

33. See for example, "United States Assessment of the Downing of Flight MH17 and Its Aftermath," United States Embassy of Georgia, July 19, 2014.

34. Matt Sienkiewicz, "Start Making Sense: A Three Tier Approach to Citizen Journalism," *Media, Culture and Society* 36, 5 (2014): 691–701.

35. Ibid.

Chapter 10: The Recruit

1. Sophie Kasiki is a pseudonym used for fear of Islamic State reprisals. Other personal details, like her country of origin, have also been altered. Her narrative from this section comes from an interview with the author in Versailles, France, on December 7, 2016. Kasiki has also written a a book about her experiences: *Dans la nuit de Daech*, https://www.amazon.fr /Dans-nuit-Daech-Sophie-KASIKI/dp/222119098X.

2. Peter A. Padilla and Mary Riege Laner, "Trends in Military Influences on Army Recruitment: 1915–1953," *Sociological Inquiry* 71, no. 4 (2001): 433.

3. Ibid., 423.

4. Google definition of *propaganda*, www.google.gr/?gfe_rd=cr&ei=IW FKWOzjJNTc8AfomLSQBQ#q=propaganda+definition.

5. Abdel Bari Atwan, *Islamic State: The Digital Caliphate* (Oakland: University of California Press, 2015), 9.

6. Ibid.

7. Ibid., 2.

8. Ibid.

9. "Letter from al-Zawahiri to al-Zarqawi," July 9, 2005, GlobalSecurity .org, www.globalsecurity.org/security/library/report/2005/zawahiri-zarqawi -letter_9jul2005.htm.

10. Bari Atwan, *Islamic State*, 2–3.

11. Ibid., 3.

12. Author Skype interview with Alberto Fernandez, March 28, 2016.

13. "Sunni Rebels Declare New 'Islamic Caliphate,'" Al Jazeera, June 30, 2014.

14. Author Skype interview with Alberto Fernandez, March 28, 2016.

15. Author Skype interview with Abdel Bari Atwan, March 15, 2016.

16. Emerson T. Brooking and P. W. Singer, "War Goes Viral: How Social Media Is Being Weaponized Across the World," *Atlantic*, November 2016.

17. Abraham Wagner, Rand Waltzman, and Alberto Fernandez, "The War Against ISIS Through Social Media," *American Foreign Policy Council Defense Technology Program Brief* 12 (September 2015), 6.

18. Hugo is also a pseudonym.

19. Author interview with Melanie Smith, London, March 21, 2016.

20. Sophie will not name the *banlieue*, for fear of identification.

21. Wagner, Waltzman, and Fernandez, "War Against ISIS," 8.

22. The author has chosen not to reference or link to any Islamic State propaganda that shows death or killing.

23. Author Skype interview with Charlie Winter, November 24, 2016.

24. Author Skype interview with Alberto Fernandez, March 28, 2016.

25. Shiraz Maher, *Salafi-Jihadism: The History of an Idea* (London: Hurst, 2016), 7. See also David Patrikarakos, "Progression Through Regression" [review of Maher, *Salafi-Jihadism*], *Literary Review*, November 2016.

26. Author Skype interview with Alberto Fernandez, March 28, 2016.

27. Charlie Winter, "Fishing and Ultraviolence," BBC News, October 6, 2015.

28. Brooking and Singer, "War Goes Viral."

29. Yaroslav Trofimov, "Radicalization of Islam or Islamization of Radicalism?," *Wall Street Journal*, June 16, 2016.

30. Again, the author has chosen not to link to Islamic State videos that show killings.

31. See Chapter 11 for a fuller discussion.

32. Reuters, "Is the Number of Foreign Fighters Joining ISIS Really Plummeting?," *Newsweek*, April 29, 2016. http://europe.newsweek.com/isis-foreign -fighters-90-percent-iraq-syria-decreasing-general-claim-453741?rm=eu.

33. "Foreign Fighters: An Updated Assessment of the Flow of Foreign Fighters into Syria and Iraq," Soufan Group, New York, December 2015.

34. Bari Atwan, *Islamic State*, 153.

35. Author Skype interview with Alberto Fernandez, March 28, 2016.

36. Author Skype interview with Abdel Bari Atwan, March 15, 2016.

37. Ibid.

Chapter 11: The Counterterrorist

1. Author interview with Alec Ross, Baltimore, June 26, 2015.

2. Alberto Fernandez, "Why ISIS Flourishes in Its Media Domain," *American Foreign Policy Council Defense Technology Program Brief* 12 (September 2015), 6.

3. Author Skype interview with Abdel Bari Atwan, March 15, 2016.

4. Alberto Fernandez's narrative in this chapter comes from three Skype interviews on March 28, 2016, October 31, 2016, and November 10, 2016.

5. In which he had warned the latter "that we are in a battle, and that more than half of this battle is taking place in the battlefield of the media." See Chapter 10. See also "Letter from al-Zawahiri to al-Zarqawi," July 9, 2005, GlobalSecurity.org, www.globalsecurity.org/security/library/report/2005/zawahiri-zarqawi-letter_9jul2005.htm.

6. See https://www.youtube.com/watch?v=O6pSAok5lxA.

7. Brendan Bordelon, "Clinton Defends Obama's 'JV Team' Label for ISIS," *National Review*, November 19, 2015.

8. https://twitter.com/hashtag/CalamityWillBefallUS?src=hash.

9. Western Europe and the Arabian peninsula are the two areas where Twitter's presence is the largest (Saudi Arabia, for example, has the highest number of Twitter users per capita in the world).

10. Charlie Winter and Jordan Bach-Lombardo, "Why ISIS Propaganda Works," *Atlantic*, February 13, 2016.

11. https://www.youtube.com/watch?v=j69ZQIXdfKM.

12. https://www.youtube.com/watch?v=LN0l4tx59FU.

13. Alberto Fernandez, "'Contesting the Space': Adversarial Online Engagement as a Tool for Combating Violent Extremism," *Soundings: An Interdisciplinary Journal* 98, no. 4 (2015): 488–500.

14. https://www.youtube.com/watch?v=-wmdEFvsY0E.

15. Indeed, sometimes CSCC's images of Islamic State violence were so graphic that YouTube took the videos down. See, for example, https://www.youtube.com/watch?v=yQqHdMk5rbw.

16. Author interview with Melanie Smith, London, March 21, 2016.

17. Author Skype interview with Charlie Winter, November 24, 2016.

18. Emerson T. Brooking and P. W. Singer, "War Goes Viral: How Social Media Is Being Weaponized Across the World," *Atlantic*, November 2016.

19. Author interview with Melanie Smith, London, March 21, 2016.

20. Sam Hinton and Larissa Hjorth, *Understanding Social Media* (London: Sage, 2013), 27 (includes quote from Gillespie).

21. For a fuller discussion, see Charlie Winter, "ISIS Is Using the Media Against Itself," *Atlantic*, March 23, 2016.

22. Abdel Bari Atwan, *Islamic State: The Digital Caliphate* (Oakland: University of California Press, 2015), 11.

23. Greg Miller, "Panel Casts Doubt on U.S. Propaganda Efforts Against ISIS," *Washington Post*, December 2, 2015.

24. Ibid.

25. Author interview with Zahed Amanullah, March 22, 2016.

26. Author interview with Alec Ross, Baltimore, June 26, 2015.

27. "A Revolutionary Message," *Cipher Brief* (blog), March 9, 2016.

Conclusion

1. For a discussion of this in the Chinese context, see Emerson T. Brooking and P. W. Singer, "War Goes Viral: How Social Media Is Being Weaponized Across the World," *Atlantic*, November 2016.

2. Sam Hinton and Larissa Hjorth, *Understanding Social Media* (London: Sage, 2013), 22–23.

3. Ibid.

4. Mary Kaldor, *New and Old Wars: Organised Violence in a Global Era*, 3rd ed. (London: Polity, 2013), Kindle ed., location 81–82.

5. Author Skype interview with Jon Snow, January 15, 2015.

6. Kaldor, *New and Old Wars*, location 358.

7. Author interview with Emile Simpson, November 19, 2014.

8. IISS, "Neither War Nor Peace: Why the Information Revolution Makes 'Forever Wars' a New Normal," November 26, 2014, https://www.youtube.com/watch?v=OAR34uz3plE&feature=youtu.be&list=UUYygxNuTTlq2neh6Fu6rP4Q.

9. Charlie Winter and Jordan Bach-Lombardo, "Why ISIS Propaganda Works," *Atlantic*, February 13, 2016.

10. Geoffrey Ingersoll, "General James 'Mad Dog' Mattis Email About Being 'Too Busy to Read' Is a Must-Read," *Business Insider*, May 9, 2013.

11. Joe Weisenthal, "Donald Trump, the First President of Our Post-Literate Age," *Bloomberg View*, November 29, 2016.

12. Author Skype Interview with Nicholas Wright, July 1, 2016.

13. Jasper Jackson, "BBC Sets Up Team to Debunk Fake News," *Guardian*, January 12, 2017.

14. Ibid.

15. Amber Jamieson, Olivia Solon, "Facebook to Begin Flagging Fake News in Response to Mounting Criticism," *Guardian*, December 15, 2016.

16. Russell Goldman, "Reading Fake News, Pakistani Minister Directs Nuclear Threat at Israel," *New York Times*, December 24, 2016.

17. Ana Swanson, "The World Today Looks Ominously Like It Did Before World War I," *Washington Post*, December 29, 2016.

18. Ibid.

19. Ibid.

20. Ibid.

INDEX

David Patrikarakos is the author of *Nuclear Iran: The Birth of an Atomic State*, a contributing editor at the *Daily Beast*, and a contributing writer at *Politico*. He has written for the *New York Times*, *Financial Times*, *Wall Street Journal*, and many other publications. He lives in London.